IMPRESARIO OF CASTRO STREET

IMPRESARIO
OF CASTRO STREET

An Intimate Showbiz Memoir

Marc Huestis

Outsider Productions

San Francisco

Published by Outsider Productions, June 2019

OUTSIDER PRODUCTIONS
San Francisco, California
outsiderpro@earthlink.net

Deluxe trade paperback edition with color photos
ISBN: 978-1-7337352-0-9

Standard trade paperback edition with black & white photos
ISBN: 978-1-7337352-1-6

E-book with color photos
ISBN: 978-1-7337352-2-3

Library of Congress Control Number: 2019935173

For my brother Henry,
who made this book possible

IMPRESARIO OF CASTRO STREET

Author . . . . Marc Huestis

Editor . . . . Jay Blotcher

Copy Editor . . . . Casey Ward

Proofreader. . . . . John Karr, Isak Lindenauer

Consulting Editor . . . . . Bob Hawk

Book Design . . . . Toby Johnson

Cover Design. . . . . Tim Lewis

Photographers . . . . Steven Underhill,
Daniel Nicoletta, Greg Day,
Rikki Ercoli, Rick Gerharter,
Marshall Rheiner, Kent Taylor,
Bill Wilson

Graphics . . . . Silvana Nova, Rex Ray

Consultants. . . . . Jim Van Buskirk, Steve Susoyev,
Jim Provenzano

Special Thanks: Burl Willes, Daniel Nicoletta, Castro Theatre,
the Nassers, Castro Theatre staff (Gary Olive, Mark Ganter,
Keith Arnold, Brian Collette, Eric Schaefer, Jeff Root, Tom Wade,
Mark Almanza-Soldryk), Hal Rowland, N. Moses Corrette,
Isaac Amala, Lulu, Lawrence Helman, Henry G. Huestis,
Hank Huestis, Michele Flannery, Ken White, Patrick Marks,
Jen Joseph, Linda Larrabee, Peter Gowdy, Karen Larsen, Kathy
Nelsen, Allen Sawyer, Penni Kimmel, Gary Hobish, Mark Kliem,
Tod Booth, Beaver Bauer, Greg Cruikshank, Helen Shumaker,
Bill Jankowski, Mark Abramson, Silvano Nova, Craig Seligman,
Twin Peaks Tavern, Alvin Orloff, Lauretta Molitor, Frameline,
Frances Wallace, Joie de Vivre Hotels, SF Hilton, Jo Licata, Ron
Williams, Greg Mayo, Karen Cadle, Mani Niall, Harry Lit, Jenni
Olson, Ronald Wiggin, Bob Hoffman, Roberto Friedman, Carol
Lynley and all the stars and performers that have graced my
stages.

Contents

Cast 5

Overture 9

Act 1
Chasing The Rainbow

Act 1, Scene 1 – Million-Dollar Baby 11

Act 1, Scene 2 – Rebel, Rebel 27

Act 1, Scene 3 – College. 38

Act 1, Scene 4 – On the Road 41

Act 1, Scene 5 – An Angel Gets His Wings 44

Act 1, Scene 6 – Showstopper 52

Act 1, Scene 7 – A First Film Festival and
Something To Vote For! 57

Act 1, Scene 8 – Awoke and Fighting Back 63

Act 1, Scene 9 – Strange Fruit. 68

Act 1, Scene 10 – Dark November 73

Act 1, Scene 11 – Lost & Found. 76

Act 1, Scene 12 – My Vagabond Shoes 80

Act 1, Scene 13 – Inside Out 84

Act 1, Scene 14 – First Love & A Big Opening 90

Act 1, Scene 15 – The Party's Over. 99

Act 1, Scene 16 – Positive 107

Act 1, Scene 17 – Coming of Age. 111

Act 1, Scene 18 – The Work Begins 118

Act 1, Scene 19 – On The Road. 123

Act 1, Scene 20 – Burying the Dead 130

Act 1, Scene 21 – Trouble in Paradise 138

Act 1, Scene 22 – Sex Is.... 146
Act 1, Scene 23 – The Theater of Sex. 153
Act 1, Scene 24 – Willkommen 159
Act 1, Scene 25 – The Sweet Smell of Success. . . . 164
Act 1, Scene 26 – After the Ball 170

Act 2
Dancing With The Stars

Act 2, Scene 1 – Impresario 177
Act 2, Scene 2 – The Ship Sails On 183
Act 2, Scene 3 – Strictly First Class. 195
Act 2, Scene 4 – A Living Doll 204
Act 2, Scene 5 – The Heiress 213
Part 2 – Daughter Dearest 221
Act 2, Scene 6 – Look at Me 230
Act 2, Scene 7 – Bad Seeds & Black Eyes 241
Act 2, Scene 8 – Intermezzo / Requiem. 255
Act 2, Scene 9 – What Becomes a Legend Most? . . 266
Act 2, Scene 10 – The Phantom Cloud
  Or The Opposite of Sex Is... 290
Act 2, Scene 11 – Class Acts 298
Act 2, Scene 12 – I Am Spartacus. 315
Act 2, Scene 13 – Living Dolls: The Sequel 325
Act 2, Scene 14 – That Final Bow. 337
Act 2, Scene 15 – Deus Ex Machina
  Out of The Streets and Into The Woods. 343

Marc Huestis Castro Theatre Events 1995-2018 . . 357

Overture

im·pre·sa·ri·o
imprə ˈ särē ˌ ō, ˌ imprə ˈ serə ˌ ō/

noun **a person who organizes and often finances
concerts, plays, or operas.**

Synonyms: organizer, producer

My name is Marc Huestis and I am an impresario.

Yes, I have been dubbed "Impresario of Castro Street."

I've come to embrace that title, but getting there has been a long, circuitous journey; rough and rocky, often full of capricious twists and turns.

In the swirl of historic events, I have often been at the right place at the right time. Even in the wrong times I tried to make them right.

I was not a silent witness; I have always been a participant—both in show business and as an activist for social justice.

And throughout, the stars have always been my touchstones. Morning stars and death stars. Shining stars from Hollywood, guiding stars high above the Sierras.

"The Morning After" from *The Poseidon Adventure* is my theme song. I've lived through a whirlwind of memorable nights and mornings after. Some mornings were filled with heartaches, headaches, and hangovers. Others brought dreams fulfilled. This book will attempt to balance all those nights and mornings—to make peace with the past. With others, and with myself. Now step right up, the show is about to begin!

ACT 1
CHASING THE RAINBOW

Act 1, Scene 1 – MILLION-DOLLAR BABY

It's twilight on a summer evening in 2008. A shiny stretch limo pulls up at the Castro Theatre, San Francisco's majestic movie palace. The door opens, revealing to the crowd a pair of gorgeous gams in seamless nylons. The crowd goes insane. The woman takes it all in, and gaily poses for the scrum of photographers crowding around her. Our eyes meet. She takes me by the arm as the paparazzi snap furiously.

Then from her ruby-red mouth come the words "Thank you for all this, Marc Huestis." This woman is the legendary Hollywood star Debbie Reynolds. And she's gushing over me!

It's surreal, a dream come true. And in this moment, all the crap in my life—all those speed-infused liquored-up lost weekends, all those AIDS deaths, all that fear of dying myself, all those career dead ends—it all instantly melted away. Debbie

Reynolds had said my name! Who would have thunk this could ever happen?

Debbie Reynolds waves to her fans as jubilant Kathy Nelsen and impresario Marc Huestis look on. Photo by Steven Underhill.

Flash back to some 44 years earlier. It's a Long Island autumn in 1964. A wide-eyed, precocious ten-year-old is taken to the movies for the first time. It was the musical *The Unsinkable Molly Brown* starring Debbie Reynolds. I don't recall the theater, but I'll never forget what I saw on the big silver screen. From the first bars of the overture, I was hooked.

It was a logical addiction. After all, show business was in my blood. My dad was an editor for NBC-TV. And my mother was a stripper. My gene pool danced. On television, in living color.

Even before *Molly Brown* wowed me at the movies, the mother's milk of my early years was the Million Dollar Movie on New York's WOR-TV. Each week—twice every evening, three times on weekends—a classic film would play, introduced by the lush "Tara's Theme" from *Gone With the Wind*.

I was introduced to Astaire & Rogers musicals, *Casablanca*, *King Kong*, *Rodan* and *Godzilla*, *The Helen Morgan Story* starring a torchy, boozed-up Ann Blyth and a trashy film called *Harlow* starring Carol Lynley. Back then, I had no idea what role these movie stars would play in my own life.

Watching the Million Dollar Movie was the ultimate bonding time with my mother. A momentary escape from a sad, sometimes violent, childhood.

As we watched these Hollywood dreams unfold in our suburban Bethpage home, my mom, the stripper, would be hand sewing beads on lavish costumes and gluing rhinestones onto her pasties.

Together we gorged on dried-up drumsticks from Swanson's TV dinners. And we shared Kleenex during melodramas. We both loved a good weepie, but when the climax came, I did try to hide my tears. Boys don't cry.

We ingested each of these dream-factory fantasias. And my mother knew a great deal about fantasy. She lived in a world of her own making.

Mom was born Matilda Bluvaite—of Lithuanian Catholic descent—and grew up in World War II Europe. Her exact date of birth and age were a mystery. Her first fantasy—one I think she truly believed—was that she had been born a gypsy princess, making me a member of royalty. It's true; I grew up to be a queen.

Matilda's childhood was better than any Million Dollar Movie. A nomad, she roamed from country to country as the war raged on. She insisted that her father was killed and she was a dark-haired ugly duckling reared by a beautiful but evil Aryan stepmother—alongside two equally beautiful blonde but evil stepsisters. Talk about a Cinderella story!

The saga continued: In her fanciful narrative—this part I had a hard time believing—she was betrayed by the Jews who had her thrown into a Nazi prison camp. She kept her sanity through these early years by singing. After the war, she *did* board a boat to the United States, sponsored by a benevolent Lithuanian refugee—

my godmother Ona Matulionis. Matilda landed in Plattsburgh, a small town in Upstate New York, a lost teenager in the new world.

The only picture of my mother (right) as a child. Here she seems happy.

There she met my father, Henry J. Huestis. Born in Brooklyn, "Hank" became a gifted radio engineer. After serving in the Coast Guard, he landed a job as a technician at WEAV, a station in Plattsburgh. Each week the station held a local talent show. My mother entered. My father was smitten by both her vocal and physical charms. Soon afterwards, Matilda was pregnant.

My father at work in the radio station.

In this era, those unmarried women who dared to become pregnant were judged harshly. My mother's only option—abortion was illegal and unthinkable—was to check into a home for unwed mothers. There my brother Henry George was born in September 25, 1951.

For whatever reason, my father decided to make an "honest" woman of my mother. They married on Nov. 1, 1951.

Honestly, they never should have married. For one, the stars were not in their favor. Both Mom and Dad were Geminis. A bond that is a total astrological no-no. It's like living with a million people.

Still, they gave it their best shot. My father landed a plum job at NBC Radio in New York City. He worked with the best in the business, editing *Weekday*, a popular radio show starring Mike Wallace and Virginia Graham.

The happy couple, Hank and Matilda.

Mom learned English in record time. She played the obedient '50s suburban housewife, producing two more children. I was born on Dec. 26, 1954, the day after Christmas (a horrible birthday!). My sister Michele followed two years later.

My mother was old Europe strict, kept a spotless house, and relished cooking.

God knows my parents tried to create the perfect *Leave It to Beaver* lifestyle. But behind this conventional '50s facade, a storm was brewing.

Dinner on my dad's lap.

Matilda had an artistic temperament that could not be contained. Tillie, as she was called, wanted to trade the perfect *Better Homes & Gardens* life for—drumroll please—a new life as a singer, dancer, and finally stripper extraordinaire.

Mom possessed movie star looks: a cross between the flaming red-haired Rita Hayworth, sultry Greta Garbo, and glamorous Joan Crawford. And she had real talent; she sang like Marlene Dietrich on Quaaludes. Mama would tuck us in singing "Lili Marlene" (her anthem to her dying day), followed by "Edelweiss" from her favorite film, *The Sound of* Music (a song that she took to her grave).

Her jump into an actual show business career started with a growing collection of sheet music, and then singing lessons. At an accelerated pace, her image became more theatrical. Tasteful shades of lipstick gave way to come-fuck-me red. Her eye shadow went from subtle to defiant; sequins and costume jewelry replaced tasteful pearls. Her mousy brown hair was dyed flaming scarlet.

Mom before her transformation from Matilda to Marija.

On frequent trips to "the city," Mama met other show biz types. Her best girlfriend Chiquita was a small Mexican woman who acted like Carmen Miranda on speed. She made my mom's stage outfits. It was a real treat to tag along with Mom for costume fittings at Chiquita's 42nd Street studio. She fussed over me, pinching my cheeks, calling me "Chico," and telling me how cute I was. I adored her.

Then there was Mortie, her agent. "Matilda," he told her, "will never sell." So Mama became "Marija, the Continental Gypsy." I'm proud that my mother was the first person I knew who changed her name for stardom.

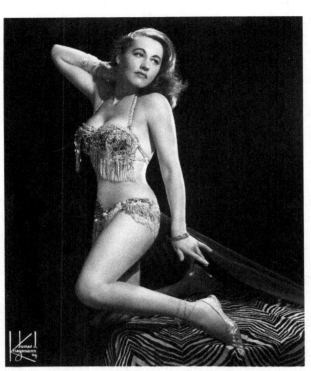

MARIJA the Continental Gypsy

Marija, in her full glory.

Meanwhile back at the ranch house (OK, it was actually a suburban split-level), I too was going through my own changes. Like Marija, I was also in love with show business. In first grade, I debuted as Dopey in *Snow White and the Seven Dwarfs*. I'd become aroused by the feel of the tights on my thin, hairless legs.

It was the first inkling of being queer.

I was a relentless tease to my sister Michele. I liked her girly things—mercilessly grabbing her Barbie, Chatty Cathy, and Tressy, the doll with amazing growing hair. Often I was so aggressively mean, I would leave Michele in a puddle of tears.

I didn't care. And inspired by my mother, I would design and execute elaborate drag-queeny gowns for Barbie, using sequins and feathers left over from Chiquita's costume creations. I even created a tight, glittery red eyelash lamé number with a fishtail of flared mesh. Very *Pink Flamingos* Divine.

I all but ignored my big brother Henry. We shared the same room, but an invisible curtain separated us. Sad and sullen, he was lost in his own world, something that would never change.

Christmas in the 1960s. I wanted the dolly,
my sister wanted the baseball bat.

My other passion was—surprise, surprise—musicals. Since my father worked at NBC, we were always the first on the block to get the latest technical innovations. Soon our suburban home was equipped with a spanking new reel-to-reel tape player. I quickly learned how to thread up the tape with the latest Broadway musical recorded off radio broadcasts. I'd spend afternoons blissfully listening to *West Side Story*, *The King and I*,

The Pajama Game and *Gypsy*. All done while rocking back and forth at a furious pace (a habit I have to this day). My favorite was *Judy Garland at Carnegie Hall*. I fantasized being in the hall with Judy staying up all night and "singing them all." Then I'd belt out "Somewhere Over the Rainbow," tears in my eyes. I was on my way to becoming a friend of Dorothy and going down that yellow brick road. With a few detours.

When Dad switched to video editing, I remember visiting him at NBC. I was a kid with stars in his eyes roaming the halls of 30 Rockefeller Center. My dad would give us a tour, often saying hello to famous folks he knew. Johnny Carson even knew him as "Hank." We'd visit the buzzing tape room, where Dad would demonstrate editing two-inch videotape with a magnifying glass and a razor blade.

His work was all-consuming and he'd clock in endless overtime hours at the network, coming home just to sleep. Yet seeing my father's name at the end of the credits of the '60s variety show *Hullabaloo*—a TV showcase for some of the biggest pop music stars of the era—gave me bragging rights at school.

My own life in showbiz began unceremoniously by putting on little spook shows at home. Around Halloween, I would elaborately decorate our newly finished basement with fake cobwebs, witches on a stick, pumpkins with flashlight eyes, and skeletons that would pop out of the closet. I'd charge a nickel, put the kiddies in my shiny red wagon, and weave them in and out of my little funhouse.

However, one year the kids stopped coming. And with just cause. Our block was primarily Jewish. And my mother was deeply anti-Semitic. (Lithuanians are reputed to be the worst of the worst in that regard—signing up for the SS in droves.) Still she tried to befriend the neighbors, particularly a Jewish woman named Sylvia.

Dad's credit on "Hullabaloo." The NBC variety show featured stars like James Brown and Sonny & Cher, backed by energetic go-go dancers.

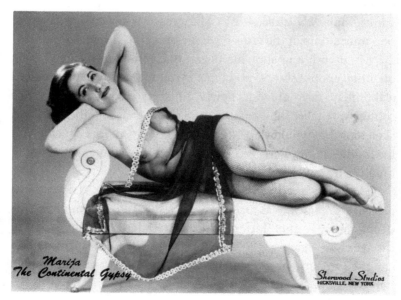

My mother after releasing her inner stripper. Not shown: her barely repressed rage.

For a while they were thick as thieves. But that changed after an early evening altercation. Sylvia slammed the door in mother's face. Furious, Mom ran into the middle of the street and howled at the top of her lungs in her thick accent, "I vish Hitler had killed you all," shot a Nazi salute and repeatedly shouted "Sieg Heil!!!" It was so loud I could hear it in my bedroom a half block away. I was so embarrassed; I placed my pillow over my head to mute the hate. After that night, most of the kids on Lex Avenue were told to stay away from the crazy lady at number 9.

Meanwhile my mother's metamorphosis into a showgirl continued, much to my father's chagrin. The smell of hairspray and spirit gum replaced the aromas of mom's cooking in our increasingly unkempt home. Soon my mother graduated to the hard stuff, slapping Stein's theatrical makeup onto her face. I still hear her voice commanding me: "Marc, I vant you to go on your bicycle to the druk store and get me these things."

The list usually included two bottles of L'Oréal's Go-Go Red No. 1, a bottle of Tabu perfume, a tube of Bain de Soleil and a small bottle of liquid eyeliner.

Each weekend, perched on the toilet seat, I watched as my mother put on her face, sprayed her hair, and penciled in her arched eyebrows, à la Joan Crawford. Two large suitcases were brimming with costumes, sheet music and eight-by-ten glossies. Mother as Marija would whisk off for the weekend, leaving three children with a string of housekeepers.

Affectionately known in the business as "Gypsy," Marija hit it big in the summer of '64. While my dad worked the Democratic Convention for NBC, my mother would work the Atlantic City clubs. And we three kids would have a two-week vacation!

Atlantic City in the early '60s was the ideal playground for a fun-loving boy. The boardwalk was abuzz with young couples with scads of of stirred-up children. The shop windows featured saltwater taffy being hand-pulled, and the sweet smell of fresh chocolate fudge perfumed the air. The famed Steel Pier featured crooner Bobby Rydell and a man on a horse who dived from a high platform into a huge vat of water. It was a picture perfect place for a convention.

Imagine my excitement when one night Lyndon Baines Johnson was helicoptered onto the boardwalk to greet people before accepting his party's nomination. I'll never forget how he flashed his big Texan smile and waved his huge hands for the cameras while the cheering crowd went wild. They say that politics is show business for ugly people, and I was hooked by the glitzy razzmatazz of the moment. No surprise that I would become a political junkie.

But the times, they were a-changing. After our Atlantic City trip my parents fought. And fought. And fought. As America's postwar ebullience came crashing down—riots, Vietnam and more assassinations—so did my parents' marriage. My father became increasingly jealous of my mother's profession and the attention she was receiving from other men. He was largely absent, and when he did come home, he was often drunk.

I grew to hate the times my parents were together. It meant one thing. There would be horrible fights. Christmas was the worst, an absolutely hellacious time in the Huestis house. One, occurring in my early teens, particularly stands out.

The turkey and all the fixings were set on the table. The candles were lit. My mom went upstairs to get my dad's dress jacket. In its pockets she found a stash of love letters with a Boston postmark from a woman named Geraldine. My mom flew into a rage, demanding to know who this Geraldine was. When my dad didn't answer, Mom picked up the electric carving knife, held it to his face and shouted, "Go to your Boston whore, you bastard!" She then repeatedly chased him around the table hurling food and epithets, as my brother, sister and I watched in horror. For my family, there was no place like home for the holidays.

My mother became increasingly abusive. At the slightest pretext, she would become enraged. Periodically she would march us three children into the laundry room and treat us to the business end of a thick leather belt. Often we didn't have the slightest idea why we were being beaten.

Like many women of the day, my mother found comfort in a daily regimen of pills, courtesy of one Dr. Lazlo. First headache tablets were prescribed. Then Miltowns, the drug of choice for many '60s moms to relieve stress. My trips to the drugstore were soon replaced by home deliveries. Twice a week, a large brown bag of prescriptions would accompany Marija's makeup and L'Oréal go-go red. She had set up residence in the valley of the dolls.

The pills also inspired a new routine: suicide attempts. After violent altercations with my father, Mom would slam the master bedroom door. Then I'd hear a grisly shriek from inside.

"Call the hospital," she would dramatically moan, "I've taken some pills." Then we three would wail, "Daddy, Daddy, make it stop... Mummy, Mummy don't die." The ambulance would arrive, and my mother would be rushed to the hospital to get her stomach pumped. Next day, we would all be carted to the hospital, where Mother, without makeup in a dingy hospital robe, would weep and tell us, "I'm verrrrrrrrrrrrry, verrrrrrry sorry. It von't happen again."

That is, until the next time.

I eventually escaped the sadness and madness of home with a potent mixture of politics, drugs and art. But first and foremost was sex.

Masturbation came early and often. At the tender age of 10, I discovered the joy of rub-a-dub-dubbing in the tub. A bar of soap, some suds, a little friction, and I was transported to exotic places. My body would convulse spastically while strings of mozzarella cheese plopped from my erect penis into the soapy bathwater.

I was initially shocked, but it sure felt good. Soon, the bathroom became my favorite place in the house. I later learned to gratify myself in the darkness of my own bedroom, using *Tiger Beat* magazine or the Sears catalog's underwear pages. My poor brother pretended not to notice.

The Boy Scouts were also a great source of sexual pleasure. When the other boys caught wind of my mother's profession, I gladly became the troop's resident stripper. Once our scoutmaster was fast asleep, the tent would come alive. Flashlights turned into spotlights, and voila, I was Gypsy Rose Lee entertaining Troop 69. I dipped and gave 'em a glove.

Real sex was reserved for the tough boy down the block. Walter was a rough and rugged boy of thirteen who cursed and smoked cigarettes. A total JD (juvenile delinquent). After I made him miniature brownies from my sister's Easy-Bake oven, he befriended me.

In the summer of '67, I pitched a tent in the backyard, and invited him for a sleepover. That night, snuggled up close together, we both whipped it out. I taught Walter what I had learned in the bathtub. "Rub it harder," I whispered. His nicotine-tinged lips drew closer to mine, as well as other aroused body parts. I experienced more pleasure that night than any boy my age.

Next morning, we parted, both of us pretending to ignore the intimacy we had experienced the night before. Occasionally we would meet after dark in secret places and attempt to repeat the pleasure, but never came close to the same thrill. The first time, I realized, is always the best.

Act 1, Scene 2 – REBEL, REBEL

1968 was a historic year. For me, it was also the year Hank and Marija, my battling parents, finally separated. My absent father became more absent, save for court-sanctioned weekend jaunts to McDonald's and putt-putt miniature golf. Honestly, it was a relief they were no longer together. Their marriage had played for years like *Who's Afraid of Virginia Woolf?* I was tired of Dad's drunkenness, Mom's suicide sagas and their violent nonstop arguments. Now, we kids no longer had to deal with all that damn drama.

But other problems popped up. My mother suddenly realized she couldn't feed three hungry children on Dad's $70 a week child support payments. So she began taking out-of-town gigs every weekend—and leaving us alone. While I initially felt abandoned, this precocious 14-year-old quickly found a way to fill the void.

About four miles from my Bethpage home was the Hicksville train station. I heard that men met in the bathroom for blowjobs. The station's "tea room" became my obsessive weekend destination.

There I was quite a popular teenager. Sure, my suitors were much older men. But I didn't care. I wanted it. I *needed* it.

I recall a gray-haired gentleman in a fancy Cadillac who lured me from the station to his apartment and threw me on the bed. His sagging body quivered as he pulled out his dentures, chowed down with his naked gums on my young throbbing cock, masterfully tweaked my nubile boy tits and got me even harder. I loved it.

But the ecstasy was short-lived. After I came, I was guilt-ridden. I would run home muttering under my breath, "I'm not a homo. I will *not* come back here ever again."

But the next weekend, I'd be back for more.

Anonymous sex wasn't my only insatiable appetite. There was a passion for the arts, too. That is, "the theatah!" A quest for personal expression driven by a need for love and attention.

That quest had been inspired by an early childhood eavesdropped conversation.

One night my father returned home from working overtime at 30 Rock. From their bedroom, I heard something rare: A thoughtful discussion—at normal decibel levels—between my parents. The subject was their children's future.

Mom asked Dad what career was awaiting my brother Henry.

"He will probably grow up to be a mathematician or an engineer like me."

"And vhat about Marc?" she queried.

"He's quite a character. Maybe he'll grow up to be a clown," my dad replied.

Though I'm sure his intention was not to be hurtful, I aspired to a higher calling than being a goddamn circus clown. So his words were like a dagger in my heart. I cried myself to sleep.

But Dad had a point. I was prone to entertaining folks with my wacky tricks. Being double-jointed, I could wrap my feet behind my head and walk on my hands. Still, I wanted to be taken seriously.

But certain personal quirks got in the way. My freakish habit of rocking back and forth earned me outsider status—plus a demerit. One teacher actually tied me down to the chair. Bound but not gagged, I transferred all my nervous energy by chewing the plastic of my Bic pen down to the core. Added to that, I was left-handed.

The goofy kid with an unusual talent.

I was just plain different. So, I overcompensated by being the best student I could.

In high school, I became a top honor student and joined the drama department. My freshman year, I had my first break: being cast by English/Drama teacher Mr. Yesselman as young Tom of Warwick in the school production of the musical *Camelot*.

My big scene came at the very end of the musical. I played my one brief shining moment to the hilt. I felt an odd thrill in getting on my knees and repeating "Yes, my lord" as the cold steel of the King Arthur's sword crowned my shoulders. And, boy, I really loved wearing that multicolored tunic and matching powder-blue tights! The whole experience was erotically charged, connecting theater and sex in my mind.

The director, Mr. Yesselman, a smart, self-assured, and inspiring figure, soon became my mentor.

With him, I had my first inkling of "gaydar." Nothing was spoken.

No boundaries were ever crossed between student and teacher, but Mr. Yesselman's attentions secretly thrilled me.

In my sophomore year, he cast me as the White Rabbit in *Alice in Wonderland*. He took it upon himself to apply my makeup. As he attached my fake white whiskers with his gentle, sweaty large hands, I had to cross my legs to hide my hard-on.

Rehearsing as the White Rabbit with bunny ears and no make-up.

Mr. Yesselman continued to nurture my talent, directing me in Arthur Miller's *The Crucible*, Sophocles' *Antigone*, and Ionesco's *Bald Soprano*. Heady stuff for a high schooler.

He also tutored me in the importance of activism and political engagement. So I walked the streets for "Clean Gene" McCarthy, cleaned Bethpage State Park for Earth Day, boarded the bus to Washington D.C. and protested the war, joining the 500,000 who attended the famous Moratorium Against the Vietnam War, Nov. 15, 1969.

I watched every second of the bloody riots at the 1968 Democratic Convention, my room festooned with "McCarthy for President" banners and balloons. After Humphrey was nominated, I wrote a passionate letter to the editor of *Newsday*, the largest newspaper in Long Island. "As a former McCarthyite, I ask disgruntled voters not to sit out the election but to write in their candidate of choice." It was published as the featured letter; the first time my name appeared in print. I was only 14.

Me in 1968 with my first cat, Muskie
—named after Sen. Ed Muskie.

The election of '68 also gave me the great opportunity to work the floor at NBC's Presidential Election Headquarters at Rockefeller Center. Although my father no longer lived with us, he procured me a one-day gig as a page for the network's election coverage, anchored by the legendary broadcasters Chet Huntley and David Brinkley.

My job was to give the anchors the projected results for each state: Minnesota's ten electoral votes will go to Hubert Humphrey, Alabama's ten electoral votes go to George Wallace, etc. I would run through the studio carrying a little piece of paper and pass it to Chet or David, so they could read the tally on-air.

On the morning of Nov. 6, 1968, I passed on to John Chancellor, NBC's morning anchor, the piece of paper that would prove decisive. It held Illinois's 26 electoral votes. Soon afterwards it was declared on air that "Nixon's the one." In my small way, I had a hand in electing Tricky Dick. But please don't blame me.

Meanwhile, back at home, things continued to deteriorate. Marija was having career problems. She was realizing that the shelf life of an "exotic dancer" (a term she preferred to stripper) was all too brief. Now in her thirties, she was past her prime. As she aged, her gigs became seedier. She went from working classy clubs in Long Island to toilets in smelly Secaucus, New Jersey. The Continental Gypsy was now go-go dancing semi-naked in wood-paneled cages adorned with tacky cardboard cutout nudie silhouettes—to the catcalls of cheap drunks.

Even worse, she was bringing home patrons of these dives: sleazy, tattooed, stupid men named "Tony" and "Joe."

At the same time, she began adopting dogs. Hoarding, actually. At one time six white German shepherds were penned up in a small fenced-off patio and stinking up the entire block. It was gross. Our once-manicured suburban home became a mini-Grey Gardens.

Her fights with "Tony" and "Joe" and other short-term lovers rivaled her fights with my father. My sister, my brother, and I would watch the battles silently, knowing it was a matter of time until she turned her violent outbursts on her children.

My poor brother Henry became the target for most of Mom's anger. "If it wasn't for you, and getting pregnant from your bastard father, I wouldn't be in this mess," she'd howl, referring to her unhappy shotgun wedding. The kid never had a chance. His choice of escape was to join the Air Force, destination Vietnam.

My mother, the go-go dancer.

And Mom quickly found my Achilles' heel. My friends and my favorite teacher, Mr. Yesselman, were all Jewish—and Mom's anti-Semitism raged deep.

"That Jew is going to turn you into a faggot," she said one day, referring to my beloved mentor. That was my breaking point. I impulsively screamed: "Shut up!" Marija was momentarily shocked at my rebellion, but then she pounced, beating the shit out me. My mother literally tore the hair out of my head.

But enough was enough. For the first time, I fought back. After that, she never touched me again.

My yearbook photo. I was voted Class Actor,
Debbie Campbell, Class Actress.

My main retreat from domestic abuse was high school theater, and the group of fellow misfits that it housed. My favorite was Cindy Seaman, a Jewish wild child who proudly donned army fatigues and no bra. She taught me the power of a strong, liberated woman. She also taught me the joys of hashish. I had never particularly been attracted to drugs. But hell, it was the '60s. And Cindy made it sexy.

During rehearsals for a production of *Oliver!* she took me aside and gave me a small lump of smelly, sticky brown stuff wrapped in tinfoil. "It's good hash. Take it home and smoke it before our next rehearsal," she purred.

The next day I rushed into the basement and lit up. After a bit of coughing, I was higher than a kite. How I got to rehearsal I'll never know, but there was a bit during "Consider Yourself" where I had to jump off a five-foot wooden bridge that was part of the set. I didn't jump; I flew. Cindy winked at me, and I laughed all the way down.

Also, I was lucky enough to be in close proximity to New York City. Mr. Yesselman had tutored me on what was the best of Broadway. In 1971, I ventured (by myself) to see my first live musical (his favorite), *Company*. In an instant I was hooked, and when Elaine Stritch belted and brayed "Ladies Who Lunch" it was a revelation. After that, I became a Broadway baby. Among the other shows that made an indelible impression were *Applause* with Lauren Bacall, *Pippin* with Ben Vereen, Tom O'Horgan's *Inner City*, and my absolute favorite, the Hal Prince production of *Follies*. I became a *Follies* groupie, seeing the show countless times and becoming a teenage stage-door Johnny. After the show, I waited for the stars so many times that both Alexis Smith and Dottie Collins took a shine to me, telling me that I was just the most adorable thing they had ever laid eyes on. By closing night, they expressed how much they would miss me. It was my first real brush with celebrity, and I loved it!

Not all my high school memories were rose-colored. Although I had found my niche in the drama department, the jocks hated me. I was always the last person picked on the team, and was the prime target during dodge ball. In the locker room, there was always a barrage of homophobic slurs (I wasn't out, but they could see the obvious).

I was unfazed by their derision and insults. They were mostly harmless. That changed one spring night in my junior year. I was walking home from rehearsal with a good female friend, someone the jocks hated because of her strength. All of a sudden, and out the blue, a group of drunken boys approached us, one of them carrying a baseball bat. I knew them as my tormenters. We tried to walk faster, but they quickly caught up and cornered us. Two of the boys threw me on the lawn, and the others grabbed my friend. They took turns getting on top of her, humping her and calling her a slut.

I tried to get away and help her, but they were too strong. They laughed and asked me, "How does it feel to be a faggot? Bet you want us to do this to you Faggot, FAGGOT!" vilely spitting out the F's.

Thankfully, the resident of the house heard the commotion, turned on the porch light and asked what was going on. The boys fled. We were left breathless and traumatized. I asked my friend if she was OK, she brushed the dirt off of her jumpsuit, picked out the leaves from her disheveled hair, and simply said, "Let's get out of here." We were silent all the way home.

They say what doesn't kill you makes you stronger, and I learned that at a pretty young age. Still loved my high school years. Precious were the bonds that were formed between budding thespians, and the nurturing tutelage from my mentor.

On Graduation Day in 1972, Mr. Yesselman penned words of wisdom in my yearbook. It's an inscription that I will always remember: "Dear Marc, I wish you great happiness, but little contentment." Even before the ink dried, these words were forever seared into my memory.

Years later, I discovered through Facebook that Mr. Yesselman was living in Palm Springs. On a whim, I looked him up in the phone book and called. "Hi. My name is Marc Huestis. You might not remember me..." "Of course I remember you!" he interrupted, his voice brimming with excitement.

A tender thirty-minute conversation ensued. Yes, Robert Yesselman was gay; he had come out at Bethpage High a few years after I graduated. After he left in 1976, he moved to New York City and became executive director of the Paul Taylor Dance Company and later Joffrey Ballet. He was the president of "Dancing for Life," a 1987 gala which was the dance community's first response to the AIDS crisis. His husband Lee had recently died and Mr. Yesselman was now ailing.

I told him about being HIV-positive for over thirty years. And how important he was to me. He cried. Teachers often don't know the influence they have on their students. But now we were contemporaries: two older gay men who had both struggled through the epidemic. And survived. I promised if I ever got to Palm Springs, I would look him up.

A year or so later, I learned that Mr. Yesselman had passed on. I suddenly recalled one thing I had forgotten to tell him on the phone: how meaningful his yearbook message was—and how it both inspired and haunted my entire life.

Act 1, Scene 3 – COLLEGE

I fucking hated college.

I didn't expect to. After all I was thrilled by the prospect of getting away from my crazy mother and derelict father.

I wanted to go to a good university (the further away, the better!). I had stellar grades. But a lack of money derailed my dreams. I couldn't attend Harvard, Princeton or Yale on a stripper's salary. And Dad wasn't likely to pay.

So State University of New York (SUNY) schools were my only option, using my New York Regents Scholarship. I chose SUNY Binghamton in upstate New York, to major in drama.

Little did I know the Binghamton Drama Department was the epicenter of the "Lessac Method" of acting. There, Arthur Lessac, the inventor of this highly unnatural vocal technique, maintained cult-like status. All drama undergrads were expected to become his devotees, and taking his training was mandatory. Ungodly sounds came from within the classroom doors. Inside, we were forced to crawl on all fours, and to repeatedly bellow "Hellllllllllllllllooooooooo." This hideous exercise, known as the "Lessac Call," sounded like cattle in heat. I wanted to be an actor, not a cow.

Disenchanted, I quickly found another calling: the bathroom next to Lecture Hall 6.

There you'd find me on my knees, sliding my dick through a two-foot opening between the wall of the stall and the floor for anonymous blowjobs. It offered temporary release. But that familiar high-school feeling of guilt afterwards always followed.

But one day towards the end of my freshman year, I accidentally saw the face of my fellow fellator. He had blond hair, blue eyes and a lithe tight body. He was *sooooo* beautiful and his lips were *sooooo* sweet. "Hellllllllloooo!" I crooned, putting my Lessac training to good use. He invited me back to his dorm room to continue our carnal escapades. After less than an hour, without even asking his name, I spontaneously uttered the words "I love you."

For the first time, after I came, I felt no guilt. Now I knew sex didn't have to be ugly. For years I had prayed that I was not gay. Now, I finally was willing to accept that I was a homosexual.

My "love" for the beautiful blond boy of Lecture Hall 6 was short-lived; I never saw him again. Nor did I pine for him. I knew there would be others around the corner. So I began to frequent the local gay bars. Binghamton's men's watering hole The Cadillac (its name an oxymoron) was a depressing dive, very *Boys in the Band*. I didn't discover love there. But I did find I could earn a little extra cash by hopping into a car circling the bar for a quickie. So it wasn't a total waste of time.

The other bar in town, The Green Onion, catered to hardcore dykes. It felt more warm and welcoming than The Cadillac. There was a sense of community in dyke bars in small towns, particularly in the early '70s, before gay liberation took hold.

My favorite Green Onion moment revolved around Paul Anka's hit song "You're Having My Baby." Right before last call, the jukebox would blast the tune. The ladies, properly lubricated, would hit the dance floor. The commandeering butch would lead, and the goo-goo-eyed femme would look up at her partner lovingly. At the chorus, the butches would sing "You're having my baby," and the femmes would chirp back, "I'm a woman in love and I love what it's doing to me." All in unison. It was so sweet and innocent.

In my sophomore year, I also had my first gay "girlfriend." William, quickly known as Ponce, was the first person besides my mother who changed his name. Ponce, he told me, was English slang for effeminate; that shoe fit and he wore it with pride. Ponce had a wild mane of jet-black hair, protruding teeth, and a soft high-pitched voice. I was not attracted to him, but we bonded over old movies. He did a mean Doris Day imitation.

We rented a funky house off-campus, along with a lovely hippie woman and two straight guys. I lived in the attic. We were both crazy about Bea Arthur, so each week when *Maude* came on, like clockwork Ponce would crawl up to my room. During the show, Ponce would slink closer to me, kneel, and slowly unzip my jeans. He'd take out my soft dick and commence chowing down on it. I never got totally hard, and occasionally I'd scold him because his Bugs Bunny teeth were scraping the skin. Then I'd go back to watching TV. It became a regular ritual. I felt these blowjobs were just the price to pay to keep the friendship. It was well worth it; I enjoyed his companionship.

Still, I realized I was bored with Binghamton, and I was itching to break free. This drama queen wanted real drama.

Act 1, Scene 4 – ON THE ROAD

By Junior year, I was jonesing to let my freak flag fly. I needed a summer break.

But I first needed some money. Ponce and I took assembly-line jobs at Landers Perfume factory, a depressing-looking brick workhouse straight out of a Dickens novel. My job was to attach small buttons on knock-off perfumes; his was to screw poodle heads onto bottles filled with hot-pink bubble bath. All while trying to keep up with the rapidly accelerating conveyor belt, just like Lucy and Ethel at the chocolate factory.

Still in a month, I managed to save up enough to finance a solo trip to Provincetown, the notorious summer hangout for bohemians, hippies and homos. P-town was the ideal destination for a young queen with raging hormones.

I hitchhiked from upstate New York to Cape Cod. The drivers who picked me up were mostly men with grabby hands and one thing on their minds. I did what I needed to do and got where I needed to go. And sometimes I got a cash tip.

I had no place to stay in P-town, but never underestimate the power of youth. Putting my backpack in a locker, I headed straight down Commercial Street—the center of the action—to the A-House.

I quickly established my bar persona, prancing around with a saffron-colored Indian bedspread wrapped around my head. I'd close my eyes and begin a wild interpretive dance: I'd kick up my legs, grunt like an animal and spin like a whirling dervish. My improvisational spectacle was a sordid cross between Isadora Duncan and Sandy Dennis in *Who's Afraid of Virginia Woolf*—"I dance like the winnnnnnnd." Whenever someone asked to dance with me, I'd look them straight in the eye, channel my Lithuanian mother, and say: "I vant to be alone!"

This pockmarked, wild-haired hippie boy soon became a celebrated A-House character.

That was the summer the San Francisco underground theater troupe Angels of Light came to P-town. One evening, a dark and handsome man from the Angels approached and insisted that I should move to San Francisco. He swore there were lots of folks "like me" there and I'd fit right in. His words would be prophetic.

Since I still lacked a place to crash, I counted on my wiles for that, too. Each night after last call, I would hit the "meat rack" in front of Town Hall, joining a line-up of men looking to score. I learned quickly to pose seductively and barter my naturally sculpted body for a bed to sleep on.

After several obligatory hotel-based one-nighters, I finally met someone with his own pad. His name now escapes me, but he was in "the theater" (translation: a trust fund baby). He had a mane of long, unkempt, blond hair, a leather jacket and tight, torn jeans. I especially remember his smell: a mixture of cigarette breath, patchouli, Crisco, and the residue of anal sex. He was alternately hot and gross. He made me an offer I couldn't refuse; he'd put me up if I put out. I now had more permanent lodgings.

His beachfront cabana was perfect, right off the main square. The sex part of this devil's bargain sucked; his fucking was often bloody and painful. Still, as I lay on the stained sheets afterwards and listened to the Atlantic Ocean roar, I fantasized I was Liz Taylor in *The Sandpiper*. Minus Dick.

I was his trophy trick, his prize piece of ass. But in public, he belittled me and treated me like I was a dumb callboy. Probably in retaliation for all the attention I got at the A-House. After all, I was young, "frisch fleisch" as the Germans say, and he was nearly thirty — over the hill in gay years.

This "relationship" lasted several weeks. After yet one more suffocating night in bed, he asked what I wanted to do with my life.

"I want to be an actor."

He burst out in dismissive laughter. "Not with that faggy voice!" Here I thought I would be the next Paul Newman, but he was treating me like Paul Lynde.

That summer of 1974 was also the height of the Watergate scandal. In between wild A-House nights and being blondie's pet, I'd sneak off to search for anywhere that had a television. I remember how excited I was at 9 pm on that humid night of August 9th as I watched Richard Nixon resign through the plate glass of a closed appliance shop. History was being made as I was experiencing the beginnings of my own personal liberation.

But summers never last. So back to Binghamton I went. It was the fall semester of my senior year, and my remaining time at university would be filled with all the required classes I had put off taking: math, science, and (ick) gym.

Mark Twain once wrote: "Some people get an education without going to college. The rest get it after they get out." A decision had to be made. I realized that my most useful education had come from the bars, bathrooms and bedrooms, not the classroom.

So, after three-and-a-half years at SUNY Binghamton, at age 20, I officially became a college dropout. Of course, the news didn't sit well with my father, but I really didn't give a flying fuck what he thought. He wasn't paying for my education and I was having a ball rebelling.

At first I had no idea where to go. Then I remembered I had been enticed by an Angel of Light at the A-House in P-Town, who assured me I would find kindred spirits in San Francisco.

Act 1, Scene 5 – AN ANGEL GETS HIS WINGS

On a cold autumn morning in 1974, Ponce and I boarded the fabled Green Tortoise bus in Manhattan for the trip to California. Ponce, I suspect, thought this trip would at last make us lovers. I loved him, but not in that way. I just wanted a one-way ticket to freedom.

The Green Tortoise was famous for bringing idealistic young folks with cross-country dreams to the Golden West. A ticket on "the hippie bus," as it was colloquially known, got you floor mattresses, psychedelic posters, a thick haze of marijuana smoke and a wild assortment of kooky characters.

It was a long, mythical, romantic trip. Simon & Garfunkel's evocative "America" was on a continuous loop in my mind as we passed wheat fields, desolate plains and snow-capped mountains. Along the way, we'd anchor in middle-of-nowhere rest stops, filled with lonesome cowboys, truckers on speed and smelly toilets. Still there was no time to trick; barely time for a tinkle.

It was onward to California and at last that moment of wonderment. The San Francisco-Oakland Bay Bridge. As we crossed it, the hills and spires of the City came into view, rising up from the sparkling waters of the Bay. I was rocking back and forth wildly, in a mixture of deep agitation and divine excitement.

Ponce and I landed at his friend's pad on Francisco Street in North Beach, the storied turf of beatnik poets and topless dancers. Our first days were filled with wonder: We strolled the neighborhood that was fragrant with espresso—in those days, an exotic concoction found only in Italian enclaves. I adored the clang, clang, clang of the trolley on the incredibly steep streets.

Zing went the strings of my heart as I encountered for the first time some of the city's other magical sites. There, on Dolores Street standing tall, the first palm tree I'd ever seen. There, the Haight-Ashbury, a kaleidoscopic neighborhood with swirling, brightly colored murals. There, queens in tight bell-bottoms and high platform shoes strutting their stuff down Polk Street.

Polk Strasse, as it was nicknamed, was the epicenter of the gay scene in the early '70s. It was lined with bars, boutiques, and side streets catering to johns looking for a cheap trick. Ponce and I both found jobs in a new gay restaurant called the QT. In my dorm days at Binghamton, I had worked as a dishwasher. That qualification—plus my tight, young ass—got the owner's attention. He pretended to scour my resume while he looked me up and down (mostly down). I was hired.

As I dodged waiters' advances, I got my first exposure to the uncensored lingo of dishy queens.

"Oh girl, she's tired."

"I betcha that tacky queen has got a big dick."

"That megasaur ass probably spends all her time on Planet Uranus."

I knew I wasn't in Binghamton anymore.

I took the day shift, and Ponce took the night shift. Our work schedules now separated us. We drifted apart. And a brand new world was about to open for me.

One day on the 7 Haight bus, a handsome man took the seat next to mine.

"Hi, remember me?"

"Ummmm," I replied nervously.

"My name is Gregory. I met you at the A-House in P-Town. I told you that you would love it in San Francisco. Well, you're here now. Welcome."

I was too shy to say anything but thanks.

Gregory suddenly mentioned that he and his friends were planning a big show. He suggested coming by 1140 Oak Street.

"Do I have to audition?" I queried with a puzzled look on my pimpled face.

"No, you'll see. Just come by," he whispered. With a wink and a chuckle, Gregory pulled the metal cord to signal his stop.

I could hardly contain myself. My first month in town, I was already being called to a life in the theater. I had no idea what the play was about, or if this was all one big scam to get me in bed.

But what did I have to lose? The next day, I dressed in hippie regalia, my signature saffron Indian bedspread wrapped around my head.

I arrived at the corner of Oak and Divisadero and stood before a huge, funky Victorian home. I nervously climbed the concrete staircase to the large entrance under a wooden arch. As I raised my hand to knock, the door flung open. There stood a drowsy barefoot hippie with a beer can. He had jet-black frazzled hair and a huge welcoming smile with a missing tooth. I asked for Gregory.

"Come on in; my name is Tony Angel," the hippie said with a slight slur. "We're in the middle of rehearsal." Then quickly assessing me, he shrieked, "Oh my god, YOU'D BE GREAT IN OUR SHOW!"

No appointment, no audition. I knew I was entering an alternate universe.

I felt like Alice entering the Rabbit Hole. Tony Angel was the White Rabbit, and the large room, lined with full-length wall mirrors and glitter-covered cardboard set pieces, held a welcoming group of eccentrics.

There were mad hatters, queens of all colors, and lots of smoking caterpillars. Many sipped herbal potions appropriate for this tea party.

They were in the midst of rehearsing their next Angels of Light extravaganza, *Paris Sites Under the Bourgeois Sea*. The plot, whispered Tony, revolved around a group of peasants, gypsies, and freaks during the French Revolution, oppressed by a trio of evil countesses costumed in overdone Versailles-style wigs topped with paper maché toilets. The peasants get the plague, ransack the chateau, carry out a revolution and liberate the people. It ends with a rainbow of ribbons and Ho Chi Minh dancers waving Viet Cong flags.

Our Town this was not. But I was intrigued. I stayed.

During a rehearsal break, an exotic creature with wild red-henna-dyed hair and a huge nose ring came rushing toward me. He was decked out in a gypsy peasant skirt that rustled with petticoats, and a gazillion jangly rainbow-colored bracelets.

"Hi, my name is Tede Matthews," he said in a high nasal voice filled with breathless excitement. "You'd be perfect as my gypsy sister."

I'd never even considered performing in drag. But hell, my mom was nicknamed Gypsy and always claimed to be a gypsy princess. What queen could resist playing his own mother? I agreed. I even had a name ready: Marija.

Tede spun like a dervish. "I love it! Marija. What an unusual name. You look like a Marija, and after I get you up in drag you'll *feel* like a Marija. Oh, you'll be such a pretty drag queen. Come to rehearsal tomorrow at one o'clock, and we'll start to write your part."

Thus began my drag career in underground San Francisco theater.

Thanks to savings from my odd jobs during college, I was able to quit my job at the QT. Then, I found a room at Haight and Ashbury, the most famous corner in San Francisco. Our flat was populated by straight stoners, squealing rodents, and giant cockroaches. It was a dump. But it was $50 a month. And it was a room with a view.

Each day I would scamper over to the Angels' funhouse to be schooled about the history and politics of the group. The Angels of Light were an offshoot of the Cockettes, an infamous avant-garde theater troupe formed in 1969. While the Cockettes were primarily gay men (the singer Sylvester was their breakout star), the Angels were a mix of men and women, both gay and straight, outrageous drag queens and devoted hippie mamas. The Angels also added leftist politics.

Most members lived at the Oak Street Commune. Each was a refugee from the straight-laced world. Many had taken new names: Beaver, Tahara, Jet, Indian, and Radha. Everyone in the collective had responsibility for rearing the children, and no one had their own bedroom. There were ever-changing sexual relationships, gay men pining for straight ones, and most women hot for the gay guys. Everyone was invited to explore every aspect of his or her sexuality. Monogamy was a no-no.

The Angels' house was strictly vegetarian. With one exception: Each time a child was born, the protein-rich placenta was fried and served at the evening's feast. It was a blessed ritual.

Day-to-day decisions were made at house meetings, and each person carried equal weight. The shows were written collectively. There was no director (although everyone was a director). Angels pooled money from various sources to finance food, clothes and show production. Plus there was a little help from the government.

Like church, the Angels believed theater was sacred and no admission should be charged. Shows were low-budget productions that combined vision, imagination, and artistry. Lavish sets were whipped up from cardboard boxes wildly painted and covered with buckets of glitter. The empty paint cans housed makeshift theater lighting.

Never before had I been exposed to such an alternative way of life. It was so sweetly utopian; *Children of Paradise* meets *Hair*. Everyone was encouraged to participate in all aspects of the theater, and each person with a specific talent was encouraged to teach classes. I taught Afro-Haitian dance, inspired by a class I took while at college. The sight of a white boy with no rhythm conducting this class was something to behold.

I was taught how to make costumes by Beaver Bauer in the basement sewing room, stitching satin tuxedo jackets for the tap-dancing penguins production number. "Beavsy" became a friend for life.

I learned more about theater and life at Oak Street in one week than I did in three years at Binghamton. And I had a new, supportive and loving family.

As the script of *Paris Sites* took shape, my part as the gypsy flower girl in the middle of the plague blossomed. I was to open the show by singing a song written by Tede with the soaring chorus: "We're tired of being hungry and poor; crusts of bread satisfy us no more. It's hard to believe that this is all real; soon you aristocrats will know how it feels."

But best of all, I got to show off the unique talent I had developed as a child. In formulating the plague scene, Radha had suggested that folks stricken by the disease become demented, possessed, and sexually crazed. She asked if anyone had any ideas.

I immediately perked up. I explained that I was double-jointed. Then in an inspired bit of improvisation, I threw my feet behind my neck and straddled the floor on my hands. Like a deranged banshee, I screamed, "Fuck me, fuck meeeeeeeeee."

The other actors broke out into applause.

But a controversy around my act soon erupted. *Paris Sites* was to be performed for two nights at the War Memorial Veterans Theatre, an historic house where the United Nations Charter was signed. We learned that city officials would be in attendance, including someone from the mayor's office. Would a crazed queen in a freakish pose (and costumed in a shitty diaper), screaming, "Fuck me" be in the best interest of the group?

An impassioned debate lasted several hours. Some argued that we shouldn't compromise our art and must resist self-censorship. Others countered that we would undermine potential fame if we alienate our audience. I simply sat silently, rocking.

Finally, they reached a consensus. The double-jointed kid shouting, "Fuck me!" in the shitty diaper stayed. The people united shall never be defeated!

*Tede Matthews and myself in the opening
scene of "Paris Sites Under the Bourgeois Sea."
That's Gregory Cruickshank peeking behind us.*

The crowds that came to War Memorial Veterans Theatre were a show in themselves. They were "dressed to the tits"—in everything from leather chaps to evening gowns; and "ripped to the titties"—high on a multitude of drugs. Peeking through a hole in the curtain, I could see they were revved and ready.

When the curtain opened, I was the only person onstage. I was met with a deafening roar from the audience—almost like a giant animal noise. No doubt they were applauding the elaborate sets and not me, but I didn't care. I was immediately hooked on the opiate of San Francisco audiences.

The symbiosis between audience and performer was intoxicating, psychedelic. And when my star turn arrived in the middle of the show, I dropped into position and crawled across the stage on my hands, screeching, "Fuck me, fuck meeeeeeee!"

The crowd went wild. A star was born.

The infamous plague scene of "Paris Sites Under the Bourgeois Sea."
That's me screaming "Fuck meeeeeee!" on the right.
Photo by Daniel Nicoletta.

Act 1, Scene 6 – SHOWSTOPPER

After my two-night triumph in *Paris Sites*, things were looking up. Tede Matthews invited me to move into his legendary Castro Street collective.

Tede's flat was at 529 Castro Street, steps away from 18th Street and smack in the heart of the bustling Castro neighborhood, which was destined to become ground zero for the queer community.

I faced a steep rent increase—from $50 to $120 month—but I was determined to find a way to afford such extravagance. After all, I loved the area; it was now the heart of Gay Mecca! The streets were bustling with bars, late-night hangouts, 24/7 cruising, and gay-owned businesses.

Harvey Milk's Castro Camera was just up the street at 575 Castro. Harvey had yet to be dubbed "The Mayor of Castro Street." But we knew that he was an up-and-coming force in San Francisco politics, and his cramped camera store was an exciting hubbub of burgeoning gay activism.

Tede's Castro Street flat was the epicenter for the farthest left of left-wing types. Lots of rebels with causes. There I also met my first dykes with beards, wannabe working-class heroes and an eccentric dressed in multicolor rags named "The Cosmic Lady" who babbled metaphysical nonsense.

Like the Angels of Light Oak Street house, we functioned as a commune, in theory a haven of egalitarian living. Yet like many political activists, Tede was chockfull of contradictions. He was always off to some "working-class caucus." Yet he did zero work around the house. And I was treated like Cinderella, before the ball—cooking, cleaning, scouring the dirty floors, and baking organic whole wheat bread.

During our weekly house meetings, we'd have a section called "criticism/self-criticism" based on Maoist tenets. It was a version of commie confession, where we'd pour out our hearts and souls and list our defects in the quest for a gay revolution. Tede would bully his way through these discussions, avoiding any critique that he was just a lazy-ass queen with a big mouth.

Early San Francisco days.
Photo by Marshall Rheiner.

To be fair, Tede exposed me to a worldview that included gay politics, feminist teachings, and alternative art, literature, and music. Although if I had to hear those damn albums by lesbian folkies Holly Near, Meg Christian, and Chris Williamson one more time…

Tede and our flat would later be immortalized in the landmark 1977 documentary "Word Is Out." Tede was the "colorful" one, decked out with oversized multicolored wooden beads; crucifixes hung upside down, a Ken doll in a tutu, etc. And if you see the film today, you can see a picture of Tede and I as gypsy sisters in the background.

Meanwhile, after my double-jointed triumph in *Paris Sites*, the Angels invited me into their next cabaret show, *Mein Kamp* at their cozy Valencia Street studio theater. Best of all, I could choose my own number.

Having already caused a small sensation playing my mother, why quarrel with success? When not scolding or beating us, my mother would sing us wonderful songs until we fell asleep. One of her faves was the Gershwin classic "Someone to Watch Over Me." And it was also sung with great drunken angst in *The Helen Morgan Story*, a "Million Dollar Movie" starring Ann Blyth.

What better tribute to both my mom and Helen Morgan (via Ann Blyth) than playing a boozy drag torch singer named Ellen Organ? I gave Miss Organ a swept-to-the-side flaming red hairdo and Mom's deep Lithuanian accent.

Unexpectedly, the older queens in the group objected to my debut solo.

"That song has been done to death by every bad drag queen in town!" they bitched.

Well, I assured them, not the way I was going to do it.

What I lacked in vocal talent, I more than made up in "give," a style of overacted, hyper-dramatic performing that made for camp. And my drag was flawless—a salmon-colored moiré satin ball gown purchased at Goodwill, topped off with a shimmering gold lamé shawl and matching orange marigold in curly hennaed hair. It screamed Ellen Organ!

The first night of the run, I was a hit.

On the second night, I was a smash—but not in the way I had hoped.

Ellen Organ in all her glory.
Photo by Daniel Nicoletta.

In the middle of the number, I lunged into a melodramatic monologue, befitting a tortured torch singer whose man had gone away. On a chair was a glass bottle filled with dead weeds and brown water. My impassioned speech went like this: "These are the flowers he gave me. Weeds! Here, take them, I don't want them anymore."

At that point I was to take swig of the dirty water and fling the flowers into the audience in disgust. But I was so out of control I flung the bottle too! It flew over much of the audience and smashed into the head of a hippie in the house. Blood splattered out of a large gash, all over his black leather jacket.

My number was literally a showstopper! An ambulance was called, and the hapless hippie rushed to the hospital where he got six stitches. (Only years later did I learn my victim was into S&M and he relished his battle scar.)

The whole damn thing was so humiliating. So I went into hiding for a week, rocking furiously in my darkened Castro Street room. Perhaps I wasn't suited to be a drag queen superstar, after all? Maybe it was time to find a new profession.

Act 1, Scene 7 – A FIRST FILM FESTIVAL AND SOMETHING TO VOTE FOR!

The flung bottle cut short my life in the theater. It was time to get over playing my mother and concentrate on other creative pursuits.

I had always loved cinema and seen my life as a series of scenes from the movies. Hell, since moving to the Bay Area, I was practically living in a freakin' Fellini film. So, why not become a filmmaker!

Gay San Francisco was filled with folks ready for their close-ups, and orbiting around the Angels was a cast of colorful people tailor-made for the movies. The most striking was Silvana Nova, who named himself after the Italian film star Silvana Mangano, Tadzio's aristocratic mother in Visconti's *Death in Venice*. Silvana was a tall, elegant bird-like creature, with a distinctive sloping nose. He was highly educated and radiated an effete touch of class.

To make movies you need to watch a shitload of them, and Silvana became a perfect partner for my cinematic explorations. We would often inhale triple features at the Times Theatre in Chinatown—watching the works of Bernardo Bertolucci, Francois Truffaut, Ingmar Bergman, Satyajit Ray, and Busby Berkeley. The most influential to my ornate taste were the Josef von Sternberg / Marlene Dietrich extravaganzas. Inspired, I fancied myself a gay Svengali with Silvana my Marlene, and thrust headlong into the wonderful world of Super 8 filmmaking.

I enrolled in film classes at City College of San Francisco and cranked out a flick once a month. What I lacked in money,

I made up for in imagination. Each class project became a drag mini-epic, with twisted titles like *Poodle Poo Miracle Mask, Cliché in the Afternoon,* and *Miracle on Sunset Boulevard.* My crowning glory was *The Basket Case,* a convoluted yet fabulous mash-up of *The Wizard of Oz, Carrie* and *The Sugarland Express,* starring Mx. Nova and her dog Pupaya. It offered no-budget spectacle, social commentary, and lots of ketchup for blood.

Now a prolific filmmaker, I needed to buy and develop vast amounts of Super 8 film. The only place to go was a half-block away from my apartment: Castro Camera, owned by Harvey Milk and his lover Scott Smith.

I had met Harvey Milk initially through Tede Matthews, who nicknamed him Marvey Cream—considering him a suit-and-tie sellout to his earlier radical roots. But there was little doubt that Harvey was a mover and shaker, and the atmosphere of activity inside the Castro Camera drew you in.

Manning the front desk at Castro Camera was an adorable young waif named Danny Nicoletta. He looked about 13 years old. Danny was a photographer and filmmaker, and parenthetically, one of my fans (he had shot my Bay Area stage debut in *Paris Sites*). Danny and I had much in common: both East Coast kids (he was from Utica, NY) with showgal moms. We were born three days apart, both 1954 Christmas babies—Capricorn sisters! The connection was instant.

While Danny and I chatted at the front desk during my visits, other Super 8 gay filmmakers would drop off films for processing and join in our discussions on filmmaking. Eventually, we decided to support each other in creating a public exhibition for emergent film projects. We called it The Gay Film Festival of Super-8 Films.

Our ragtag group of hippies, nerds and filmmakers included Danny, Bern Boyle, Ric Mears, Wayne Smolen, Billy Miggens, Greg Gonzales, and David Gonzales. We formed a loose collective and met in my Castro Street flat.

I'd like to claim that I co-founded the festival out of some altruistic, utopian vision of a burgeoning new gay culture. But really I just wanted my ego stroked and my damn movies to show. And there was safety and power in numbers.

Our fledgling festival was loosely curated. Show up to a meeting and your film was most likely in. With one glaring exception. Rob Epstein's submission, which featured his lover John Wright naked in a bathtub, intercut with shots of his cat cleaning herself. The group decided his short was "not gay enough" and rejected it. Of course, Rob would eventually go on to win two Oscars for his groundbreaking documentaries: 1984's *The Times of Harvey Milk* and 1989's *Common Threads*.

My life was now dedicated to organizing the festival, writing press releases on a battered manual typewriter and copying them on a dilapidated Xerox machine. Silvana Nova designed the fire engine red poster and Neighborhood Arts donated the printing. Soon every telephone or streetlight pole on Castro Street was covered with our agitprop art advertising the festival.

The festival had a distinctive Mickey and Judy flavor. Instead of a barn, however, we booked (for next to nothing) a funky community space at 32 Page Street, run by gay activist Hank Wilson. Danny Nicoletta contributed a rickety Super 8 projector. We couldn't afford to rent a screen, so we hung a funky white bedsheet. I even ironed it!

On February 9, 1977, the festival was held. Echoing the Angels' philosophy, admission was free. Two hundred people arrived for a space that could only accommodate 100. The overflow was turned away. (Except for Harvey Milk, whom we ushered in.) Tobacco smoking was absolutely forbidden, but the sweet smell of pot perfumed the air. We ran the films, coping with the numerous film splices that broke and the audiocassette soundtracks going out of sync. The audience didn't care; they were there to see images of the lesbian and gay community, something rarely addressed by the Hollywood machine.

The poster for the first festival, designed by Silvana Nova.

Our maiden voyage spawned three other screening events that year and would later evolve into Frameline, now the oldest and largest LGBT international festival in the world. We had created something special.

1977 was also a benchmark year in San Francisco gay politics. Progressives had demanded and won the right to elect their supervisors by district. This ensured that their representatives would be more sensitive to the needs of their expanding multicultural and diverse neighborhoods, instead of beholden to downtown moneyed interests. Harvey Milk decided to make a bid for his neighborhood seat. Film drop-offs to Castro Camera became all the more exciting as Milk's supervisor campaign cranked into high gear.

Although Harvey's main competitor was a conservative gay businessman named Rick Stokes, the streets of the Castro became festooned with posters and placards from a slew of candidates representing the free-for-all nature of this first district election. One campaign poster featured a hunky mustached man in a flannel shirt, sitting atop the rocks of Twin Peaks. His slogan was "At Last Someone to Vote For," as if his bona fides for office were that his cojones were bulging out of his Levis.

This was the height of the Castro clone era, when most gay guys wanted to look super masculine, just like the Marlboro Man. No fats, fems or freaks allowed. I did not move to San Francisco to look like a lumberjack. Or a cop, or a soldier. To me, this whole butch thing was rather oppressive. And I was not alone.

So in response to the butch clone in the supervisor's race a few of us revolted. Our candidate for District 6: Silvana Nova!

Silvana was photographed in the same rocky summit of Twin Peaks. He was decked out in the highest of heels, a short, pleated black skirt hoisted high around his neck, black tights, a Pebbles Flintstone ponytail, and an exuberant Patti Labelle pose. As a rebuke to the clone slogan "At Last Someone to Vote For," ours was "At Last!! Some Thing to Vote For."

Late at night, poet Aaron Shurin, photographer Marshall Rheiner and I hit the Castro and plastered the hood with 11 x 17 Nova for Supervisor posters. Morning came and our gay dada street art was everywhere.

Come Election Day, of course we all voted for Harvey. And he was elected our first gay supervisor. That night there were real celebrations across San Francisco. History had been made.

Poster by Silvana Nova.
Photo by Marshall Rheiner.

Act 1, Scene 8 – AWOKE AND FIGHTING BACK

"Rights are won only by those who make their voices heard."

—Harvey Milk, The Harvey Milk Interviews

Although I was firmly planting roots in San Francisco, I was also itching to see other parts of the world. I was in the prime of my life and I wanted new experiences, new faces, new surroundings.

With my dwindling savings plus a small government subsidy, I booked a three-month sojourn to Europe. Off I went, with my student Eurail pass and my used Canon Super 8 camera in hand.

First stop, Gay Paree. I did the standard sight seeing. I dutifully visited the Louvre to get a glimpse of the smiling Mona Lisa. But my *real* destination was the adjacent Jardin des Tuileries, the famed cruising area. I spent days on the benches there, smiling and searching for sex. And finding it in spades.

I hit some of the other great ports of call in Europe: Vienna, Venice, Rome, Mykonos. And I became an expert on the many parks, beaches, and dank dark rooms where horny men were in ready supply.

But as I was fucking my way across Europe, there was disturbing news from the home front. Proposition 6, nicknamed "the Briggs Initiative" for the right-wing state senator who spearheaded it, would ban gays and lesbians from working in California's public schools. It was scheduled to appear on the 1978 statewide ballot.

John Briggs had been emboldened by the successful campaign to repeal a gay rights ordinance by "orange juice queen" Anita Bryant in Dade County, Florida. Early polling suggested Prop. 6

would pass, threatening to spark a national movement of oppression of gay and lesbian people. It had to be stopped.

Here I was, on the continent far away from home. What could I do? Well, I did have my Super 8 camera. I decided to weaponize it. I made an unplanned stop to the grounds of the Dachau Concentration Camp. As I entered its gates, the spirits of the dead, including those of the many exterminated homosexuals, haunted and empowered me. I felt possessed.

I shot close-ups of the weathered train tracks, barbed wire fences, empty barracks, extermination ovens, rusted showerheads, and photos of the ill-fated prisoners that covered the walls in the austere museum. Then I shot contrasting images of the present tranquility at the site: skipping children, smiling tourists, even a baby in a carriage staring blankly at the camera in front of the crematorium.

During that day of filming at Dachau, I would often break out crying. But a slogan, etched in a stone museum monument, empowered me. It simply stated "Never Again." I saw parallels between the Nazi treatment of gays, forced from their jobs and made to wear pink triangles, and the situation of California teachers being called out of their classrooms, fired, and ostracized from society.

On the plane trip home, I conjured a fictional storyline to crosscut with the documentary footage from Dachau. It involved two now-elderly men reuniting in 1978 and reminiscing about one shared night of sex in 1930s Berlin and their subsequent incarceration in a concentration camp. I titled the script *Unity*.

I quickly got to work. I asked friends to act as players in the elaborate cabaret sequence where the two lovers meet. I would shoot the silent film in cheap, grainy, high-speed black-and-white Super 8, recreating the look of early German Expressionism. For the soundtrack, I would use Samuel Barber, Dietrich and the Adagietto from Mahler's 5th.

I realized this was a highly ambitious project for a City College student with little professional expertise, but I didn't care. It was a labor of love and passion.

I shot *Unity* at a feverish pace. Literally. Just before filming the complicated cabaret scene, I learned I had syphilis. I was immediately given a heavy dosage of penicillin. Under the hot lights and amid the frenzy of setting up multiple shots, I began sweating like a pig. My syphilitic fever, which had climbed to 103 degrees, was breaking right there on the set. My clothes were dripping wet. Funny, the cast of 20 thought it was artistic passion causing me to sweat buckets. Only I knew otherwise.

Shooting the cabaret sequence of "Unity" with Lulu.
Photo by Daniel Nicoletta.

The whole film was shot for $250. Again, Castro Camera developed my footage. The store also served as a key meeting and strategizing place for the "No on 6" activists. Opponents of the Briggs Initiative knew they were in the fight of a lifetime, and Harvey was the general to lead the battle.

It was during this intensely politicized period that I had a momentous face-off with Mr. Milk.

Remember that this was a time before Harvey became Saint Harvey Milk. While he was still alive Harvey was someone who could be challenged. And I was just the young, opinionated firebrand to do it.

Our fight centered on Harvey's strategy for the upcoming Pride March. One day Supervisor Milk, our de facto leader, dictated to everyone in the store, that due to the upcoming Briggs Initiative, all Pride marchers should be "presentable" to the masses. That is, toned-down versions of our regular exuberant selves.

He lobbied for a massive makeover: All men should dress respectably—preferably in suits and ties, and carry signs announcing their place of origin, as a visual reminder that we were everywhere. This would make us relatable to the straight world, since we desperately needed their votes. There should definitely be no drag queens or leathermen out in front, lest the news media zoom in on the "outrageous elements" within our ranks. And maybe it might be best if they stayed home.

To me, this was hogwash. Drag queens and outsiders populated my world. What was the point of our rights, if those rights were only for people who conform?

I got up the courage to contradict Mr. Milk, launching into an impassioned tirade about how some of us didn't want to dress down to be "normal." He listened to me, his signature smile intact, and then responded.

"This year, this is the way we need to move forward; otherwise we'll lose the election," Harvey stated.

"If we do that, we give up our individuality and honesty, and we lose," I said.

"You are wrong, my dear," Harvey countered.

"Don't condescend to me," I snapped, foam forming at the corners of my mouth.

And on and on went this *la ronde* of an argument, the volume rising between each point and counterpoint. Poor Danny Nicoletta sat quietly at the front desk, unwilling to get involved in a battle between his boss and his friend.

Harvey's thinking won the day. The 1978 San Francisco Pride Parade was both more blatantly political and decidedly toned down. But our little argument became a microcosm of an issue that persists to this day. Assimilation vs. self-expression. Projected reality vs. actual reality.

Harvey is remembered historically as an unabashed radical. But he actually was willing to bend toward the side of caution. And Harvey spoke passionately and convincingly during the campaign against Prop. 6, rallying the troops and influencing the hearts and minds of the mainstream California voting public.

I'll never forget the September evening our community packed an auditorium to watch a televised feed of a Prop. 6 debate taking place in Walnut Creek. Harvey and his historically under-appreciated debating partner, the eloquent San Francisco State Professor Sally Gearhart, squared off against the opposition. We all cheered boisterously as, point-by-point, Harvey and Sally destroyed John Briggs' dangerous agenda. At that moment, my earlier fight with Milk seemed insignificant. We were all in this together.

Act 1, Scene 9 – STRANGE FRUIT

Upon my return from Europe, I moved away from the frenzy of the Castro collective to Silvana Nova's large tasteful flat on Beulah Street across the street from Golden Gate Park.

Our Victorian home became the epicenter of my movie making. We christened it Beulahwood Studios. Silvana hung a hand-lettered sign proclaiming, "Give so more can live" alongside a picture of Italian actress Anna Magnani. This became our motto, and Magnani became our guiding goddess.

I continued churning out one film a month. Campy little chestnuts shot in glorious "tack-nicolor." Here too, I finally finished editing *Unity* on a teensy-weensy Super 8 splicer from Thrift Town. When I unveiled the 15-minute piece to a small group of friends, they were all in tears.

Since the Prop. 6 battle was in full fury, my film needed to be exhibited immediately for maximum effect. By this point I had also amassed an assortment of Beulahwood Studios shorts and a group of actors hankering to tread the boards.

So together we decided to put on a show! There would be skits and poetry, plus my short films—the centerpiece being *Unity*.

Strange Fruit became the show's title. Its theme—resistance to homophobic oppression and playful reimaginings of conventional identities by sissies, drag queens and dykes.

Our dedicated group for the evening included: Mx. Silvana Nova (and yes, Sil used the honorific Mx. decades before it was used to question binary gender identity); Reno, a boisterous East Coast dyke with a thick New Yawk accent, later to become a renowned performance artist; and Roseanne Johnson, a pioneering lipstick lesbian partial to thrift-store dresses and rhinestones. From the Gay Theater Collective came funnyman Tommy Pace and swanlike Michael Starkman.

"Strange Fruit" poster designed by Silvana Nova.
Photo by Daniel Nicoletta.

And then there was Lulu. I had met Lulu at the Albion Fair—a country gathering of hippies, rural homos, bikers, stoners, fats, femmes, fairies, fruits and fags, where people camped out in festooned tents dolled up like gypsy caravans. A precursor to Burning Man.

That night I dropped a tab of acid—something I did every six months for "spiritual cleansing." Under a crescent moon in the Albion forest, Lulu emerged, dressed in Moroccan-style flowing pantaloons, dark kohl accenting his sparkling blue eyes. He was a femme genie that popped out of a bottle. As I was peaking, Lulu morphed into a fierce, raging creature, with an infectious laugh that pierced the night. He became a kindred soul, a girlfriend for life. And one of my valued stock players.

With our group of artistic misfits in place, we gathered to write *Strange Fruit*. The script fucked with the rigid roles of gender, explored androgyny, and created exciting and colorful new modalities. I was the only man in the group that didn't do drag, stemming from my disastrous debut as Ellen Organ. But while outwardly butch, I felt like a drag queen trapped in a man's body, spawned by a mother that was a drag queen trapped in a woman's body.

One day during rehearsals, the postman delivered a letter from mama Marija. Inside was an audiocassette. Mom had a history of sending bizarre recordings to me, so I knew we were in for a treat. "Get a load of this," I hinted and played it for the group.

In the breathiest of Lithuanian-accented voices, she sang "Lili Marleen." It was eerily incestuous. She followed with the classic "I Wish You Love" and concluded with a personal message.

"Maaaaarc, alvays until the twelfth of never, I vish you much, much happiness. I miss you so sooo much. Auf wiedersehen my beautiful son, love always." And then, in a come-fuck-me voice, she signed off with "Mooooommmmm" as if she were having an orgasm.

The group shook their heads in disbelief. I simply shrugged, adding, "That's my mom." My strange fruit bona fides had been firmly established.

Like Mom, I had a touch of the poet. A few of my poems were published in the most radical gay journals of the era, including *Fag Rag* and *RFD*. So, I got to work revising the lyrics of the Billie Holiday classic "Strange Fruit" as an anthem denouncing the oppression of drag queens. It was to be the show's somber opening number.

Afterwards, Candidate Nova would jubilantly burst through a paper screen, cracking a few jokes about his rival for supervisor, Harvey Milk: "I'm not bitter. After all, only in San Francisco can a true wreck run for office—and win."

Reno and the brilliant Tommy Pace—and I keep using that adjective to describe him, as he was one of the few comic geniuses

I have ever met—would then perform a satirical confrontation between a dyke and drag queen set in the ladies' room.

(Tommy is applying makeup in the mirror)

RENO (brusquely to the drag queen)—Hey, this is the women's room. Why don't you go to the men's room where you belong?

TOMMY (sweetly)—Because, darling, the men's room is dirty and the men's room is smelly and the men's room has a lousy mirror.

RENO—Yeah, so you can put on makeup and dresses that make fun of women!

TOMMY—Oh honey, I'm not making fun of women.

RENO—Then what are you wearing a dress for?

TOMMY—Well dear, someone's got to do it.

I also contributed an anti-clone screed to the show. Here's a taste:

"It's like sleeping with the enemy," I said
"Gay freedom meaning to you release of cum from that hard gun
Forming bullets sticky white on your suppliant mustache," I said
He said, "Why the cynicism, bitch, fit in you've got the mold"
I said, "I fit that mold sir but I'm burning in its stinking plastic"

Our cultural work seemed important, done at a time when our community was percolating with new ideas and fierce creativity.

And just upstairs from the theater of the Gay Community Center at 330 Grove Street, *real* gay history was being made. On the top floor, community artist Gilbert Baker was creating and stitching together a massive rainbow flag. We watched the process in awe. On breaks from rehearsals, we'd clock its progress and cheerlead Gilbert and his buoyant crew, their hands dripping with dye. Little did we know this eight-color banner would become the symbol of our movement and that Gilbert would become the community's Betsy Ross.

Strange Fruit was a smash—sold-out, held over, and playing several venues. It fostered a conversation on gender, which would only flourish in the coming years. I consider it the fairy godmother to *RuPaul's Drag Race*.

Act 1, Scene 10 – DARK NOVEMBER

November 7, 1978, was a joyous day in California. By a substantial margin—58.4 percent to 41.6 percent—Proposition 6, the anti-gay Briggs Initiative, was defeated. Months before, polls suggested that the initiative would easily pass. But through the grassroots efforts of the LGBT community and our allies, we brought together enough voters to overcome this threat and score an important victory. San Francisco had helped turn the tide on homophobia, and shown the world how to create a more inclusive world. Or so we thought.

On November 18, just nine days later, in Guyana, South America, the Reverend Jim Jones instructed his primarily Bay Area followers to drink poisoned Kool-Aid from a large metal vat. In the end, 918 people died, including 276 children. The Jonestown Massacre would become the largest mass suicide in history.

Before Jim Jones's Peoples Temple had migrated to Guyana, the mother church was located at 1859 Geary Blvd., blocks away from the Angels of Light commune. I'd often look out the windows of the 22 Fillmore bus on Sunday afternoons, and spot worshippers in their colorful hats and festive finery. Joy seemed to surround them. Churchgoers were also actively engaged in San Francisco politics, bussed in to rallies for progressive candidates, including Mayor George Moscone and Supervisor Harvey Milk. Just like the Angels, the Peoples Temple flock had visions of changing the planet.

But after the congregation left San Francisco to build their new utopia, the dream became a nightmare. And in one fateful day, all their hopes were shattered. The gruesome images out of the Guyana jungle were haunting: grotesque, swollen corpses of men and women—even babies and grandparents—dead in this real-life heart of darkness.

How could this have happened? How could we have all been so blind to the megalomania of Jim Jones, a charismatic leader we once respected? How could something that started out as a visionary social dream turn into such a ghoulish horror?

An introspective sadness hung over San Francisco. We all looked to escape from the lunacy that had gripped the city. And fuck, I just wanted to have a good time.

So just nine days later, November 27, I boarded the 71 Noriega bus for Sproul Plaza in Berkeley to attend a free concert by the up-and-coming band Talking Heads. I was obsessed with their infectious, irreverent, and edgy hit New Wave single "Psycho Killer." Its lyrics seemed apropos to this particular moment in our history.

It was a beautiful crisp autumn day, perfect for an outdoor event. Folks on the half empty bus were going about their daily business. Many were reading the *San Francisco Chronicle*, absorbed in the latest turn of events from Jonestown, As the bus turned the corner of Steiner and Page, a man stormed on with a portable transistor radio. "The mayor and Harvey Milk have just been shot at City Hall," he cried out.

People immediately stopped what they were doing. There was an audible gasp. My mouth fell open, but nothing came out. Instinctively I jumped off the bus and ran several blocks to City Hall.

The gathering crowd was standing in stone-cold silence, heads shaking in disbelief. Zombie-like. Directionless. The numbers swelled as the shocked and saddened spontaneously congregated. Even Tede Matthews, often critical of Harvey, was there.

Grief-stricken, we stood in front of the golden dome of our spectacular City Hall. Rebuilt after the 1906 earthquake, it was both a reminder of past resilience and a symbol of the gay community's hard-fought freedoms. Now we were experiencing the aftershock of an existential emotional earthquake. We all felt numb.

Board President Dianne Feinstein announced the suspect in custody was Supervisor Dan White—a political adversary to Milk and Moscone. Beyond the human toll of two lives taken in their prime, White's murders were also deeply symbolic: he had murdered both our first elected gay official and the most progressive mayor in a generation.

First Jonestown, then this. A dark cloud had enveloped San Francisco, swallowing it whole. San Francisco had been our Emerald City. But Oz died that day.

As dusk descended, we marched in unison, tens of thousands, down Market Street, led by somber, mournful drums. Each of us carried a candle. We hoped so many small candles could magically become a blinding beacon of light. But magic eluded our aching town. Shivering and cold, we held each other.

On the steps of City Hall, Joan Baez, our own Joan of Arc, belted out "Amazing Grace." Her inspired voice echoing through the cavernous city streets.

None of us wanted to leave City Hall that night; going home would be a sad and lonely journey. As we blew out our candles, we knew a light in our fair city had been extinguished that day. Things would never be the same.

Act 1, Scene 11 – LOST & FOUND

It was July 15, 1979. Wrapped only in a towel, eating my reheated Dinty Moore stew from a vending machine, I was glued to a TV set next to the sauna at the Club Baths. President Jimmy Carter, elected in a wave of optimism, was now speaking of the malaise that gripped our nation. His somber words: "We can see this crisis in the growing doubt about the meaning of our own lives and a unity of purpose for our nation."

This deep despair might have reigned supreme in the outside world, but it was abandoned when you entered the Club Baths. Every Tuesday night there was a two-dollar special. It was the best bargain in town—entitling you to a locker, a steam room, porno on a large screen, a smorgasbord of sexual opportunities, and the best music in town.

And it was there at Eighth and Howard Streets that I had a life-changing experience. It started innocently enough. High on pot, I walked from my locker down the long hallway, past mirrored rooms where men lay in seductive poses, many with their asses up in the air, ready to be plowed. I entered into the sea of darkness that was the orgy room. As I groped strangers, I suddenly heard a strong female voice through the speakers. It began reciting quiet prose that gave way to the pulsing, pounding beat of hardcore rock and roll.

And it was speaking directly to me.

Hearing Patti Smith's "Horses" for the first time, in this setting, was a religious experience. That orgasmic song, filtered through the rush of poppers, with naked male bodies writhing all around, was like living in a Hieronymus Bosch painting. I didn't know whether it was *The Garden of Earthly Delights* or *The Last Judgment*. Heaven or hell. Or a mixture of both.

Patti's music was transportive, transgressive. It gave a loud, energetic middle finger to the present-day malaise. It was a kick in the ass and a kick in the balls. When I finally saw the cover of her LP, I found her divinely androgynous look—man's shirt and undone tie, looking straight into Robert Mapplethorpe's camera—revolutionary.

I became a born-again punk rocker. I bid farewell to my free love, hippie mindset and embraced the hard edge of leather jackets and fuck-you attitudes. Accordingly, I chopped off my soft Pre-Raphaelite curls and soon sported a severe, *Eraserhead* bouffant. Shaved on the sides, puffed high in the middle, and dyed jet-black.

I eschewed the politically correct didacticism of gay liberation and the hardcore left in favor of the multiple freaks and artists in my midst. Life became exciting again.

My friends and I leapt into the revitalized underground San Francisco scene. It was ablaze with activity, concerts and endless edgy events. Monday nights we'd go to the Cafe Flore, a boho hangout in the Castro, for a twilight gathering of punks. Then it was off to the Stud, a legendary gay bar, for Punk Night, where we'd pogo our asses off in the mosh pit screaming "I Wanna Be Sedated." Tuesday, the Club Baths were filled with a growing cadre of art fags lured by the mind-blowing music DJ Alan Robinson was spinning. Other nights we'd frequent the Mabuhay Gardens, a Filipino restaurant in North Beach turned punk palace. The "Fab Mab" featured early concerts by later-famous groups like Devo, X, and the Ramones. It also nurtured homegrown acts: Dead Kennedys fronted by Jello Biafra, the Nuns, and Crime.

The rest of the week featured parties, openings in funky galleries, wild industrial installations created by mad scientists like Mark Pauline. And concerts at the On Broadway, I-Beam, Deaf Club, everywhere. They were populated by an eclectic mix of artists, straight and gay, not segregated by the stifling monikers of sexual preference.

Friends were forming bands of their own: Tuxedomoon, Pink Section, the Wasp Women, Indoor Life, Factrix, Voice Farm, and Noh Mercy.

My film work was also given new inspiration. Beulahwood Studios had been disbanded. The era of collective creativity had come and gone. I was now living alone on the corner of 18th and Guerrero, a more neutral neighborhood, away from the constant energy of the Castro or the Haight. I found introspection suited me.

Meanwhile *Unity* began to screen at international film festivals, even winning several awards, most notably in Caracas, Venezuela. It was named 1st runner-up at the Student Academy Awards (losing to an up-and-comer named Eddie Muller). And I got an out of the blue phone call from Tom Luddy of Francis Ford Coppola's American Zoetrope studios. He'd just previewed *Unity* for the San Francisco Film Festival and found it impressive.

"It reminded me of classic movies from the German Expressionist period. I think you are on your way to become quite a strong filmmaker." Luddy continued: "We would like to screen your film at the Castro Theatre as part of the Bay Area Filmmakers Showcase."

I was on cloud nine. Luddy was well known in international film circles and a co-founder of the Telluride Film Festival. He'd just produced Philip Kaufman's remake of *Invasion of the Body Snatchers*. He knew film, inside and out. If he thought so highly of my no-budget short, then I had found my calling. And my movie would be on the big screen at the legendary 1400 seat Castro Theatre!

The Showcase's catalog write-up lifted my spirits: "*Unity* is Marc Huestis' fine prize-winning short. A film of texture and mood... an elegiac memory piece." (I had to look up "elegiac.")

This screening gave me strength and confidence for new film work. In the early days of my filmmaking, I fed off the power of the activated gay community. Now I found fresh inspiration in punk rock.

The first influence of this new music on my films came in a convoluted working-class vampire short called *Transfusion*, followed by *X-Communication*, a bizarre, Cocteau-inspired fever dream about a tortured young artist who kills himself by eating a piece of glass. Very graphic, very experimental. And very, very silly.

Still, these films gained enough attention to get me named one of "the enfants terribles" of San Francisco's underground movie scene and to appear on the cover of an influential punk publication with fellow filmmakers Erich Brogger (who had also starred in *X-Communication*) and Mary Bellis. Inside, an extended interview allowed me to babble on about my philosophies of life and film. It was pretentious stuff. But it was also exciting.

Puffed up, I decided to take Erich's, Mary's and my films on the road. Erich had befriended Ann Magnuson, who managed Club 57, right in the heart of the East Village in lower Manhattan. Located at 57 Saint Marks Place, this converted Polish church basement-cum-nightclub featured countercultural events spotlighting up-and-comers Madonna, Cyndi Lauper, Klaus Nomi, the B-52s, John Sex, and Joey Arias, as well as wild theme parties such as Putt-Putt Reggae miniature golf. Based on Erich's reputation, Magnuson agreed to screen our films there one night! I was hankering to make a brand new start of it in old New York.

Act 1, Scene 12 – MY VAGABOND SHOES

I arrived in NYC in the summer of 1980 primed for the Club 57 gig. Although I had grown up in Long Island, and made many trips to visit my dad at the NBC tape room inside 30 Rock, I felt like I was discovering Manhattan for the first time. I was now an adult.

Just as Tony Angel opened the door to my enchanted experiences at the Angels' commune in San Francisco, he was about to open the curtain on a brand-new world in the big city. Tony, who was straight, was proudly bicoastal. He spent his summers creating sets for the street shows produced by the Theater for the New City, one of the leading Off-Off-Broadway theaters—and, as fate would have it, a block away from Club 57. "Why don't you come to New York and help paint the scenery? And you can crash at the theater."

Upon dropping anchor at Theater for the New City, I was introduced to Crystal Field, one of its founders. She was a short, rotund and energetic woman with a thick mane of curly hair.

"I feel like I know you from somewhere," I found myself blurting out.

"Did you see the film *Splendor in the Grass?*" Crystal responded. "I played Hazel. Natalie Wood's best girlfriend. I'm in the last scene in the car before she meets Warren Beatty at the farm."

"I make movies too," I replied, quickly realizing how stupid and self-serving that sounded. Crystal smiled and welcomed me into the New City family.

In the theater's wardrobe room, Tony had set up a makeshift dorm. Several mattresses were splayed across the unswept floor, and the room reeked of mold and make-up. There were a few other San Franciscans headquartered there: *Strange Fruit* alum Tommy Pace; Phillip Russe, a handsome but wackadoodle character with whom I had had a brief affair in San Francisco; and Annie Crawford, an ex-junkie with a heart of gold who had to be the ugliest woman I had ever met. It was a roomful of misfit toys.

Each day was brimming with boho adventure. Around noon, Tommy would serve as my human alarm clock. He would bend down and whisper a phrase he had picked up at the piers from a Puerto Rican street queen. In a thick *chica* accent, he'd purr, "Did he beat you, girl, did he beat you? He's not a real man unless he beats you." As I opened my eyes, Tommy would switch to a falsetto version of the Debbie Reynolds hit "Tammy." I'd roll out of bed in hysterics and ready to greet the world.

We'd "breakfast" at B&H Dairy, chowing down on warm buttered challah or overstuffed cheese blintzes. Afterwards, we'd attempt to paint the sets. Tony would already be on his fifth beer, and we'd all be entertaining each other with our various routines, so we'd get precious little work done. Humid nights were reserved for Italian ices at the air-conditioned Veniero's Bakery. After a stroll down St. Mark's, always bursting with free-spirited energy, we'd take a disco nap.

Our late-night destination was often Danceteria, one of the hottest destinations for clubgoers. I knew doorman Haoui Montaug, a former San Franciscan who had performed in one of Tede Matthews' street theater skits. I also knew DJ Iolo, who had briefly lived with Silvana and me at Beulahwood. So, the red velvet ropes would open freely to our San Francisco entourage. Sometimes club owner Jim Fouratt would give us free drink tickets. Other New Yorkers would have killed for such carte blanche privilege. But the crew at the club saw us as kindred West Coast spirits.

Danceteria was a whirlwind of sounds and images: multiple floors framed by roving lights, wild dancing, an eclectic mix of music and video, and live shows.

The most memorable of those spectacles featured Nico. In the '60s, the Warhol superstar had been a slender, seductive, German-born blonde and deep-throated vocalist for the Velvet Underground. Nothing would prepare me for the Nico I saw that night. Onstage came a haggard, overweight frau in a muumuu, with dirty hennaed hair. Seated at a harmonium, she began to sing. Miraculously, her powerful voice filled the room, colored with deep melancholy. Her former majesty arose like the chords from her bizarre instrument, as her current state of dishevelment seemed to fade away. She was mesmerizing; and this performance, unforgettable.

When nightclubbing was over, urban nomads would arm themselves with posters, staple guns, buckets filled with wheat paste, and hit the streets. After all, this was the era of do-it-yourself self-promotion. With my upcoming show at Club 57, I joined their ranks to post flyers plugging my event.

On one such late-night Manhattan odyssey, on the corner of St. Mark's and First Avenue, I spied another artist furtively at work. A lanky man with curly hair and wire-frame glasses was spray-painting sidewalks in day-glo orange with the stenciled initials FAFH.

Not wanting to disturb him, I waited for him to finish. I then struck up a friendly conversation. I told him about my screening at Club 57. He told me he had some art pieces hung there.

I asked the graffiti artist what his tag, FAFH, meant.

"Fags against facial hair," he said, with a smirk on the nerdy, adorable baby face.

I immediately perked up. Being anti-clone, I was glad to meet another brother in the struggle.

"Why don't we meet for lunch?" I queried coquettishly.

"I'd like that!" He then offered a wheat-pasting tip. "Try using a spray bottle filled with Borden's condensed milk to put up your posters. It's indestructible."

Before he left, he shared his name. But I didn't have a pen or paper and quickly forgot it.

Next day we met for lunch at Dojo's, a vegetarian cafe on St. Mark's. My heart was going pitter-pat. He had a distinctive, oddly sexy look, reminiscent of the *Felix the Cat* cartoon character Poindexter. I definitely had a crush on this man. Of course, in those days, I had a crush on almost anyone under forty with two legs and a penis. But there seemed to be something special about this guy.

I ordered the tempura; what's-his-name had the famous $4 soy burger. He told me he grew up in Pennsylvania and loved drawing from an early age. He moved to the city to study painting. Beyond his current FAFH obsession, he was a struggling artist—picking lettuce in Long Island during the harvest season to make ends meet.

Between the noshing, I babbled on about my life story: Mother stripper, theater in San Francisco, underground filmmaker. Blah, blah, blah. It was a delightful afternoon; he was kind, smart, sensitive. A true gentleman. But I soon could tell that this brief encounter would be just a lunch between a pair of homos who hated facial hair.

As we parted, he reminded me to check out his work at Club 57. And I did. His art consisted of stick figures in motion. Cute, I thought, but rather elementary. Any child could do this; he'll never go anywhere. Then I peered at the small placard under the art. It read "Art by Keith Haring."

My film showing at Club 57 was anticlimactic. For all those evenings spent plastering the streets, only twenty people showed up. But I had made my mark.

And this New York summer had been magical, inspirational. I was meeting dynamic creative people and experiencing things that couldn't be found in San Francisco. My battery had been fully recharged.

Act 1, Scene 13 – INSIDE OUT

Upon returning to San Francisco, I decided to make one last go of my educational career—this time in the film department at San Francisco State University. Based on the strength of *Unity*, I was allowed to skip three grades and be placed as a senior with the added perk of visiting filmmaker Academy Award-nominated documentarian Bill Jersey becoming my mentor. And best of all, I would have access to 16mm equipment complete with sync sound. At last, talkies!

But funds were low and I didn't have film for my camera. That changed with a phone call from my dad.

"Hey Marc. I just heard that the news department at NBC is going completely to tape. They are getting rid of all their 16mm film. Could you use any?"

Like manna from heaven, courtesy of the National Broadcasting Network, I now had twenty hours of free color film! The rub was that its expiration date was rapidly approaching. I needed an idea for a film and I needed one quick.

Then, another light-bulb moment. A few years before, I had snatched up a cache of 16mm films from an open trashcan on Haight Street. Out of curiosity, I decided to project a few. Most were junk, but within the stack was an amazing find—a campy chestnut titled *The Outsider*.

This fifteen-minute black and white gem was produced by Young American Films, which specialized in '50s educational shorts with "important" messages for budding teenage minds. These were the kind of films you were forced to view in health class as you were dodging spitballs lobbed by the jocks.

The Outsider turned out to be an unintentionally funny cautionary tale, preaching conformity at all costs. It followed the trials of poor little Susan Jane Smith—a reclusive, tortured high school student with bad skin, even worse hair, no friends, and zero self-esteem.

Voiceover: "Susan? Susan Jane? What's the matter with you? Why is everyone else having such a good time when you're not?"

Enter Marcie Clark, a gregarious goody-goody with a southern twang. Determined to show poor Susan Jane how to "join in" and have a good time, warm-hearted Marcie invites her to "the Big Party."

Voiceover: "Well, Susan Jane, this is your big moment. You've fixed your hair and have on a pretty dress. And you've made up your mind not to act like an outsider. But is this enough? Will it work? Will the gang accept you, Susan Jane?"

The Outsider spoke to me. I *was* Susan Jane Smith. For several years this silly little film and its characters ruminated in my mind. Now the stockpile of free NBC film would facilitate their release.

My premise for the film was this: What if Susan Jane had grown up and moved to San Francisco, a city chock-full of outsiders? And what if stay-at-home Marcie Clark abandoned her straight-laced lifestyle to seek out her old friend?

The plot came together quickly. San Francisco, circa 1980. Susan Jane, who has changed her name to Sujana, is now a bohemian artist, running with poets, drag queens, and other assorted weirdoes. Yet like her teenage years, she remains discontent—an outsider among outsiders.

High school friend Marcie Clark, now a suburban housewife, decides to escape her life in Virginia and reunites with her friend in San Francisco. At first *she* is an outsider in Sujana's world. But after a few beers and tokes, Marcie becomes the life of the party, and in drunken abandon even fucks a drag queen. The next day, contrite over her evening of excess, and egged on by a phone call from her husband, "Big Dick," begging her to come back, Marcie agrees to return home. But her eyes have opened to a whole new world.

The actual script was written in a matter of days aided by journalist Edward Guthmann and Andrew Hayes. I'd shoot this present-day San Francisco story in color, and use the flashbacks from *The Outsider* as a sardonic framing device. In a hat tip to the 1962 Joan Crawford and Bette Davis camp classic, the film was titled *Whatever Happened to Susan Jane?*

For Sujana, I selected my dear friend Francesca Rosa, who actually resembled the character from the '50s film. But casting Southern housewife Marcie proved a challenge. I did not know many people like her.

But fate intervened when one day I ran into friend Ann Block, then a waitress at the mega-popular Savoy Tivoli bar. She looked "normal" and had a Southern accent, just like Marcie. In the course of conversation I discovered that Ann was a real drama queen. At the time, she was in the midst of an EST training—an intense self-help program that was all the rage. Ann began to babble about her emotional breakthroughs—and then broke down, sobbing uncontrollably. As I hugged her, I thought, "Goddamn what an actress—she can cry on cue. She'd be perfect as Marcie!" My instinct proved correct.

The person I was the most zealous about including in the cast was local drag legend Coco Vega—who we nicknamed Cuckoo Vega—a street creature with wildly ratted black hair and a rose tattoo on her hairy chest. Coco dressed in a tattered black lace slip, wore hideous smeared makeup, had really bad breath and worse body odor (which she tried to hide with splashes of patchouli and Tres Flores pomade). You could hear her a mile away—speaking sometimes in English, sometimes in Spanish, and sometimes in a language all her own. When she wasn't loopy on 'ludes or "gorilla biscuits" (Tuinals), she was high on black tar heroin. And if you tried to fuck with her, she had a knife in her purse and would cut you up. Coco was the ultimate outsider, with shamanistic ability to cut to the quick, speaking the truth and reading any queen in a snap.

The first day of shooting "Susan Jane."

Originally, I cast Coco as Sujana's best drag queen girlfriend, but she was constantly fucked up on drugs and forgetting lines. Instead, I gave Coco several improvised scenes where she could simply play Coco. Reliable ol' Lulu quickly stepped in, and we revised the script to cater to her unique personality and talents.

I crammed every friend I could into the film. Among the cameos was Tommy Pace channeling the Puerto Rican queen from the New York piers, offering up the film's most famous line, "Did he beat you, girl?"

The first day of shooting at Cafe Flore occurred on November 4, 1980, the morning after Ronald Reagan was elected the fortieth president of the United States. Little did we know how much he would change the world (and all for the worse). Still we had no time to truly let this ominous news sink in—gaily turning the Flore into a wild film set, and clearing the space for a frenzied go-go dance high atop a table featuring Coco and Lulu.

For the big party scene at San Francisco's Project Artaud, a cavernous warehouse theater, I combed the bars, clubs, cafes and streets for interesting-looking extras, personally handing out flyers to "be-in" a fabulous new underground film. I envisioned the scene to play out like the famous party in *Midnight Cowboy*, featuring Warhol superstars.

The night of the shoot, over 500 showed up, dressed to the nines in punk regalia.

I was able to snag my SF State professor Bill Jersey to act as second camera. He quickly plunged into the helter-skelter licentiousness of the bash, particularly excited to shoot the hetero naked "love act." There he was on his knees, like a kid in the candy store breathlessly zooming in on Nancy Carol King's bare boobies. There was only one problem: Bill got so into the action that he forgot to load film into the camera. He was literally shooting blanks (and having a ball doing it!). Of course, I was one to talk. By the end of the party I was filming the Wasp Women's closing number "Fuck You, You Queen" plowed out of my senses on cheap vodka.

*Tommy Pace, Francesca Rosa, and Lulu
in the "Susan Jane" party scene.
Photo by Marshall Rheiner.*

The morning after, I had a fierce hangover and hours of fabulous footage. I was convinced that I had a jewel of a film.

Act 1, Scene 14 – FIRST LOVE & A BIG OPENING

At the start of the '80's, I was immersed in music, film, and politics. But in my late twenties I experienced another watershed experience: I fell deeply in love.

Before this, my sexual encounters were largely limited. Hundreds of men came my way. I came and went. With no emotions attached. Worse still was a gnawing feeling something had gone awry in this culture of easy sex; a concept consummated at a New Year's party hosted by bad boy filmmaker Curt McDowell.

Curt was infamous for libertine films such *Stinkybutt*, *I Suck Your Flesh*, and his cult hit *Thundercrack*. He was also a local art star, and I was honored to be one of the select few invited to his year-end soiree.

However, I knew there might have been an ulterior motive. For months Curt had been sniffing me out for a pounce. Still this was *the* party to be at, and it was a step up the underground film ladder. All those bohemian celebrities together in one room! When I arrived, my insecurity kicked in. I was nervous about the impression I'd make. So how did I calm my anxiety? I got smashed. I wound up passed out on his lumpy thrift store couch surrounded by a sea of my vomit.

Who knows how many hours I was lying there limp? But when I awoke all the guests were gone, and Curt was fucking me, hard. Between his thrusts and grunts, I was sure he was the devil impregnating me with Rosemary's baby. And his twisted smile telegraphed that I was another notch on his belt, another conquest he could brag about. I didn't fight him off, but after he finished, I fled. I can't say it was an experience that scarred me for life, but Curt's rape just made me feel cheap, violated, dirty and empty. As I hobbled home to greet the sun and a new year, I prayed for a miracle to alter my life's course.

Then that spring, in front of the Pentecostal Church near Market and Church streets, I saw a young angel. He had delicate alabaster skin, deep vulnerable brown eyes, dimples for days, and a mischievous smile. My heart was pounding double-time as I dragged Phillip Puckett off the street, into my bed.

After the perfunctory sex, I discovered I had deep feelings for him. I started to fantasize about having Phillip as part of my life.

At nineteen, Phillip was a lost boy in need of tender, loving care. He was the son of Pentecostal missionaries (he saw our meeting in front of a church as a pre-ordained cosmic occurrence). Throughout his childhood, his loving yet strict parents roamed rural Mexico to do the work of the Lord. Homosexuality of course was top on their list of mortal sins. Phillip rebelled, running away to the city of Saint Francis.

And in this new city, he thrived, becoming quite a charmer. Even the most jaded melted under Phillip's boyish, puckish spell. Though not old enough to work in bars legally, he managed get a fake ID and procure a job as a DJ at The Headquarters, an infamous after-hours dive frequented by every speed freak in town.

Phillip Puckett and me, circa 1980.

Heartbreakingly, Phillip soon developed his own speed problem. And he had no permanent home. So within days of our meeting, Phillip moved into my apartment, and I made it my life's mission to wean him off drugs. At 26, I became his protector—more of a foster parent than a lover. I relished the role.

We bucked convention, holding hands in public. Together we even rescued a white kitten from the SPCA and called her Queen Kitty. Until now, I had carried an armor of cynicism throughout life, protecting me from my fear of abandonment. When I fell in love with Phillip, that armor melted. I became vulnerable. The sex wasn't great, but I didn't care. I loved watching Phillip sleep after a hard night's work DJ'ing. I dubbed him "The Little One" or "Lits" for short.

"The Little One" Phillip Puckett waking up.

There was even a day when we passed Mission Dolores and fantasized about getting married there. Well before that was an option.

I had never experienced true happiness with another man before. Phillip gave me renewed purpose in life. Getting *Susan Jane* finished became more relevant. I couldn't wait to hold my lover's hand at the opening! All I needed was $20,000 in completion funds.

It seemed like twenty million dollars.

I wrote fundraising letters, brainstormed about benefits, and spent sleepless nights wondering where the money would come from. During that time, in order to make ends meet, I also took a day job. I became a ticket taker and "popcorn pusher" at the Clay Theatre.

Located in San Francisco's tony Pacific Heights neighborhood, it was one of five art houses owned by film exhibitor Mel Novikoff. The office for his small Surf Theatres empire was right across the street from the Clay. He'd make numerous dashes every day for a fresh cup of coffee. Mel didn't need the caffeine. He was a short twitchy man with boundless nervous energy. And a true passion for film.

I was happy to be under Mel's tutelage. Within the Clay's cramped small box office, we'd often have heady, heated conversations on the state of the current cinema. Mel would become quite perturbed when I would criticize the lesser works then being produced by masters Truffaut, Fellini, Kurosawa, and Godard. And when I touted John Waters, he would go apoplectic, the hairs on his mustache bristled and he'd spill his coffee. Still, he respected my opinion. It helped that Mel was fond of my short *Unity*, having seen it when it screened as part of the Bay Area Filmmakers showcase at the jewel in his crown—the Castro. And he'd often ask about the progress of *Susan Jane*.

At the Clay we'd host star-studded movie events. At a sneak premiere of *Lust in the Dust* I met Divine. Out of drag, Glenn Milstead was achingly shy and seemingly lonely. At another gala for Howard Brookner's *Burroughs: The Movie*, I escorted the star, legendary beat writer William Burroughs, down the aisle.

Afterwards, I propped up the crusty old man for a photo op, as he snarled, "Take the goddamn picture." He couldn't wait to leave!

Propping up William Burroughs for a photo op.

For the first time in my life, I felt like I was clicking on all cylinders: I had a major film project, a job I liked, and a man I loved. This got me through post-production on *Susan Jane*, which would last two years.

Cutting the film became an obsession, as I channeled my dad's editing genes. I spent days and nights in a darkened editing room, where time was suspended. I had no more time to look for money, but luckily the finishing funds for the film came through a $5,000 loan from Ann Block's mom.

Through my connection to Mel, I booked, at discount rates, the Castro Theatre for a midnight screening premiere on Saturday, February 13, 1982. My feature-film dream debut was about to become a reality at San Francisco's most beautiful movie palace.

As the film neared completion, I became a self-promotion machine. Taking a cue from Keith Haring, Phillip and I spray-painted sidewalks at night in bright red letters that asked the cryptic question "Whatever Happened to Susan Jane?"

Several weeks before the big opening, we held a press screening. As local critics and journalists filled the screening room, an unexpected guest entered the room: my American Zoetrope supporter, Tom Luddy. By his side was German director Volker Schlöndorff, whose *The Tin Drum* had won an Oscar for Best Foreign Film. Luddy introduced us, calling me one of the most promising filmmakers in the Bay Area.

I placed myself near Luddy and Schlöndorff to gauge their reactions. During the screening, the local critics were laughing at all the right places. But in the Luddy corner, I heard muted groans and watched the pair sink into their seats.

When the lights came up, almost everyone had smiles on their faces. But not Luddy and Schlöndorff. They avoided my eyes, and quickly slipped out a side exit. I imagined the apologies Luddy would make, after seeing a local protégé lay a big fat egg on-screen.

No matter. I feverishly forged forward.

Just as the final plans were being made for the big Castro opening, I received a frantic phone call from Lulu. He had devastating news. Coco Vega was dead. He had been taken down by "the dragon" (as he called heroin)—found with a needle in his arm after shooting up a lethal dose. Even with his diminished role in the film, Coco was the heart and soul of the film: the truly bohemian spirit of our local underground. As I finished editing, it was spooky to see Coco so vibrant on film, dancing on a tabletop at the Cafe Flore. (He would become the first of many dead people who would populate my films.) I dedicated the film to his memory.

On a cold, drizzly night in February, high-voltage klieg lights pierced the skies. The World premiere of *Whatever Happened to Susan Jane?* was a majorly sold-out event—1400 in attendance. Those unlucky souls who waited till the last minute to snag the hottest ticket in town were on the street begging for cancellations. Our film's debut attracted San Francisco's finest drags, punks and New Wavers to the Castro Theatre. There were limo entrances galore. (Actually, the same stretch picked up cast members two blocks away, making it seem like multiple cars were rented for the occasion.) It was the culmination of two years of sweat and toil.

That night I felt on top of the world. And the crowd loved it all!

The Wasp Women on opening night for "Susan Jane."
Photo by Greg Day.

After floating on cloud nine the entire weekend, it was hard to come back to work at the Clay. I was thrilled when I saw Mel Novikoff crossing the street to greet me. But Mel had a sour look on his face as he barged into the box office. "Well, Marc, congratulations," he begrudgingly harrumphed.

"What did you think of the film, Mel?" I asked with a big smile on my face.

"Honestly I was shocked, shocked to see so many people coming to see that... that, that *monstrosity,* and no one coming to see the Truffaut here at the Clay." (A minor Truffaut film, *The Woman Next Door,* was a major flop at the theater.)

I think Mel was equally perturbed that he had rented the theater to me at a deep discount, thinking no one would show up.

Susan Jane went on to several sold-out runs at the Roxie Theatre, a funky beloved 300-seat art house in the heart of the Mission. These screenings became mini-events. One night I caused quite a stir by falling flat on my face, drunk, as I introduced the opening act, the Fabulous Four Beauties.

Susan Jane was invited to several film festivals. In Chicago, Roger Ebert proclaimed it "a hot ticket." There our posse schmoozed with the likes of Franco Nero, Rex Reed, and Ann-Margret. Then off to Italy, where the streets of Florence were plastered with festival posters with my name (misspelled) in big block letters—alongside those of David Lynch, Charles Burnett, and Slava Tsukerman, director of the cult sensation *Liquid Sky.* On to Rome, where the film screened to a huge crowd at the ancient Circus Maximus, where chariot races once reigned. Then Los Angeles, for a commercial run at the Vista Theatre, attended by punk rock goddess Nina Hagen and her baby daughter Cosma Shiva.

The Advocate proclaimed it "the first cult classic of the 1980s." But truth be told, many deemed *Susan Jane* "too San Francisco." For some out-of-town audiences, it played like some weird home movie.

Still its legacy has grown stronger with time. This 1983 review best summed it up: "Its historical interest should increase as the years pass." Indeed it has. It still sells on Amazon, and I'm told that rock icon Robert Smith, lead singer from The Cure, now lists it as one of his all-time favorite films. And with the gentrification of San Francisco, *Susan Jane* holds up as a time capsule in living, breathing color, capturing one last gasp of fun-fueled innocence of the party before the plague.

Nina Hagen and moi at the Los Angeles opening of "Susan Jane."

Act 1, Scene 15 – THE PARTY'S OVER

It was March of 1982. At the corner of Castro and 18th the stenciled fire-engine-red letters inquiring Whatever Happened to Susan Jane? were fading, worn out by time and traffic. Something new was demanding the attention of passersby.

In the window of Star Pharmacy, a local activist named Bobbi Campbell had scotch-taped handmade notices about a frightening new skin ailment. Posted were multiple Polaroids of his feet spotted with purplish blotches, similar to bruises, but raised and hardened.

Campbell soon started writing a column in the San Francisco Sentinel on this mysterious new condition. It became known as gay cancer, but the more technical name was "gay-related immune deficiency," or GRID. Friends and I, terrified, could only call the condition "it." We had no idea who would get "it," or whether you could get "it" by just breathing the air.

At a party in June of 1982, a friend told the crowd that doctors had determined "it" was a sexually transmitted disease. The look on people's faces—of fear, shock and horror—was unforgettable. We became obsessed with "it." Soon afterwards people no longer touched, stopped sharing glasses of water, towels or toilet seats, and started greeting each other with air kisses.

Theories and value judgments abounded. It was the leather queens who were going to get "it," or people who used poppers, or the bathhouse or sex club sluts.

Before I met Phillip, I was the slut of all time. Compulsively picking up men on the streets, in leather bars, and at the baths, including a raunchy and wild establishment called the Slot, where the unwritten rule was anything goes and everything went. For years, I had indulged in whatever was my pleasure, as extreme as my imagination would carry me.

Even before I fell for Phillip, I was getting sick of my addiction to hedonism. Stalking the darkened halls of the baths for sex had become demeaning. I felt reduced to a slab of meat. There were few smiles on people's faces. Sex was now serious business. And no matter how much sex I'd have in a night, I would leave less satisfied.

And often I'd exit the baths with something extra. Syphilis, several bouts of the clap, hepatitis A and B, crabs, scabies, you name it. A trip to the VD clinic in those days was a social outing. As you waited for your number to be called, you'd see friends and tricks alike, seated in the uncomfortable metal folding chairs. Sometimes you'd smile or wave, catch up on the latest dish. Or even cruise. We knew that a simple shot would cure our transmitted malady. Till the next one.

But with the advent of "it" we were dealing with a more nefarious stalker.

No shot would cure "it." "It" was life threatening. And "it" soon had a more permanent new name: Acquired Immune Deficiency Syndrome. AIDS.

I became obsessed with reading everything I could about AIDS. Remember before the Internet, when people had to physically go to newsstands and libraries to peruse papers and magazines? Coverage was mostly in the LGBT rags or occasionally in small articles on page 27 of the *Times*. Many reports were dry; but a deafening alarm sounded in the March 1982 issue of the *New York Native*. A front page piece titled "1,112 and Counting" by journalist Larry Kramer. The lead sentence: "If this article doesn't scare the shit out of you, we're in real trouble."

I wasn't only scared, I was petrified.

I checked my body obsessively for purplish lesions. Every new bruise or rash, I was certain, was a sure sign of impending doom: the beginning of the dreaded Kaposi's sarcoma (KS), the rare skin cancer that ravaged the bodies of gay men. I frantically measured each marking daily, convinced they were enlarging or hardening. I was constantly running to the doctor, only to be reassured I did not have KS.

More AIDS-related symptoms were named: swollen lymph nodes; thrush, a white fungus of the mouth; and hairy leukoplakia, a raised white corrugated squiggle on the tongue. I was sure I had them all. At the Clay, I'd spend my break in the men's room at the mirror, convincing myself I had thrush. And if I didn't see anything, I'd scrape the insides of my mouth until I manifested its symptoms. I'd return to the candy counter in a cold sweat, avoiding eye contact with customers and fellow workers. I couldn't shake the image of the wheel of misfortune spinning and landing on me.

And my relationship with Phillip was also falling apart. My AIDS obsessions were turning him away. I was also used to being the star of the duo. But with *Susan Jane* dimming from folks' memories, and with Phillip's star in ascent as DJ at the Stud—a hugely popular gay nightclub—I became bitter, envious. I also became drunken and abusive.

At the same time, Phillip was back on speed, having free access to lines put out by adoring clubgoers. And tricking with many of them afterwards. After nearly two years together, he moved out.

After several weeks apart, Phillip came to visit our child, our beloved cat Queen Kitty. We spoke of getting back together. And we had a session of "make-up" sex.

Phillip loved to get fucked. I never liked doing it—it was so smelly and messy. But I begrudgingly obliged when we first got together (before the HIV virus was discovered to be sexually transmitted). But on this night of reconciliation, he implored me to fuck him again. Desperate to do anything that would keep us together, I acceded to his wish. I forcefully came inside of him, the most memorable orgasm of my life. I was hoping my stream of ejaculate would bind us together like crazy glue. But crazy glue doesn't work on broken hearts. And all the king's horses and all the king's men...

It was a desperate, vainglorious attempt to pick up the pieces of our shattered relationship. When I pulled out, I knew we would be forever apart.

After Phillip left for good, I realized my life was going nowhere. And now I was scared to death I'd soon be dead. I needed something to get me back on track.

I joined a gym. Being a man of limited means, I found the cheapest one. A no frills, non-gay establishment aptly named the Universal Club. With every weight I was lifting, I'd visualize that my body was ridding itself of a piece of the virus I was sure was swimming inside and eating me alive.

One day, while doing my bench presses, I noticed a man with a naturally sculpted buffed body and perfect teeth, waiting to take over. He was striking. Although he had a masculine veneer, he also had a soft quality that made him pretty. And he looked very familiar. Perhaps he was an ex-trick.

"Do I know you?" I flirted.

"Hi, my name is Phil. We've never met. But didn't you do the film *Whatever Happened to Susan Jane?*" he replied in a distinctive Australian accent.

"Wait a minute. I've heard that voice before. Are you Doris Fish?"

The butch man turned nelly. "Well, love, I've been sprung!"

Doris Fish, aka Phil Mills, was one of the most famous drag queens in town, and star of the notorious group Sluts a Go-Go. The group included Miss X, self-proclaimed "heiress to the Brand X fortune," and Tippi, "the oldest living child star in captivity." They were performing at the Hotel Utah, as well as making guest appearances with the glam-rock group the Tubes. They were also making the gender-bending sci-fi thriller *Vegas in Space*.

Although the sensibilities of the Sluts were less political than mine, they were a force to be reckoned with. And I needed an art project. Perhaps working with Doris and company would be the jolt of energy I craved. I asked Doris if she would like to collaborate.

We exchanged phone numbers (for work purposes only). Although Doris was quite attractive, the thought of having sex with a new girlfriend/possible art colleague vanished from my mind.

Our collaboration began in the heart of the Tenderloin, the seediest neighborhood in town. In the '80s, 181 Eddy Street was home to the 181 Club, a hotspot that attracted lounge lizards, club kids, transvestite hookers and drug dealers. It was a glamorous mixture of the Cotton Club, a Fassbinder film and a beatnik coffeehouse. My first friend in town, Greg Cruikshank, was booking acts that varied from porn star Leo Ford to singer John Sex to an up-and-coming drag queen named RuPaul. I approached him with the idea of a new Huestis/Fish show. He was game.

But what would Doris and I create together?

During this period, the TV soap *Dynasty* was all the rage. For an hour each week, we cheered and hissed at its camp vulgarity; our queer eyes glued to the set as we watched the war between the Carringtons and the Colbys. The catfights between Alexis and Crystal were just the catnip we needed to momentarily forget the grim reality of AIDS. *Dynasty*, or *Die Nasty* as we called it, demanded a queer send-up.

I came up with a monthly drag queen/beatnik soap opera titled *Naked Brunch*. In honor of our new TV muse Joan Collins, we called our new theatrical troupe "The Alexis Carrington Colby Players." The coterie from the Sluts a Go-Go joined up with my stock group of actors and several newbies—including Arturo Galster who would become an important player throughout my showbiz career.

We scheduled the first episode for January of 1984, with the plan to write and rehearse a new episode every month. Writing sessions would take place at the House of Fish, Doris' large Oak Street flat. The address was the perfect setting to nurture creativity, with constantly changing decor. One week its rooms would be done up with day-glo green fake fur; the next week classic Grecian with kitschy statues of nude males, faux-marble walls and garish gold-painted moldings. The constant would be Doris' large day-glo self-portraits that suggested Van Goghs with Keane eyes. They stared at you wherever you went.

We'd gather midday in the television room, where the latest technical wonder had been hooked up—a bulky Betamax VCR. Now we could watch and rewatch every episode of *Dynasty*. We must have seen the Alexis/Crystal slugfest at the lily pond a hundred times. Our goal was to rip off every line and bit from these shows and incorporate them into our scripts, augmented by renowned lines from classics like *A Streetcar Named Desire*, *Who's Afraid of Virginia Woolf?*, *Valley of the Dolls*, *Peyton Place*, *Caged*, and others.

These sessions would be periodically interrupted by the telephone. If the pink Princess phone rang, Doris would answer it in her queeniest voice, "Doris Fish speaking." If the beige ATT phone rang, a phony-sounding butch voice would say, "Hello, this is Phil." Doris would then excuse herself to don her tightest tank top and torn jeans to accentuate her gym-toned bod, bulging crotch and buns of steel. A half hour later, the doorbell would ring, and Doris would be called away to entertain a stranger in a special room set aside for "professional" purposes. It all seemed very odd behavior from San Francisco's most outrageous drag queen.

Rehearsals for *Naked Brunch* soon began in earnest at the glamorous Club 181. Except in the light of day, it was really quite a dump. Often, as we'd rehearse a dance number, we'd see rats scamper across the stage. And the place also literally stank. (Later we learned that two dead bodies had been stashed in the rafters years before, and were decaying right above our kick-line.)

Naked Brunch proved to be a huge hit. The audiences got bigger with each episode, so much that one night the fire marshal threatened to shut the show down. That made us happy! The scripts got better, too.

A poster for "Naked Brunch, Episode III."
Poster designed by Silvana Nova.

Our script writing and performances were all-consuming. We had little time to think about the menace of AIDS lurking just outside the House of Fish. But still it was ubiquitous. At each show meeting there was always the news of another diagnosis or another death among a rapidly contracting circle of friends and colleagues. Each time I would attempt to bring up the subject in any depth, I would be greeted with a curtain of silence. Drag was glamorous, and the queens didn't want realism. They wanted magic.

Still AIDS was impossible to totally ignore. Before each meeting, Doris would drink a green spirulina shake, allegedly a powerful potion against any intruding viruses. This concoction, plus an organic vegetarian diet and regular exercise, she said, would surely protect her.

But the disease really hit home at the end of the run of Episode III of *Naked Brunch*. Throughout his performances, Tommy Pace wore full-length gloves over his multiple costumes. Odd, I thought, Tommy never wore gloves before. After the final show, I popped my head into his dressing room cubicle to pay tribute to his brilliance. I noticed the gloves were off—and on Tommy's arms were several raised purple blotches. He had been hiding the fact that he had the beginnings of KS.

Act 1, Scene 16 – POSITIVE

After *Naked Brunch*, I crashed and burned. And AIDS again became my constant worry. The door was bolted, the shades were shuttered. For months, I barely went out. What was the point? Each time I'd venture into the streets, I'd see friends and acquaintances that either talked about "it" or, worse, had "the look": drastic weight loss, gray skin pallor, or purple spots, when just weeks before they had looked fine. Castro apartments had a plethora of "For Rent" signs in the windows. A neighborhood once vibrantly alive with hotties on the prowl was now populated with emaciated men hobbling on canes. Our San Francisco was becoming a city of Dead Men Walking.

Throughout my life, I suffered from periodic depression. But now it was deeper and darker. Why go on living, I felt, if you knew you would be dead in a few years? Making matters worse, our community now felt isolated from the rest of humanity. We were experiencing societal cognitive dissonance. Each day we would see or hear of multiple loved ones dead or dying, and the outside world went about its business as if nothing was happening. Articles about AIDS would sometimes appear toward the back of the major newspapers, if at all; but in our lives it was the main headline, each and every day. And the biggest abomination of all was having a president, Ronald Wilson Reagan, who had yet to utter the word AIDS. It was criminal.

Adding to my constant anxiety, I was now flat broke. My minimum-wage job in a movie theater was not cutting it, and it wasn't like the royalty checks for the few theatrical screenings of *Susan Jane* were lucrative.

I needed a new better paying job and was lucky enough to get one. Due to the generosity of former Castro Theatre manager Allen Sawyer, I was hired as a clerk at Captain Video. Allen was a tall, lanky, quiet, and warmhearted soul, a true film aficionado, super-smart behind his horn-rimmed glasses, and one of the few folks who didn't think I was too crazy to hold down a "real" job. And this one paid a hefty $7.50 an hour plus health benefits! In keeping me afloat, Allen was an unsung hero in my first act.

Located on Market and Castro, Captain Video was the hottest video emporium in San Francisco. These were the early days of video rentals, before there was a video store on every corner. At our shop, there were lines out the door, and lines of cocaine for (some of) the managers counting the wads of cash in the office. Our crackerjack staff prided ourselves on our vast knowledge of movies, old and new, in VHS or beta. I also quickly became as much an expert on porn, and I was put in charge of procuring smut. It actually was fun purchasing and pushing titles like *In and Out of Africa* and *The Sperminator*. And I felt I was doing my community a service. After all, in the age of AIDS, adult films were a welcome masturbatory escape—a safe way of getting off.

The star-studded clientele at Captain Video in the Castro made going to work fun. The singer Sylvester would often fly through the doors, dripping in white chinchilla and tons of bling. (When he stopped coming later, the rumor quickly spread that he had "it.") Noted gay film historian Vito Russo, whose lover Jeffrey Sevcik worked at our store, would often pop in and chitchat about movies when he was in town. Robin Williams, then a resident of the hood, was also a regular. In he'd walk quietly, head bowed, as Marcia, the nanny of his child and then secret lover, did all the shopping. He'd lethargically look at the new releases, radiating an aura of sullen sadness. I felt sorry for him. Off-screen, he was not the funnyman we had grown to love. My former boss Mel Novikoff also became a regular customer, though we'd no longer argue about the merits of the latest Truffaut. Instead he'd ask for my recommendation on what was the hottest new release in gay porn.

This full-time job helped break me out of my depression. Added to that, I also took in a live-in lover. Tony was a young, extremely good-looking, fun-loving kid I had rescued from the streets, just like Phillip. Tony loved watching old movies and sometimes dressing up in drag and becoming the characters. He particularly enjoyed playing a Stepford wife, dressed in his flouncy dress and little apron and saying over and over, "I haven't baked anything today, I haven't baked anything today."

Honestly, our connection was not deep. Sometimes I felt I was babysitting. And there were no bodily fluids exchanged. I was now adamant about having safer sex. Still it was companionship, and he kept my mind off of heavier thoughts.

The question of HIV loomed large when the first test for the virus became available. I was initially opposed to taking it. Deep down, I knew I was positive, so why bother? But Tony wanted us both to take it. He convinced me that regardless of the outcome, we would still be together.

So on a lovely spring day in 1985—the first day the test was being offered—we walked hand in hand to the Community Health Center on 17th Street. How romantic! Surprisingly, there were not many people in line. We were both led to separate cubicles to get our blood drawn. My hands were shaking.

Several weeks later, we went back to the Center for our results. Tony got his results first. He was negative. Again, he adamantly assured me that, whatever my status, we would remain bonded. Through thick and thin, in sickness and in health. I was instructed to come back the next day.

When I returned I was told that I needed to first see a counselor, and the wait seemed forever. Finally I was face to face with my future. "I'm sorry to tell you that your first test came back antibody positive," the man said. "However, we should do it again to make sure it isn't a false positive."

As I walked home, everything around me was a blur. Despite the fact that this was the news I was convinced I was going to get, it still didn't seem any easier to take. And Tony needed to be told. At dinner, I broke the news. "I'm positive. I always knew it." Tony gave me an uncomfortable hug; it now seemed like there were miles between our barely touching bodies. We quietly ate and went to sleep.

I awoke the next morning to an empty bed. And a note. Tony was leaving me. He had met someone at work, had fallen in love and was moving in with him. He assured me my results had nothing to do with his decision. He would come back and pack his bags when I wasn't in the house.

"Whatever," I thought, rolling my eyes. Honestly, I knew this was a dead-end relationship, so perhaps it was for the best. I didn't feel hurt, just numb.

To this day I don't blame him for his quick exit. That was the nature of the times, and you had to be there to understand. Tony and I are now Facebook friends.

Act 1, Scene 17 – COMING OF AGE

After Tony moved out, I took renewed solace in my energized community. In the early days of GRID, we had lived in fear and isolation. Many felt alone. But as we got a grip on the day-to-day reality of AIDS and understood the magnitude of what was happening, we came together like never before.

Suddenly, new nonprofits and support groups sprang up to aid the sick among us. If the government wasn't going to tend to our needs, we would do it ourselves, creating new models of palliative care.

By helping others, we found something within ourselves: a humanity that slashed through the despair. Fear was replaced by action. Lesbian separatism ended; sisters came to the aid of brothers. Doctors befriended biological families *and* extended families alike. Circles of friends met to schedule quality time with stricken comrades. We held hands at bedsides, cleaned soiled sheets, cooked meals, bawled at corny old movies, savored our weekly fix of *Dynasty*, laughed and then cried some more.

The virus would also fuel my artistic expression. And kismet again came into play, this time in the personage of Chuck Solomon.

I had known Chuck for years. He was part of the Gay Men's Theater Collective that produced the groundbreaking *Crimes Against Nature* in the late '70s, and an early founding member of Theatre Rhinoceros, the world's oldest queer theater. He had a ringside seat at the fateful Angels of Light cabaret when I stopped the show as Ellen Organ. "I loved you from the moment you flung that bottle," Chuck would joke. We'd also periodically rub eyeballs on two-dollar nights at the Club Baths, dish and smoke a doobie before starting our separate hunts.

One autumn day in 1985, I spotted Chuck slowly making his way down Market Street. After exchanging obligatory pleasantries, I looked into his eyes. It was obvious that he had "it." I helped him to his customary corner outdoor table at the Cafe Flore where he lit up a cigarette, coughed, and began talking.

He proceeded to share the horror of his last few years. First, his older brother Howard, his only sibling, had died of AIDS. Weeks later, his lover Scott was diagnosed and quickly passed. Then Chuck learned he had full-blown AIDS. My heart sank.

Chuck seemed both resigned and relieved about his own diagnosis, quipping, "I don't know which is worse, turning forty in several months or having AIDS." After we parted, my head was spinning. I was devastated by his news, yet moved by his courage.

Chuck had been an inspiration to me and many others for decades, both for his cultural work and his personal strengths. Now he was dying. We all had been to *so many* memorials for our dead. I asked myself: Why wait for a memorial to express our love, affection and admiration for Chuck. Why not throw him a party while he was still alive? A celebration of his life that would fill a room with healing energy? (Yes, I had become a Californian.)

I called Chuck with this idea. He took to it immediately, but insisted it not become a pity party. Instead, the event could mark his fortieth birthday. And he'd foot the bill.

I sprang into action, pitching the idea to Chuck's Cafe Flore cohorts. But most found it morbid. I referred them to Chuck, whose power of persuasion ultimately moved folks to embrace the concept.

A party committee was formed. We reserved a sweet room with a small stage in the California Club, capacity 200. Menus were planned. Talent was booked among the many performers throughout Chuck's theatrical career including comic and politician Tom Ammiano, Doris Fish, the SF Mime Troupe, poet

Aaron Shurin, chanteuse Esmerelda, Silvana Nova, and the cast of *The AIDS Show*.

It felt like something special was happening. So two weeks before the party, I also decided to film the proceedings. Although I had never made a documentary before, how hard could it be?

With lightning speed I assembled a production team, composed of collaborators old and new. *Susan Jane* co-producer Wendy Dallas immediately came on board—a godsend easing my workload. We had no money, but we had drive, and everyone, it seemed, wanted to help. Equipment was rented at a deep discount; crew members donated their time, we got tape stock from AT&T and even obtained a second camera gratis, courtesy of local porn impresarios, the Mitchell Brothers. They too had been deeply hit by AIDS. All hands were on deck.

Chuck's birthday party occurred March 10, 1986. The show portion surpassed all expectations. Each performer was not only at the top of their game, giving the best of their talents, but also opened their hearts to their dear friend and colleague. As Sandhal Hebert, in a blonde wig, and shimmering in sequins, serenaded Chuck just like Marilyn Monroe singing "Happy Birthday" at JFK's Madison Square Garden bash, there wasn't a dry eye in the house.

Wiping tears from his glasses, Chuck mounted the stage and addressed the throng: "To think that this many people love me makes me feel like Sally Field. Seriously, I feel so honored and blessed and moved. And you're all invited to my 50th birthday. So start shopping!"

Sitting close to her beloved son was Chuck's mother Bette. She had already lost one son to this horrible virus, and now her only other child was ailing. We all imagined what she must have been thinking. Yet there she sat, proud and dignified, quietly taking in the proceedings, moved by the all the testimonials, lovable and loved.

Chuck Solomon and his mother Bette.
Photo by Marshall Rheiner.

Later, when I reviewed the party footage with my team, we knew we had captured something defiant, joyous and hopeful. And at this point in the epidemic there were no documentaries on AIDS coming from within the gay community. This story needed to be seen by the world at large. And it needed to be expanded to include Chuck's singular personality and moving life story.

Shooting the rest of the piece reminded us of the grim reality of the disease. At a Cafe Flore shoot, just before cameras began rolling, Chuck had a grand mal seizure—one of the manifestations of toxoplasmosis, a parasitic brain infection common at the time among people with AIDS. His body stiffened, his eyes rolled into the back of his head, and he lost consciousness. Soon his muscles began to spasm, and then his entire body flailed, causing him to fall off his seat. After calling for an ambulance, we sat helplessly while the seizure took its course. It lasted no more than a few minutes, but it seemed forever. It was the most frightening thing I had ever observed.

At the moment the seizure started, I quickly instructed our director of photography Fawn Yacker to stop filming. The thought of shooting his convulsions seemed ghoulish. When the paramedics arrived, Chuck ruled out going to the hospital. I was ready to cancel the rest of the shoot, but Chuck would have none of that. He demanded we continue. As the camera rolled, he looked directly into the camera, calmly explained what had just happened, then matter of factly began to reminisce about his childhood.

After we wrapped, Chuck asked if we had shot the seizure. No, I said; I didn't think it appropriate. Chuck being Chuck was disappointed, curious about how the seizure looked as it took over his body.

Our final shoot was an intense, exhaustive, and exhilarating four-hour, sit-down interview. Chuck charted his inspiring personal history, in ways mirroring our community's own. And ending with his wise words: "When my father found out I was gay, he said I was going to be a lonely, bitter old man. And I am anything but a lonely, bitter old man! And at the party, my family saw what an amazing community I have, that I will never be alone. None of them have been in a room with all those queers, all those loving people. And I didn't want a memorial after I was gone. Give me one that I could enjoy, please!"

When we wrapped, we were exhausted. But Chuck was invigorated. He looked like a kid who had just strolled through a magic museum—each step revealing a hidden treasure of his life journey.

In post-production, Wendy Dallas and I worked at breakneck speed, determined to have Chuck see the finished piece in his lifetime. The clock was definitely ticking. But the project gave Chuck a reason to live. And gave me a sense of purpose.

The Ninth Frameline Lesbian and Gay Film Festival was in late June. Michael Lumpkin, the festival director, had seen some footage. Based on its strength, he invited us to premiere the film there. It seemed like a near impossible task to create a feature documentary in three months' time. But I knew Frameline was the perfect venue for its premiere. And Chuck was still in decent health. Guided by our editor Frank Christopher, we created an hour-long documentary, *Chuck Solomon: Coming of Age*. The title was a reference to Chuck's fortieth birthday, and a metaphor for our community's newfound maturity during the crisis.

The premiere was held June 29 in the Video Free America screening room. Despite advance raves in important papers, the tiny screening room was half empty. Everyone was incredibly supportive of the concept of an AIDS film, but no one actually wanted to see one. They were living it, and wanted movies that were a momentary escape from the grim reality outside.

As the film started, I grabbed hold of Chuck's hand, not letting go throughout the course of the film. As the end credits rolled, we were all blubbering like babies. A standing ovation ensued. I felt proud, particularly for Chuck. He now knew that even after his death, his words and spirit would live, through the film.

Several weeks later, I got a phone call. The connection was fuzzy, full of crackling sounds. (This was in the days when long-distance landlines still sounded like long distance.) Between the dropped words and static, a deeply accented voice on the other end emerged.

"Hello, my name is Manfred Salzgeber and I am the director of the Panorama at the Berlin Film Festival. My assistant Wieland Speck saw your documentary in San Francisco and spoke most positively about it. May I see a copy?"

I had goosebumps at just the thought of being included. I immediately Fed Ex'ed Salzgeber a copy.

He called again a week later. In the middle of the night. I was barely awake as I picked up. This time, the connection was strong.

Salzgeber had just seen the film.

"Marc, your film is very important. It needs to be seen. I vould like to invite you to the Berlin Film Festival. Jah?"

"Jah," I sputtered. "JAH!"

Act 1, Scene 18 – THE WORK BEGINS

The *Internationale Filmfestspiele Berlin*, held in the dead of winter, is one of the major film festivals in Europe, along with Cannes and Venice. It was especially known for launching important gay and independent films; I was quite honored to be invited. And Berlin, more than any other world capital, held great allure for me. It was the city of Brecht, Dietrich, Fassbinder and of course, Sally Bowles.

In 1987, Berlin was still a divided city—east and west, communist and capitalist—both coexisting on a razor's edge. West Berlin was an oasis for artists and outsiders surrounded by a sea of red. This precarious arrangement made the city all the more exciting. Everywhere there were cafés, coffeehouses, odiferous alleyways and shawarma stands, Turkish baths, gay bars and fabulous thrift shops. Berlin was a gray city and not pretty; you could almost feel the pain and destruction it had endured throughout the ages. But the falling February snow obscured some of its ugliness.

I marveled at the city's historic markers. As I ran through the archways of the elevated U-Bahn, I was tempted to let out a loud, primal scream, à la Liza in *Cabaret*. The Berlin Wall, a concrete monster that snaked through the maze of Kreuzberg streets was, to my mind, a great work of modern art. The fourteen-foot-high slabs were covered for kilometers with graffiti left by tourists, provocateurs and artists alike. Indeed, my New York crush Keith Haring, now a major art world star, had recently spray-painted a 330-yard stretch at Checkpoint Charlie.

What a perfect place to introduce our film to a world audience! And at the Berlin Film Festival, we had the ideal advocate. Manfred Salzgeber, our host and supporter, was known for discovering young gay filmmakers: Derek Jarman, Gus Van Sant, Rob Epstein, and Rosa von Praunheim all had their work shown first in his Panorama section. He was a singular person in the world of film.

Salzgeber was a dark, bearded, leather-vested man with a gruff deep voice, boundless energy, and an encyclopedic knowledge of film. He made things happen. He was also democratic with a small "d," treating the famous and the not so famous with equal aplomb. It didn't matter if you were Marc Huestis or Tom Cruise. And he was equally at home cruising the dark room of Tom's Place, the local leather bar, or schmoozing at a chic festival soiree. I nicknamed him "Manfred the Magician."

I'll never forget my first visit to the Panorama office. Our posse of four—Chuck Solomon's on-screen interviewer Ann Block, producer Wendy Dallas, sound person Lauretta Molitor and myself—green to such international gatherings, all walked in, wearing our *Coming of Age* T-shirts. Salzgeber let out a belly laugh. He thought we were so American—walking advertisements for our film—but decided it was cute. He gave us five minutes of his valued time, then offered his apologies.

"Oh shit, I have to run to a screening, I have my Spanish filmmaker here with his star. Let me introduce you. This is Pedro Almodóvar and Carmen Maura." The pair gave us polite Euro smiles. I had no idea who they were, but politely smiled back.

We were then invited to attend the premiere of Almodóvar's *La Ley del Deseo* (*Law of Desire*). It was a sold-out mob scene. Scores of disappointed cinephiles, left outside, pounded on the thick wooden doors, shrieking and screaming in multiple languages to be let in.

*Manfred Salzgeber and Wieland Speck at the 1987 Berlin Film
Festival/Panorama.*

Alas, our screening was hardly riotous. Our film was coupled
with a moving short by Stanford student Tina DiFeliciantonio
titled *Living With AIDS.* It was a poignant account of twenty-two-
year-old San Franciscan Todd Coleman's day-to-day battle with
the disease.

To sell the film, *Chuck Solomon: Coming of Age* had been
pitched as uplifting and inspiring. Nice try, but it seemed the poor
attendance at screenings in San Francisco was not an anomaly.

The Berlin screening—despite the buzz surrounding both films—was more than half-empty.

But Salzgeber, ever the optimist, counseled us that it didn't matter how many people were in attendance. It mattered the *type* of person. Indeed, he was right; a large press contingent from around the world attended.

Screen International's Nick Roddick wrote, "In a Berlin Festival dominated by worthy but dull works from established directors and films that should never have been let out of the can, *Coming of Age* shone out for its integrity, its humour and the sheer power of its emotional impact."

David Robinson, in *The Times of London*, said, "There is a gallantry and courage in these two films that transcends the specifics of the sickness."

Even the notoriously bitchy American critic Rex Reed cornered me afterwards outside the Panaroma office. He told me how moved he was by the film, and profusely thanked me for making it. It was ironic, since in the documentary Chuck dishes Reed's poison-pen review of his show *Crimes Against Nature*.

The screenings also affected me on a personal level. The newly formed AIDS activist group ACT UP declared Silence = Death. I was determined to play my small part in breaking this silence, coming out as HIV-positive at the Q&A's and multiple press interviews. In 1987, this was a rare confession. Few people revealed their HIV status publicly. There was a huge stigma associated with HIV, and those infected usually stayed quiet, fearful of losing jobs, apartments, family, friends, lovers.

Unfazed, I revealed my status with religious fervor, presenting myself as healthy and artistically active. God knows how long I was going to be alive. But if I was a walking time bomb, I certainly wasn't going to go down without a fight. And I had a big mouth.

Our first generation AIDS films offered a call to arms to a new breed of filmmakers, without obstacle. And more radical. What Hollywood would fail to do with their multimillions, we dedicated independents could do on our shoestring budgets.

But it required heart and soul, fire in the belly, and hard work; persevering against commercial and public resistance.

I promoted *Coming of Age* like a missionary on the frontlines. Thanks to Manfred Salzgeber my work was now on an international stage. And I had finally come of age in one of the greatest cities in the world.

With movie critic Rex Reed at the 1987 Berlin Film Festival.

Act 1, Scene 19 – ON THE ROAD

Manfred Salzgeber's zeal for exhibiting important films extended well beyond the Berlin Filmfestspiele. After the festival, he brought Tina DiFeliciantonio and I on a 20-city whirlwind German tour with *Chuck Solomon: Coming of Age* and *Living With AIDS.*

Manfred's trusted assistant Wieland Speck took the wheel—neither Salzgeber nor I knew how to drive—and we four fearless filmsters journeyed on the autobahn through the many burgs of Deutschland: Nuremberg, Heidelberg, Freiburg, Augsburg, Hamburg. Over the Rhine, across the Elbe, toward the blue Danube. In between our film's playdates, we slept on floors, bunked in dorms, and stayed in cheap hotels.

On the East German border en route to Berlin, I was detained by the Stasi, the notorious secret police, and held in a locked, concrete bunker. They rummaged through my bags and quickly unearthed press reports on my film and me. Being gay and HIV positive was certainly a red flag. But it didn't help that I was such a slob; my passport was in tatters, and I had glued my photo back on my documents with rubber cement. While I was being interrogated, guns cocked in my direction, poor Tina was forced to sit alone in the van for hours, listening to the same four songs played over and over on the tape deck. When I was finally released, I was shaken and perturbed, yet undaunted.

Often, after long days of traveling, only two or three people would turn up for the program. So much travel, so few people. Still I came to believe that our efforts were all worth it. The discussions after our screenings were achingly intense. The Germany of

1987 was two years behind America in terms of their epidemic's severity—and progress. People were just beginning to know of loved ones with diagnoses. Help was often only an anonymous voice on a bureaucratic hotline.

At each of the German screenings, I would come out as being HIV-positive, then I would open the floor to the audience. Silence. Then more silence. Finally, someone would politely raise a hand and begin speaking, haltingly in broken English. Out would come a heartfelt often tearful tale of how the epidemic had touched their lives.

Other times, I would be taken aside by a gay brother, away from earshot of others. He would whisper, "I have a friend who is positive." From his frightened look, I would know that he, himself, was "the friend." I would do my best to offer a receptive ear and caring heart.

Elsewhere, *Chuck Solomon: Coming of Age* was garnering a measure of success at numerous film festivals. Internationally, the film aired on the UK's Channel 4, TV Toronto, and Spain's Channel 3, and stateside on local public television stations in San Francisco, Los Angeles, and New York. But PBS National decided not to televise it, for a bizarrely politically correct reason: Executives were fearful of being criticized for portraying AIDS as a gay disease. To me that was absurd. AIDS was a gay disease. Point of clarification: AIDS was not *just* a gay disease, but it *was* a gay disease nonetheless.

In 1988, although *Chuck Solomon* was almost two years old it was accepted into the Sundance Film Festival (then called the U.S. Film Festival). I was in disbelief; Sundance normally prefers new works. But director Tony Safford, acknowledging the importance of the issue and the paucity of AIDS films, programmed it in the prestigious documentary competition.

We had a modest hope of scoring a prize, but even that was quickly dashed when we received inside jury information. Documentary filmmaker Richard Leacock, the jury president, had taken a distinct dislike to our film. One mole whispered that

Leacock, director of the 1960 classic *Primary* and a *cinema verité* purist, bristled at the film's talking-heads format. But our source also suggested another reason.

I decided find out exactly for myself.

At one of the festival parties, I cornered Leacock, a gray-haired, well-bred, slightly unkempt patrician man in his sixties. We had just come from a screening of Jennifer Fox's *Beirut: The Last Home Movie*. The documentary depicts an aristocratic Lebanese Christian family apathetic to the civil war that surrounds them—even taking tea in their palatial home as bombs destroy their upper class neighborhood.

"Some people are calling Jennifer's film decadent," Leacock opined. "But to me, *your* film is decadent."

I politely prodded, "Why is that?"

"Because, my dear, it is a portrait of a dying culture."

Fuck you, I thought. Despite—or perhaps because of—the death that surrounded us, our culture was more alive than ever. Leacock's comment demonstrated that even within highly intelligent circles, homophobia could rear its ugly head. Needless to say, our film came up empty-handed at the awards ceremony.

The final screening of *Chuck Solomon: Coming of Age* occurred July 1989 in the most unlikely of places—the Moscow Film Festival. The former Soviet Union was in the midst of glasnost and perestroika, marking a new era of openness in both politics and culture. In this spirit, the Moscow Film Festival had tasked the San Francisco Film Festival to curate a pioneering series under the rubric, "Sex in the American Cinema." Titles included *Blue Velvet, The Unbearable Lightness of Being, Desert Hearts, Beyond the Valley of the Dolls,* and *sex, lies and videotape.* Plus *Chuck Solomon.*

I was invited to attend, joining directors Philip Kaufman, the Coen brothers, Donna Deitch and Russ Meyer. So I begged, borrowed, and scrounged up the money for the trip.

Thus began a memorable flight to Moscow on Aero Jugoslovenski. After a meal of warm stewed sauerkraut and pig intestines, frantic stewardesses suddenly were running down the aisles with oxygen tanks. An announcement was made in broken English, sounding very much like Boris Badenov from the *Rocky and Bullwinkle* cartoons: "Attention, we tell you about possible plane malfunction. Please to forget violent situation and to remain calm!"

The plane began rocking back and forth. Oxygen masks ejected from above. We were doomed.

Despite all the indications that this plane was going down, after a while, it stabilized, and just like the happy ending of a '70s disaster pic, we eventually made it to Moscow.

At the end of the flight, I felt deliriously ill. I was immediately escorted to my festival digs, the renowned Rossiya Hotel. Once the jewel in the crown of proletarian architecture, it was now a communist relic, and an eyesore. Rodents scurried throughout the 5,374-room building. Toilets didn't flush. Half the light bulbs were broken, plunging stretches of hallways into darkness. The whole place stank of cheap disinfectant.

After the flight from hell, I hardly cared. I fell onto the bed, nauseous, and into a deep sleep.

Hours later, I was awakened by a loud, continuous banging at the door. The light switch didn't work. I felt my way towards the door and opened it. A Russian woman in a filthy torn housedress greeted me. She was toothless—and had *huge* breasts. When I blocked her way into the room, she stood in the doorway and proceeded to massage her ample bosom, make lip-smacking noises, and wink at me. "You want? You want?" she repeated. Sweet Jesus, her breath stank.

Then suddenly it dawned on me. She was a prostitute.

"Nyet, nyet, I don't want!" I frantically replied. I tried to explain I was gay, announcing repeatedly "GAY ... gaysky ... homosexual, homosexskia." Then I realized what would do the trick.

"AIDS," I said. "AAAAAAAAAAAIDDS!"

She ran out of there like a bat out of hell.

Night and day blurred together in Moscow, 1989.

I was stuck in bed for several days. I was scared to death I'd die in this Russian dump, with no available care for HIV. I fought off a homeopathic quack who tried to parcel out pills that contained green liquid that looked like Linda Blair's puke from *The Exorcist*. Luckily, I recovered in time for my screening.

When I got there, I was in a state of shock. The theater was packed. Nearly a thousand people! Perhaps Russians had a deep, humanitarian interest in AIDS.

That illusion was quickly shattered. As the film unspooled, there was a stony silence. Not the type you get when an audience is enraptured. The only reaction came when there was an on-screen display of same-sex affection. Folks began squirming in their seats. And when they saw two men kiss, people audibly gagged.

When the film was over, the audience fled.

"Why," I asked my translator Basil, "did they come?"

"Because, they will come to see *anything* from America."

Looking around Moscow, I could understand why America held such allure. Here, the streets were dirty, the buildings in disrepair, the market lines long, despite little on the shelves. People were perpetually drunk on cheap vodka. Workers seemed like the beaten-down proletariat in *Metropolis*. Perestroika and glasnost could not hide the air of collective despair. Although I was a veteran leftie, my time in Moscow made me an ardent anti-communist.

There were, however, respites from this grayness. It was July in the land of the midnight sun. At 11 p.m., as dusk slowly settled on the multicolored swirls and spires of St. Basil's Cathedral, I witnessed the historic majesty of this country. Everything before me turned magical, golden, transcendent, Chekhovian.

I decided to do some exploring. Canadian gay filmmaker John Greyson had told me the best cruising spot in Moscow was the park adjacent to the Bolshoi. It was filled with men of all types: Queens, hustlers, and bodybuilders, all playing a cat-and-mouse game with the police patrols. Despite Gorbachev's reforms, homosexuality was still illegal under the Politburo's penal code. Because we were all forbidden fruit, there was something exhilaratingly dangerous about the atmosphere. An outlaw, clandestine subculture, like in 1950s America.

"You gay?" one queen whispered in the dark. When I answered in English, word spread like wildfire that there was an American in their midst. I was immediately popular, having my pick of the litter. I chose a beautiful alabaster-skinned boy who resembled my angelic Phillip.

The boy made it clear he spoke little English, so I simply pointed into the distance and said "Rossiya." On the way he pulled me into a dark alley and gave me one of the most passionate kisses I ever experienced. In his mind, I was some rich American who would whisk him away. Whatever he was thinking, his thick hard-on showed he was seriously aroused. When we got to the hotel, I had him walk several steps behind me, not wanting to get him busted by the secret police lurking everywhere in the Rossiya.

Making sure the coast was clear, I immediately pounced. But his thoughts were elsewhere. He kept eying the room and gesturing to the shower. Odd, I thought; I had just showered that evening. I couldn't possibly stink. Then he pointed to the soap with a look of longing on his face.

I finally understood. There was a soap shortage in Russia. He then proceeded to undress. He stepped into the shower and soaped himself up, his beautiful body glistening, his eyes sparkling. Suddenly sex was not the most important thing on my mind; I was plagued by a realization much deeper and sadder. For too many people, happiness comes down to a simple bar of soap.

Act 1, Scene 20 – BURYING THE DEAD

Death was our constant companion for much of the '80s. By the end of the decade, the epidemic was spiraling out of control, with no end in sight. My work with AIDS films kept me immune from thinking too much about my own mortality. While on the road, I wanted to present a positive image of a person with HIV. And I tried to convince myself that my own virus was insignificant compared to the larger AIDS crisis. Still, I knew my HIV was not a mere sojourner; it was a permanent, silent enemy swimming through my bloodstream, waiting for the right time to attack. Not a day went by when I was not reminded of my possible fate. I was a helpless witness to colleagues resembling concentration camp victims who stared blankly from their hospital beds in the AIDS ward. Then they were gone. It was just a question of time before I'd be one.

The face of AIDS was grotesque. I think of my dear, wickedly funny, brilliant Tommy Pace. The man who incited tears of laughter that magical New York summer of 1980. Tommy's malady was the cruelest. It started slowly, with the smallish KS lesions I first spied in 1984 as he peeled off his gloves after a performance of "Naked Brunch." It rapidly progressed.

Tommy, a man who once could seduce you with a glance, now could not look you in the eyes. He radiated inner turbulence. Conversations became fleeting; he would abruptly terminate the exchange and retreat.

The lesions on his arm were soon matched by a single raised purple lesion on his nose. Tommy covered it up with makeup. Until there was a crop of them. The lesions, now swollen to almost double their size, soon covered his whole face, obscuring his once-glistening eyes. Tommy became unrecognizable.

Even before KS covered his body,
Tommy Pace was in emotional retreat.

Through the course of the epidemic, I had come to realize the process of death would either bring people to a higher or lower place—bringing out the more elevated spirits or the darkest demons. It was never predictable which direction the stricken would go. But Tommy, once the sweetest, gentlest soul, became monstrous. Sadistic and spiteful.

We all tried to turn the other cheek and form a support circle around our dear friend. We tried to take Tommy away from himself, but he did not make it easy. He was constantly fighting back, lashing out hatefully. An occasional outing became unbearable. A trip to the movies attracted unwanted attention.

No matter how big the hats and oversized Jackie O sunglasses were, or how many scarves he wrapped around his neck, people would point and whisper. He looked like a freak. And he knew it. When he caught people staring, he would howl in the most guttural, brutish voice, "Don't look at me, DON'T LOOOOOK AT MEEEEEEEEEEEE." It was heartbreaking.

Beaver Bauer recalled a time Tommy was taken to a dog show in a hoodie wrapped so tightly around his face that he could barely breathe. The sweat was pouring down; the makeup that tried to cover up his lesions began dripping. As a Dalmatian pranced in front of him, he whispered with unbearable black humor, "I have spots too."

Tommy was hurting financially, so we banded together to produce a benefit to raise monies and lift his spirits. We all owed him that. When asked what the title for the fundraiser should be, Tommy caustically replied, "Give Me the Damned Money!"

The event was held at Project Artaud, where *Susan Jane* was shot, the same site where dear Tommy uttered that famous line, "Did he beat you, girl?" Now he was the one who had gotten a beating.

The performances were stripped of artifice, pulsating with depth and raw naked love. Compatriots also stricken by this disease arose from their sickbeds to perform. Angel of Light Rodney Price, once an exquisitely sculpted and gifted dancer, now emaciated in his wheelchair, performed a parody of a Kurt Weill song entitled "I've Got Less Time Than You."

At the end of the song, Price's feet broke into an energetic tap dance, using the metal platforms of his wheelchair as his floor. He dove into it with gusto, like a happy Harryhausen skeleton, rattling every bone in his trouper's body.

Tommy couldn't bear to be seen that night, and was secretly escorted to the catwalk above, where he spied the proceedings. He was a gay phantom of the opera, watching the curtain fall on the final performance.

Tommy's only request that evening was a sing-along to the classic cowboy folk song "Red River Valley." We all thought that was corny, but complied. But as we sang its lyrics we began to convulsively cry. They were heartbreakingly appropriate.

> *"From this valley they say you are going*
> *We will miss your bright eyes and sweet smile*
> *For they say you are taking the sunshine*
> *Which has brightened our pathways a while."*

Tommy died shortly after the benefit. Gone was our queen of comedy.

Rodney Price died soon thereafter. And Doris Fish, who had looked the picture of health at Tommy's benefit, soon began to get "the look." Her full, fearless face turned gaunt, her piqued skin tone became ash gray.

Unlike Tommy, Doris responded to AIDS gallantly, with a full generosity of spirit. She no longer played the bitchy queen or mistress of the sardonic retort. She frequently quoted Joni Mitchell lyrics. Her softer side emerged.

Her showbiz family rallied and became caretakers. Well, most of them. Some from her inner circle of drag friends were scared to visit her during her illness; they couldn't come face to face with Doris's diminished beauty and were petrified the same fate awaited them.

However, it was easier to make a public demonstration of their love and support from a stage. So another big tribute was planned for November 3, 1989, entitled "Who Does That Bitch Think She Is?" The Doris Fish benefit brought together San Francisco's entertainment demimonde, packing the 480-seat Victoria Theatre to capacity.

Fortunately, Doris got to see it. Her weight loss was significant, but she donned a white muumuu that made her appear bigger than life. Perched in a throne in the front row, regal in her rhinestones, Doris never looked better; strangely, an aura of happiness glowed from within. At the end of the evening, she gave the most gracious speech, finding humor even in the darkest of moments.

"Although I am ailing, I'm not planning on dying right away. Of course, it would be very embarrassing if I do live through the epidemic. Five years from now, we'll pass on the street and you'll say, 'I gave that bitch 20 bucks cuz I thought she was going to die.' Anyway, if I am lucky enough to come back and perform for you again, it will be because of your support this evening... I know this will last me a long, long time."

Doris then launched into a lip-synch version of Shirley Bassey's "My Life." A slide show of her many looks was projected onto her muumuu, allowing her life to literally flash before our eyes as she mouthed defiantly, "Let me live, Let me live!"

Doris Fish in her final performance, November 1989.

After this rapturous evening, Doris' health declined. She became blind in one eye, yet ironically—or maybe not—she saw more clearly than most. Hospital visits were often akin to visiting the Oracle of Delphi. In her final days, often while on morphine, she morphed into a clairvoyant soothsayer imparting wisdom and kindness. She died peacefully. Her passing made the front page of the San Francisco Examiner. Above the fold. Damn, she would have loved to see that!

Days after Doris' death, I had a phone conversation with the love of my life, sweet Phillip Puckett. A mutual friend had reconnected us. Soon after he left me, he took another lover. They both moved to New York and became junkies. Phillip developed full-blown AIDS. Later, he contracted CMV retinitis, an opportunistic infection that causes blindness. My invincible, dimpled altar boy could no longer see. But he could still hear. Our last call was filled with deep love and mutual forgiveness. Phillip died weeks later.

Some of my bitchier friends tried to tell me I had given him HIV. Maybe; maybe not. Before we met in 1980, both of us were sluts. Phillip had already used injection drugs. And…OK, here I'll stop. What purpose would be served by isolating the moment of infection? Or by placing blame?

There's that haunting moment in *A Streetcar Named Desire* when Blanche concludes the opposite of death is desire. I understood this conceit all too well. With all this death in my life, I found solace in anonymous sex. But instead of cruising the parks, bathhouses or tearooms, I simply let my fingers do the walking. The digits 976 became my best friend. Chat lines of desperation and sexual addiction were now just a click away. The ground rules were few: Ritualized dialogue uttered in a fake butch voice. Crucial questions: "What do you look like?"

"What are you into?"

"Top or a bottom?" (The wrong answer meant a hasty hang-up.)

Sometimes I'd recognize the voice of a friend on the other end. *CLICK.*

A lot of phone work might lead occasionally to a hookup.

And while in public I was openly and defiantly HIV-positive, in bed I was not so forthcoming.

Hear me out.

At first I would tell my sex partners I only engaged in safer sex. Then I would disclose my HIV status. That led to a hard-on buzz kill, then my tricks were out the door faster than you could say "AIDS."

These guys were willing to have sex with me before the A-bomb was dropped. But when they knew my status, the thrill was gone, and with a vengeance. So my deal with the devil was to have safer sex, with absolutely no bodily fluids exchanged, and simply ditch the conversation. Unless they asked. Then I would never, ever lie.

I can't say that these quick sexual liaisons were satisfying or fruitful. But for one brief moment an orgasm with an anonymous man took me to a better place—not a dark world of enveloping death. The booze and poppers helped.

And I was not ready to die. I toned my body and ate healthier. I educated myself on every potential drug, Western or alternative, which was in the pipeline. It didn't matter how far-fetched they sounded: megadoses of vitamin C, Chinese cucumbers, African tree bark, whatever.

Project Inform, the local group focused on identifying new HIV treatments, touted Ribavirin as a possible solution. But it was not approved by the FDA and was unavailable in this country. So, I went to Puerto Vallarta, Mexico, where the small blue and white pills were sold over the counter. I raided numerous *farmacias* to form stockpiles, then prayed to Our Lady of Guadalupe for help to smuggle the contraband across the border.

Stateside, I was accepted into one of the first trials for AZT. Many people suffered from the nasty, sometimes deadly side effects of the drug, but I felt none. The only downside was the monthly visits to the trial site, where I was subjected to a barrage of mental acuity tests: ink blots, memory tricks, pencil mazes, etc., to determine whether the drug was making me cuckoo.

I was on this trial for several years. At my last visit I was told, "Thank you for your participation." When I asked where I could go to continue to obtain AZT, there was a blank stare. I began panicking as I walked out the door.

At the statue of John Huston in Puerto Vallarta.

I made a bunch of frantic phone calls, but met dead ends. Then someone mentioned a clinic opening at St. Mary's Hospital. I took the next bus. A nurse named Joan Sneider greeted me. She walked with a limp, but flew into action like an angel. She immediately enrolled me in a new program that let me continue AZT. My T-cells remained relatively stable. And much to my surprise, I stayed healthy. "Let me live!" became my new mantra.

Act 1, Scene 21 – TROUBLE IN PARADISE

When I told folks I was writing a memoir, some who loathed me (and there are more than a few) would comment with smug superiority, "I can't wait to read the chapter about *Men in Love*."

So, here goes. The chapter about my big, fat film flop.

First, a little recap of late 1980s gay history. Along with the growing street activism of ACT UP, there was a burgeoning movement of spiritual awakening. This was best exemplified by the motivational teachings of Louise Hay. With affirmations such as "My mind and body are in perfect balance, I am a harmonious being," Hay was attracting a significant gay following. As the epidemic expanded, so did her circle of disciples.

Much of the larger activist community greeted her with accusations of fraud and quackery. Although I was not a follower, I was adamant that political action and spiritual wellness were not mutually exclusive. I might have pooh-poohed the alleged healing power of crystals. Still, I felt inner peace could help get us through the madness. Whatever worked!

Enter producer Scott Catamas with the idea of a film that would champion the healing power of tantric sex for those affected by HIV. *Men in Love* would be a spiritually enlightening gay love story set mainly in Hawaii, full of sensitive souls, hot hunks, hibiscus flowers, kittens, candles, and AIDS.

Scott was a fellow Capricorn, born on Christmas Day. He often joked that like Christ, he had a messiah complex, determined to change the world through the power of love. He was also a straight male ally. And heaven knows we needed all the allies there were.

Scott had scoured the gay independent film community to find a director who could helm this "visionary" project. The usual suspects had declined. However, several colleagues pointed Scott to the cheap and available, HIV-positive, go-to director for hire. That would be me.

Though I scoffed at being sloppy seconds, a paying gig sure sounded appetizing.

Our initial meeting did not go well. There I was, a leather jacketed, rubber shirted, cold cynic, questioning the New Age premise of the film. But Scott pushed back, saying that a skeptic could see the film's faults and make it stronger. Dismissing my doubts, he ended our discussion with "Why don't you think about it and we'll meet again?"

For our second go-round, I decided to bring in my trusted cinematographer, Fawn Yacker, who felt right at home with candles and crystals. Fawn wore her best tie-dye outfit to our next pow-wow. She and Scott took an immediate liking to one another. That's when Scott began reeling me in; he proposed an extended weekend gathering for all of us to sniff each other out.

So we packed our bags and headed north to the Mendocino woods. Destination Camp Winnarainbow—a circus and performing arts camp for kids run by Wavy Gravy, the clown prince of the hippies. The camp also offered a program for adults who had "forgotten how to lighten up and let loose." Well, I grumbled, that's me!

Every day, Fawnsy and I would report to the rec center for theater games. We'd be working with a group of sweet inner city kids, many from foster homes and underprivileged neighborhoods. Scott wanted to see how open I would be to new experiences. And I was actually beginning to warm up to Scott; he had a natural gift for taking any situation and creating some sort of joy.

The most memorable of Scott's games was a trust exercise: Holding hands with your partner, looking them in the eyes, dancing in a small circle, and singing:

"I know that you know that I love you,
But I want you to know, that I know
You love me too!"

"Oh brother," the devil on one shoulder whispered, "how humiliating!"

"Don't be an idiot," the devil on the other shoulder hissed. "It's a job, *fool!*"

So I gave in, dancing up a storm, and singing my guts out. Fawn was proud of me for unleashing my inner hippie and letting go. We secretly christened ourselves with New Age names. I was Dark Cloud and Fawn was Silver Lining.

My performance that weekend must have been convincing. I got the job.

At that point, *Men in Love* was in the beginning stage; it was just a film treatment, a mere sketch. Actual dialog had not been written. The plot: Steven is a San Francisco AIDS activist who just lost his lover, Victor, to the disease. Steven jets off to Maui to spread the ashes on the palatial Pacific Ocean estate lorded over by Victor's rich, New-Agey friend Robert. Class differences prevail, and Steven and Robert instantly detest each other. In the tropical heat, Steven meets Peter, the hot and hunky native groundskeeper. Peter teaches Steven the joys of tantric safer sex. They have lots of it. Steven has a catharsis in a cave and gives up the ghost of Victor, as well as all other negativities. Robert and Steven hug it out. Ashes are spread. The end.

Oh, Christ.

The only seasoned actor in the cast was Doug Self, who played Steven. The rest were non-professionals—mostly buffed pretty boys. I kept insisting to Scott that not having written dialog while working with amateurs was a recipe for disaster, but he just shrugged it off. Don't worry; we'll compose the "script" through improv, he kept repeating. Well, John Cassavetes I was not, and the players were hardly Gena Rowlands.

A real-life, wealthy man named Emerald Starr was to play the fictional rich man Robert. True to the script, we immediately disliked each other.

And alas, poor Emerald had a face for radio. I rallied for a real actor to be cast. But whether he could act (he couldn't) or have one iota of on-screen charisma (he didn't) wouldn't have mattered; Emerald was a co-producer, and the picture would be filmed at his estate, Hali Akua. Case closed.

Ironically, the part of Peter (the native Hawaiian Steven falls for) was cast outside the island. Emerald's community in Maui was mostly white folks. To our great luck, in San Francisco we found Joe Tolbe, a non-professional with a mixture of Spanish/Filipino/Chinese blood. What he lacked in actor's training, he made up for in his demeanor. He had a calm, sweet, natural quality, an open face and a beautiful sinewy body. And unlike Emerald, the camera loved him. Joe was the picture's saving grace.

The piece was to be shot in state-of-the-art video and blown up to 35mm film. "It'll look like a million bucks," Scott assured us. The funding, $350,000 in total, was secured, and we were on our way.

From Day One of the shoot, we realized the challenges ahead. These tantric New Agers were not that popular with some on the island. As we drove down a long, winding dirt road, we would see warnings put up by belligerent neighbors in big bold handwritten red letters: "This is NOT Hali Akua. DO NOT ENTER." Aloha and goodbye!

The first night there, we all were introduced to executive producer Richard, an heir to a powerful Boston banking family. After the meeting, Richard spent the evening alone, blowing on a conch shell and braying loudly at the moon. He ruined everyone's sleep, making the crew angry and agitated at the next day's early call. They demanded a meeting to air their grievances.

But there must have been something in the Maui water. After a rough first start, the crew actually started to love being in Hawaii and shooting this wacky film. And since there was a good deal of hot flesh exhibited by the cast, everyone started to get really horny. And not in their usual ways. Lesbians were coupling with straight men, monogamous married folks were having clandestine affairs, and nights off were filled with the sound of sex and happy endings.

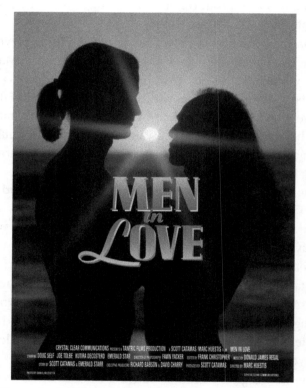

*The poster for "Men in Love." Designed by Silvana Nova.
Photo by Daniel Nicoletta.*

I wish I were having as much fun. As director, with no written script, I was making things up on the fly. I had no idea what the fuck I was doing. Moreover, the unskilled acting of most of the cast resulted in a series of unintentionally campy moments. The heavy-handed overly earnest hot tub scene where Robert chews out Steven for releasing balloons at the San Francisco memorial, scolding "Did you know that the dolphins can mistakenly swallow those balloons and die" was classic! And *not* in a good way.

At the wrap party aboard a rented yacht, Scott congratulated everyone on a job well done. Ever the optimist, he was convinced the film would "win lots of awards." As a farewell present, tabs of ecstasy were made available to the now-oversexed crew. I declined the gift. Once the drug took effect, everyone breathlessly told me how much they "loved me" before going off in twos, threes, and multiples to do…whatever.

Afterwards, on the mainland, I was forced to try and make something of this mangled mess. It wasn't easy. By the time of the final cut, I tried to convince myself that the picture wasn't *that* bad.

Then the first critics saw the movie. At the Roxie Theatre press screening, *San Francisco Chronicle* reviewer Peter Stack locked himself in a bathroom stall during the climactic cave scene. "Peter," I cluelessly suggested, "get back in there, you're missing the best part."

Little did I know he was hiding. He hated everything about the film and couldn't bear watching another second. His review was zero stars out of four.

But Scott shrugged it off. "Screw the critics. I just know audiences will love this."

The film *was* marketed beautifully. A love story, full of naked boys, ravishing sunsets, beautiful scenery, and real sex. One has to remember that in that period of the AIDS crisis, when the news was so grim, sex had become a four-letter word. *Men in Love* was an alternative to the depressing reality of our plague. Any movie that embraced gay sexuality, and tugged on romantic heartstrings was bound to draw a crowd.

And the crowds *did* come. The gala opening night at the 1,400-seat Castro was completely sold out. At the buzz-filled pre-show cocktail party, I met gay philanthropist James Hormel—

affectionately known as the Queen of Spam—and a friend of Emerald's. He pulled me aside, saying, "Please come to me with your next project, I'll be sure to help you out."

Yippee!

We all buoyantly took our seats. The lights went down, and the film's title filled the screen. Thunderous applause.

I should have left then.

As the picture unfolded, you could feel the audience squirming. By the middle of the film, there were groans. After the dolphin diatribe, gales of guffaws. By the time Victor's ashes were spread, I was slumped so low in my chair, I was practically on the floor.

The day after, I fled to Mexico.

Still, an investment had been made. Scott, perpetually sunny about the film's chances in the broader market, convinced me to return and employed me to promote the film during its multi-city screenings. After the critical impaling *Men In Love* had suffered in San Francisco, I was skeptical I could truthfully promote the film, but… Again it was a paycheck, Jack. So again I deluded myself of its merits.

Based on our San Francisco box office, we got excellent bookings in New York City: the Bleecker Street and Carnegie Hall cinemas. I had to admit, it was kinda thrilling to be playing at Carnegie Hall!

My excitement was short-lived. The New York reviews came out.

Kathleen Carroll in the *Daily News* called *Men in Love* "A love story that's a bore…absurd…moronic."

Titling his review "Zithering Idiots," Elliot Stein of the *Village Voice* blasted the film: "A limp, gay New Age soap opera, ineffective to the point of embarrassment."

In a twisted way, I got a kick out of this skewering. These reviews were howl-out-loud funny, and thankfully none of them mentioned my name. So I got off easy. And oddly, the sole positive notice we got was from The New York Times; Caryn James praised the film as "more direct in its treatment of homosexual love in the age of AIDS and more moving in its portrayal of grief than any mainstream film has managed to be."

The opening night party was thrown by NYC event promoter Chip Duckett. Everyone invited had read the reviews and/or saw the picture. Nobody showed up; the cavernous club was empty except for the hired go-go boys, half-heartedly gyrating in their tropical sarongs. So I did what any humiliated director would do: I got blotto on the free drinks. In an alcoholic haze, I staggered to the Spike, my S&M bar of choice, made a scene, got into a brawl, and was 86'ed. For days afterwards, I sported a shiner, a souvenir of my big New York opening.

Still the film did brisk business in New York. Ironically (or maybe not) it was the last picture to screen at the Carnegie Hall Cinema before it closed. (We stunk up the joint, then shut it down.)

Meanwhile, the picture continued to draw crowds nationwide, despite the continuous barrage of bad reviews. Sex sells, even when covered with flop sweat.

OK, you ask, why did I make *Men In Love*? I can be a bitch and tell you it was for the money. Partially true. Still I got to work with a real budget on someone else's dime. And my softer side still thinks that despite its hackneyed view of spirituality, it did inch the dialogue forward toward an embrace of sexuality in the time of AIDS. Of that I can take a bit of pride and solace (although *Men In Love* is a film that *never* appears on my resume).

An artist should always learn from his or her flops, and the lessons learned would guide them towards future success. Which, as fate would have it…

Act 1, Scene 22 – SEX IS...

Just as the first generation of AIDS warriors was wearying, a second generation came onto the scene. The cavalry had arrived and they were energetic, angry, and adorable.

Both ACT UP and Queer Nation formed San Francisco chapters. The streets were alive again with leather-jacketed, Doc Marten-wearing, multi-earringed, newly inked, totally queer kids. Instead of retreating behind closed doors and fear, they were itching for a fight. And they made it sexy!

Galvanized by this new social and political energy, all sorts of adjunct activist activities were springing up. Suddenly, lamp poles and plywood siding everywhere were displaying large 11x17 Xeroxes of homoerotic art. Two frequently seen slogans, created by the underground guerrilla queer art collective Boy with Arms Akimbo, were JUST SEX and SEX IS.

I loved their work. It was putting the sexual back into homosexual.

Concurrent with this new graphic activism was a blast of repressive government action targeting the arts. The culture war was on. Archconservative Senator Jesse Helms ranted, and federal grants were rescinded, shows canceled. Artists were now the enemy of the right. But if the government thought we were going to lie down and play dead, they had another thing coming.

Out of this crucible came the idea for my next film. Inspired by Akimbo's art slogan, my thought was to go one step further. I transformed SEX IS. with a period into *Sex Is...* with three dots. Instead of a definitive statement, sex would be open to interpretation.

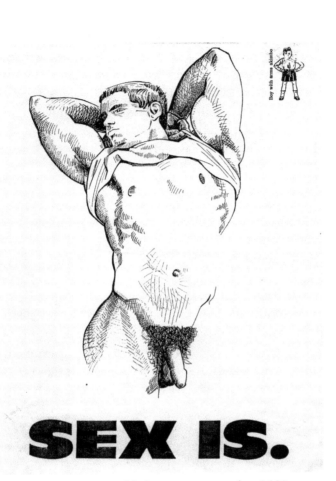

Boy with Arms Akimbo street poster, circa 1989.

My new work, I decided, would be a natural progression from the disastrous *Men in Love*. I'd still embrace its core message of healthy open sexuality. But I'd strip the new film of hot tubs and kitties, and get to the meat of things. Instead of a fictional format, I'd create a documentary that would allow a multitude of voices to speak their truths about their own sex and sexuality.

I realized I couldn't go it alone. And kismet would again bring the help I needed.

One afternoon I was at the corner of Castro and 18th, staple-gunning posters for the first fundraiser for *Sex Is*.... From out of nowhere came a dark-haired, blue-eyed stranger with a thick New York Jewish accent. He offered to help. I noticed that he wore his keys on the left (signifying he was a top), and wondered what type of help he was offering.

"My name is Larry. I've been a fan of your work since I saw *Whatever Happened to Susan Jane?* at the Thalia in New York."

Larry had good taste.

"My name is Marc," I flirtatiously volunteered.

"I know that, idiot!" Larry shot back with a laugh. Snark. I liked that.

"Well, would you like to have a cup of coffee sometime?" I proposed.

"I hate coffee, but sure!" Larry even had a tongue!

My coffee date with Larry Helman at the Café Flore was fortuitous. We had between us an amazing amount of connective tissue. Larry had gone to SUNY Binghamton right around the time I had. He even trolled for dick in the same bathroom by Lecture Hall 6! Who knows, maybe we even had sex together.

Bizarrely, Larry had also worked a summer job at the Landers Perfume factory, though we worked on different floors.

And the topper: As kids, we both had the same rare blood disease: Idiopathic thrombocytopenic purpura (ITP). The annual incidence in children is estimated at 25 to 50 new cases per million!

Fate brought us together. Despite my initial physical attraction, Sally Bowles's line in *Cabaret* came to mind: "Sex always seems to screw up a friendship if you let it. So we won't let it." God knows I had enough tricks to last a lifetime. But this man was too much of a catch to let go. I decided on the spot that Larry would be a perfect co-producer for *Sex Is*....

Thus, my closest business partnership was born.

Moving forward, I spent hours scouring the town for interview subjects—determined to find a group of gay men who represented the full spectrum of our sexual experience, from monogamy to explorative, from vanilla to hardcore. I wanted folks who were not stereotypes of their race or demographic, but were non-didactic, fully fleshed-out, complex and contradictory human beings. Racial diversity was imperative. But that didn't come easily; almost all of my friends were white.

Imagine my delight when I met Wayne Corbitt, an acclaimed African-American poet with AIDS who was into S&M—as a masochistic "slave." In our pre-interview he floored me when he spoke of the pleasure of getting whipped by a white South African. "My politics were telling me one thing, and my dick was telling me another," he revealed.

Bit by bit, I put together the cast. They represented the panoply of gay sexual experiences, ranging from an 18-year-old "slut" to a 75-year-old Presbyterian minister. They were: Larry Brinkin, Danny Castellow, Alex Chee, Wayne Corbitt, Jim Glyer, Miguel Gutierrez, Bob Hawk, Gerard Koskovich, Bambi Lake, Lulu, R. Wood Massi, David Perry, Brad Phillips, and Madame X.

I was also part of the cast, wanting to make sure the intent was not voyeuristic but collaborative. (OK, maybe a little narcissism was in play; I loved being on camera.) The film's slogan: "Sex Is... Exploring the Meaning of Sex and Sexuality in the Lives of Gay Men." (Today, cast members Bambi Lake and Madame X might be classified as trans women, not gay men; but that discussion was still years away.)

Most of the *Men in Love* crew came onboard for a fraction of their going rate. Maybe that tab of ecstasy at the Maui wrap party had paid dividends after all.

One new crewmember joined the production before the shoot. A trick had recommended a handsome new kid in town as the perfect intern.

Peter Gowdy showed up at my house, a native son of Massachusetts, Vassar graduate, and incredibly polite. And yes, rosy-cheeked, freshly scrubbed and incredibly good-looking.

The interview went well. Just as we were ready to wrap up, Peter said he had something that he needed to tell me that might be a deal breaker. Sheepishly, he disclosed, "I'm ummmm... straight." It was the most adorable moment. I patted him on the back and said, "That's OK, I'm looking for an intern, not a boyfriend. You got the job." Smiling, Peter rode off on his scooter like a mod extra from *Quadrophenia*. I nicknamed him "Scootsy." He became a decades-long valued player in my career.

With cast and crew assembled, we used Danny Nicoletta's photo studio as our location for interviews. It provided a safe harbor for intimacy and vulnerability. Each person had a two-hour slot to explore his personal and sexual history and philosophy. Since the piece was shot in video, we could allow for longer, fuller, richer sessions. These interviews were shot in the course of three days, again by the talented director of photography Fawn Yacker.

Sometimes a set becomes a sacred space where the production unit and talent become one. This set was such a place. When a cast member told a funny story, we'd hold our laughter until the command "cut." Then, in unison, we'd all break out in a roar, tears streaming, snot bubbling from our noses. When the men were revealing the most intimate details of their lives, one could hear a pin drop. Over those three days, you could feel the cast and crew bonding.

The grace note of the shoot came when Wayne Corbitt, the spiritual center of the film, described his suicide attempt:

> *"I picked up a razor blade and just started cutting. And my lover David grabbed my arms back, trying to hold the blood down and started kissing me. And I started to kiss back. And then the wrestling turned into something else. It wasn't wrestling anymore, we were now feeling each other's bodies, and he was still trying to hold on. It got so wild so fast; all of this is in thirty seconds.... It became the hottest sex we ever had. Everything in that relationship was encapsulated in that battle. I was trying to kill myself and he was trying to stop me. I hated myself and he was saying, 'I love you.' (Long pause, Wayne starts to cry) I miss him."*

It was the single most beautiful moment I have ever experienced as a filmmaker. David, Wayne's love, had died of HIV-related causes, and Wayne himself had full-blown AIDS. The raw humanity, fueled by a memory so rooted in sex, was exactly what I had been hoping for. At that moment, I took off my director's hat. I stopped shooting and just hugged Wayne tight.

After the three days of *Sex Is...* stories, each unique and utterly captivating, we were all exhausted and invigorated. We had become a family; none of us wanted to leave each other. We had created and lived through something special.

Then the post-production grind began. For almost three years, we struggled to find finishing funds. It was a labor of love. But as any woman will tell you, labor can be prolonged and painful. We tried everything to raise the $60,000 budget.

We threw countless benefits. Larry, a veteran caterer, poured lots of bubbly and chopped a lot of cheese. One house party held in Los Angeles boasted A-list guests: Lily Tomlin, cabaret star Michael Feinstein, Yippie activist Jerry Rubin, and Deborah Walley, star of *Gidget Goes Hawaiian*. It was all very glamorous. But we didn't make more than $100.

To add insult to injury, when I came home tired and depressed from this fundraiser, I found my cat lifeless on the couch. P.S., your cat is dead.

The moneyed disinterest in my film about gay sex continued. I reached out to philanthropist James Hormel. I thought he would be a slam-dunk after he cornered me at the opening of *Men in Love*, asking to be involved in my next project. Well, the Queen of Spam was not interested in this project. Phone calls, letters and faxes all went unanswered.

Money be damned, we pushed forward with editing the video. *Sex Is...*, a piece about gay male sexuality created in San Francisco, was actually cut by two foreign-born lesbians. Lara Mac was a bright, young, spike-haired, cocky British dyke. When she could no longer work on the piece, she recommended Icelandic colleague Hrafnhildur Gunnarsdottir—yes, that was her name!

"Hrapsy," as I nicknamed her, was a force of nature. A big-boned, big-hearted Amazon, full of spice mixed with ice. And quite lovable. She also brought a more radical vision. After a series of work-in-progress screenings, she realized that something was missing from the picture: sex.

She began filling the picture with real man-on-man sex. And lots of it! Hard-ons, blowjobs, penetration, ejaculation, the works. There were times even I was a bit shocked. "Take that out!" I implored. "No!" Hrapsy barked back. "It's perfect."

She was right. After all, the picture was called *Sex Is...* It would be hypocrisy to have a bunch of gay guys *talking* about sex, without having the *cojones* to actually *show* what they were talking about. Her additional edits were not gratuitous, they were illustrative. And titillating. Hrapsy had made *Sex Is...* sexy!

Once we had the proper mix of talking heads, old newsreels, archival footage, vintage erotica and pure porn, the video was locked. We had already been invited to the 1993 Berlin Film Festival, by old ally Manfred Salzgeber, who had seen an early rough cut. Now we were ready for the on-line edit. But we didn't have the money to pay for it, even at a significant discount offered by friend Clyde Wildes.

So Lawrence and I did what many a desperate filmmaker is humbled to do: We borrowed money from our parents. Lawrence from mother Gladys, me from father Hank. At last we were on our way back to Berlin.

Act 1, Scene 23 – THE THEATER OF SEX

In the midst of the creative whirlpool surrounding *Sex Is...*, another life-changing moment occurred: I discovered crystal meth.

Not that you asked, but let me offer a candid history of my substance intake (what would any memoir be without it?). OK, I occasionally smoked grass, I popped a few pills. In the '70s I did LSD maybe 10 times as a "spiritual cleansing." But the reality of the '80s quickly put a stop to this. Nothing spiritual about seeing a dear friend covered with KS while peaking on acid.

My drug of choice was booze. I was a binge drinker—though usually a disciplined one. There were the occasional fuck-ups: Like the time, after Macy's Passport (a glitzy AIDS benefit), when Lulu found me in the bushes puking my guts out, then blithely chanting "H – I – V! ... I've got H – I – V!" again and again, like an obnoxious high school cheerleader.

When work was involved, I typically abstained. I would never show up sloshed in the editing room or at a meeting. If there was a strict schedule (and being a Capricorn I liked those), I would be sober. Of course when the work was done, I'd make up for lost time. All those Vodka gimlets would get me into a lot of trouble.

Despite being a part-time boozehound, the drug culture of the gay community had passed me by. Or rather, I had bypassed it. Because, believe me, I was surrounded by it—particularly in the leather scene, which after I broke-up with Phillip, I often frequented. If a line of cocaine was offered before sex, I would decline. I never actually liked it (though I always needed my poppers to seal the deal). Compared to many of my peers. I was relatively clean.

That all changed one fateful, liquor-ridden night in the early '90s. On the prowl in Ringold Alley—the destination point after the Folsom Street bars' last call—I caught the eye of a man that I had been interested in for some time. He was not classically handsome; in fact, he was kinda butt-ugly, with an undeveloped flabby body, anemic-looking white skin, and wisps of dirty blond hair under his biker cap. But he oozed raunchy sex. He was hardcore, dressed in head to toe black leather, the accoutrements of his fetishes hanging down from his left side: handcuffs, whips, rope, slave collar, even a large wooden paddle. This total top was a total turn-on.

My friend, art critic David Bonetti, once told me that I really didn't want sex; what I desired was the *theater* of sex. This man was the perfect actor for my fantasy passion play.

I had cruised him before and he never seemed interested. Until that night. Maybe it was because I was dressed in tight Spandex, the contours of my butt shining in the streetlight. Maybe because he was high and the hour was hitting 3 a.m. Desperation time in the dark alley.

So we met.

His name was Charles. After our respective laundry lists of sexual proclivities were exchanged, he whispered in my ear, "Do you like crystal?"

"I've never done it," I replied. "Let's go! "

After a quick ride on his motorcycle, we entered his apartment, which smelled like rancid Crisco and was filled with dirty dishes, greasy porn tapes, and a cornucopia of sex toys. On the cluttered dining room table was a large mirror with six *huge* lines of white powder.

I tipped my head to the mirror and snorted my first line of crystal through a glass straw.

The room began to spin. The rush felt mind-expanding and tingly. I became *really* hungry for this man.

"Do anything you want with me," I urged him, my words drooling through spittle. "Just as long as it's safe; I'm HIV-positive."

"No problem," he eagerly retorted.

Master Charles tied me tighter to a bed than I had ever been tied before, and beat the shit out of me, employing a ritualistic series of whips, paddles, rubber hoses, and canes. I would count out each lash as it hit my body. At first in series of tens. "One, sir, thank you sir. Two, sir, thank you, sir."

The result was a night of utter debauch. Brutal. Dangerous. And I loved it.

After each of the beatings, he'd untie me and we'd do another line of crystal. When the six lines ran out, I begged him to put out more.

"OK," he said. "But that would cost you a hundred lashes. Uninterrupted. "

"Yes, sir!"

"Tina"—code name for crystal—became my new best girlfriend.

At one point, Charles stuffed me in a closet, for who knows how long. When I was let out, there was a huge, muscular black man tightly bound on his bed, and obviously fucked up. I watched Charles beat him. I seethed. The drugs made me so jealous; I wanted my "master" all to myself.

After the other man left, Charles ordered me to put on my spandex, collared and leashed me, and took me on a pre-dawn Sunday stroll through Buena Vista Park, demeaning me and talking dirty the whole way. As the sun was rising, he chained me to the fence of the tennis court and caned me, ordering me to count the blows out quietly, so as not to attract the homeless that slept in the bushes. Then he led me to a thicket and beat me some more. The sun was now blinding, my heart racing a mile a minute. "T"—another nickname for crystal—made it all seem so right, romantic even.

The scene with Charles must have lasted 10 hours. No bodily fluids were exchanged. In fact, none of us even got erections. And I'm sure the T wreaked havoc on my T-cells. But who gave a shit? This magic powder had released all inhibitions and opened up a new world for me.

By the time Charles drove me home I could barely sit down. He scribbled his phone number on a paper napkin.

I was now alone in my apartment, and I desperately needed to cum. After a few hours of stroking, watching porn, sweating bullets, and still not climaxing, the Tina hangover began to creep in. At first, my sheets were so drenched I couldn't sleep. After I stripped the bed and drank a whole quart of vodka, I finally went into a deep slumber. I slept for a full 36 hours, getting up only to binge out on food and fluid.

When I finally awoke, the world was enveloped in a pea-green haze. I began hallucinating demons. And I became severely depressed. I had my fun, now the piper needed to be paid. And the aftereffects were horrible. Ungodly. Crystal was the drug of the devil. I swore I would never do it again.

Until the next time.

A few weeks went by. I told myself I was doing fine without it. Then I began to crave it. I called Charles. He was thrilled to hear from me. We'd see each other every three months. After working hard on *Sex Is…* I looked forward to the danger and licentiousness of these wild escapades. There was a joy and excitement in the humiliation—and a hunger for the accompanying drugs. Charles also loved seeing me. In fact, he got off on our time together so much, that by the end he was paying me $200 for 200 very harsh lashes in tight bondage. This exchange of cash for ass turned me on. It made me feel like I was worth something. Thus evolved several years of periodic and evolving sex sessions.

When you're having sex on crystal, you're not having sex with the person but with the drug. This proved true with the subsequent "PNP" (party and play) hookups with men outside of the hookups with Charles.

It didn't matter what the men looked like. Some were hot, some were hideous. But when you become a "bag whore," all that matters is the shiny white powder they supply. I smoked and snorted. I watched men jab needles into their veins. I swore I'd never go that far. Mainlining was for addicts and I was certainly not one of those.

Me at the Crystal Wall in the Castro, an outlet for people to post their thoughts about the party drug wreaking havoc in the gay community.

I was not a regular user, I assured myself; after all, my work schedule disciplined me. When I could find a clearing on the calendar, I'd call Charles, or get on the phone lines. Then, with the advent of Craigslist, I'd get online. There, fellow T users employed an obvious code in their postings—"looking to geT off," "feeling greaT," "have an exciTing time?" eTc., eTc.

Make no mistake, for me crystal was the best drug for sex. But following an exhausting drugged-out sex session, my mood swings were fierce. Often I became a monster, very Jekyll and Hyde.

Tina would become, for almost a decade, my covert companion, a dark camouflaged part of my life.

Act 1, Scene 24 – WILLKOMMEN

After three years of hard labor, Sex *Is…* would have its world premiere at the Berlin International Film Festival.

Nothing, however, comes easy. Due to festival rules, we needed the video master to be transferred to 16 mm film. Larry Helman (who now wanted to be known as Lawrence) had flown down to L.A. to supervise the job at Image Transform, the same lab that had done the tape-to-film conversion of *Men in Love*. As he handed accounting the first check, it was quickly returned.

"Our company policy is that we do not show any penile erections or insertions of any kind," the lab's vice president made clear. Lawrence asked to see the company policy. The VP countered, "We do not have it in writing. That's our internal company *opinion*. Whereas *Men in Love* had gay sex scenes, there was no anal penetration." "That's funny, you never said any of this as we were sending you materials on the film. And it's friggin' called *Sex Is….*" Lawrence was quickly shown the door.

Panic set in. We were less than a week away from our first Berlin screening. Three of the four labs specializing in this process were either unwilling or unable to do the job. The fourth allowed scenes of female frontal nudity, but no male. But just when we were ready to give up, help came—from Detroit.

An obscure lab named Film Craft was willing to take a look at the film. But after careful review, more bad news. They would have to pass on the project. We were desperate. We begged, pleaded, cajoled. We explained that given the AIDS crisis, the film might help save lives. That Berlin was a respected festival not known for showing smut. We deluged the lab with a list of prestigious advisors and sponsors. The lab finally agreed to do the job.

Even though we had no film print, I had already flown to Berlin to lay the groundwork for the opening, joined by our editor Hrafnhildur Gunnarsdottir, the woman responsible for the hardcore penetration scenes. "A fine mess you got us into, Hrapsy—you goddamned Icelandic dyke! You wanted all that fucking and now we're screwed!" She let out a big guffaw.

Our Berlin team fearlessly plowed forward. We became schmooze-aholics, working every room, and becoming the life of every party. Festival folks proudly featured our bright yellow *Sex Is...* tee shirts, and the buzz on our film was terrific. Even though no one had actually seen it, many were thrilled the floodgates surrounding sex were opening at last. The first screening sold out almost a week ahead of time.

Each day we would nervously await the next fax from Lawrence at the lab in Detroit. The clock continued to tick. I was rocking double-time.

Two days before the big international premiere, the news came chugging out of the Panorama's fax machine:

Good news, transfer is done and it looks great. See you tomorrow in Berlin. XOXO, Lawrence.

We were in business! And the icing on the cake: Film Craft, which originally asked that their name not be associated with *Sex Is...*, had added a short leader with the company's name and phone number.

Wieland Speck had taken the reins of the Panorama section of the festival from Manfred Salzgeber, whose HIV disease had rapidly progressed. We were told he would be unable to attend. But, half an hour before show time, who should I see strutting down the back entrance to the theater? Manfred, like Lazarus rising from the dead and looking spry as a fox.

The Zoopalast Theatre was alive with energetic anticipation. The SRO crowd was young and old, mostly male, très gay and very cruisy. Noted film professionals also attended, including indie giant John Sayles and Albert Maysles, co-creator of one of my favorite documentaries, *Grey Gardens*.

Lawrence Helman, John Sayles, and Marc Huestis
after the Berlin premiere of "Sex Is..."

As Wieland introduced the screening, I could barely hear his words. It was just like one of those moments you see in old black and white Hollywood movies, when actual sounds fade out and people's voices turn into underwater garble. Your inner monologue takes over: "Three years of toil and here you are. And it was all worth it!"

As our freshly minted film print hit the screen, the normally critical German festival audience laughed and cried in all the right places. The applause at the end was loud and sustained.

The world premiere of *Sex Is...* had gone magnificently.

Still, I was awaiting the verdict of the one person who really mattered: Manfred. I could see a concerned look in his eye. He had only seen a rough cut months beforehand, before Hrapsy added all that sex.

"Oh, Marc, so much fucking!" Then a pregnant pause. "Well, you have made the film much more...*radical*. I wonder how the bosses at the festival will react?" Another sly pause. "Shit, what do I care? After all, I'm *dying!*"

Manfred needn't have worried; his colleagues in the festival's hierarchy embraced the film. And after our screening, we received a shitload of other festival invitations from around the world. They all were clamoring for the picture. But no distribution offers. Our man on the ground from Harvey Weinstein's Miramax, *the* major distributor at the time, called our work "brilliant," yet quickly changed the subject when we steered the conversation toward business. Another major distributor of gay films liked the film, but hated my guts. So *that* was going to go nowhere.

By the end of the week, we had no film deal to sweeten our Berlin triumph. Fuck it. We quickly decided to forego a distributor and just do it ourselves. After all, how hard could it be?

Before leaving Berlin, there was one final major festival event we were obliged to attend. Manfred and Wieland had created the Teddy Awards in 1987 to honor LGBT films in the festival. Throughout the years it had become quite a respected prize. Still a mole told us that we would not be winning the juried award for Best Documentary. Nonetheless, part of the job as a filmmaker is to just show up and put on your best face. I did, congratulating all the winners. Just as I was about to leave, Manfred pulled me aside. "Shit, Marc—stay."

Wieland then announced, "We have one more Teddy to give out. The non-juried Audience Award for Best Film of the festival. We have just counted all the ballots, and to make positive, counted them again. The award goes to (pregnant pause) *Sex Is...* von Marc Huestis!"

I was stunned. I climbed the stage, and blabbed like a fool. I did manage to thank "my Guardian Angel, Manfred Salzgeber." But as the house lights went up, I realized I had not thanked my partner-in-crime Lawrence Helman. As he came forward to congratulate me, I apologized profusely. "Don't worry, honey," he reassured me. "I'm so proud of you."

Because *Sex Is...* had won a Teddy, I was invited the next evening to the prestigious Golden Bear ceremonies in the Grande Salle of the Zoopalast. It was filled with heavy hitters in the international film community. I looked around in wonder. There was Gregory Peck, there Catherine Deneuve. And two rows in front of me sat a god of the cinema: Billy Wilder. Yes, BILLY. FUCKING. WILDER, director of one of my all-time-favorite films, *Sunset Boulevard*.

I began to cry uncontrollably. Several years ago, I had given myself up for dead when I learned I was HIV-positive. Yet somehow I survived. And here I was face-to-face with my all-time idol, Billy Wilder. In the 1930s Wilder left his homeland to escape the Holocaust. I, too, was a survivor of my community's Holocaust. And at this moment, I was so, so happy to be alive.

And there's this fun postscript. A few years later, Image Transform—the lab that refused our job on "moral" grounds—went out of business, largely due to press reports of the *Sex Is...* contretemps in the trades. And Film Craft, the only lab that would do the transfer, experienced a huge boom in their business.

Act 1, Scene 25 – THE SWEET SMELL OF SUCCESS

The stars were in perfect alignment for the release of *Sex Is*.... Finally, *finally* after the election of 1992, the long nightmare of the Reagan/Bush presidencies was over. Folks were brimming with optimism at the inauguration of our energetic new president Bill Clinton. ACT UP and Queer Nation had transformed the community's social landscape, and rumors abounded about new AIDS drugs in the pipeline. Trials of these promising combination therapies were well under way. And we had only to look around to see that some of us HIV-positives were surviving.

We could also hear the reassuring voice of Glinda the Good Witch once more, chirping, "Come out, come out, wherever you are." And we did, this time to our nation's capital.

The March on Washington for Lesbian, Gay and Bi Equal Rights and Liberation was slated for April 25, 1993. With over a million people expected to descend on the city, Lawrence Helman and I scheduled the U.S. premiere of *Sex Is...* at D.C.'s Biograph Theatre.

That remarkable spring week the whole city was abuzz. And besides making a political statement, everyone was actually having *fun* again. Topless dykes were dancing atop the Dupont Circle fountain. Semi-nude men gyrated with a sexual abandon not seen in years. The zeitgeist seemed ripe for a film celebrating gay sex.

Still the Biograph's opening weekend run of *Sex Is...* drew only a modest crowd and polite applause. We began to get slightly apprehensive. Was Berlin a fluke? But come Monday, after the frenzy of the weekend of activities ended and there was little to do in DC, our box office exploded.

The following month, our weeklong engagement at San Francisco's Castro Theatre set a box-office record for an independent documentary. A line of happy gay guys snaked around the block before each showing. During the making of the film, we were constantly questioned—and questioned ourselves—as to whether such a gay film, obviously not targeted to a mainstream (i.e. straight) audience, could be a success. The answer was now clear.

The icing on the cake was this article in *Daily Variety*:

Variety headline, May 25, 1993.

"New exclusive releases found it very tough to gain a foothold as the majors' summer releases started pouring off the assembly lines. A notable exception was Outsider Productions' documentary *Sex Is*...with a very strong opening at San Francisco's Castro Theatre earning $24,234 in its first weekend."

Through Sande Zeig, our booking agent, we scored a New York premiere engagement at the indie art house Cinema Village.

A one-week run was extended to one month due to our strong grosses, fueled by positive reviews. Stephen Holden of *The New York Times* heralded the film as "so welcome. It addresses male homosexual intimacy with a refreshing directness. At a moment when gay sexuality is often glibly equated with AIDS, it is firmly but responsibly pro-sex."

Theater bookings poured in. Next stop, the NuArt in Los Angeles. Again, boffo business and another *Variety* headline, playfully proclaiming, "Indy B.O. goes limp, but '*Sex Is...*' great in L.A."

Variety headline, November 16, 1993.

Our B.O. was beginning to emanate the sweet smell of success. We were warned self-distribution could not be done. Yet we were proving the skeptics wrong. Lawrence's one-bedroom apartment on 17th Street became *Sex Is...* central headquarters. It was crammed with papers, schedules, and ad-slicks designed on our spanking new Macintosh Quadra. The phone was ringing at all hours, from time zones around the world. The fax machine was purring overtime.

Granted, our operation was not a financial honey pot. After the theater rental was deducted (often 65% of the gross), and paying the costs for 16mm prints, shipping, booking, travel, promotion, and publicists, we were left with little. But we accrued a modest salary—after we paid back our parents.

Best of all, our film was being seen, not just in metropolitan centers on the coasts, but across America: the Deep South, the

Midwest, in thriving college towns, and beyond. *Sex Is...*screened in over 65 locations in the U.S.

While a few conservative critics skewered the picture, most of the reviews were effusive. Betsy Sherman in the *Boston Globe* called the film "significant and sad. It generates light, heat, noise and very nearly smells." In *Rolling Stone*, Peter Travers heralded *Sex Is...* as "responsible, raunchy and always riveting." Kevin Thomas of the *L.A. Times* declared *Sex Is...* "a landmark film."

There were a few critical quibbles: In the age of AIDS, shouldn't there be more of an emphasis on love, less on sex? Why weren't there more warm and fuzzy couples like the monogamous bears?

Still, crowds showed up. Often, we would donate opening day receipts to a local LGBT or AIDS not-for-profit. And I got to connect with lot of new people, celebrate our openings at festive club parties in numerous cities, rub elbows with local celebrities, and delight in the kindness of strangers. Best of all, I heard of others that had met at a *Sex Is...* screening. Even one of the stars. Brad Phillips met the love of his life William through the film. William first saw Brad on-screen in Cincinnati, then moved to San Francisco, spotted him at a night club, and got up the nerve to ask him, "Weren't you in *Sex Is...*?" That was Valentine's Day 1998 and they have been together ever since.

And speaking of Brad Phillips... Lawrence had his favorite story from the road, occurring at the Montreal Film Festival. In the lobby after the film a very straight-laced woman dressed in business attire approached. She thanked us for making *Sex Is...* and was particularly effusive about Brad, the porn star interviewed in our film. When Lawrence asked her how she knew Brad's name, she replied, "I see a lot of him at my job." Taken a bit aback, Lawrence queried, "What exactly do you do?" "I work for the Quebec censor board," she officiously replied. "I watch pornographic films all day to make sure they meet community standards. If they do, I give them an official seal of approval. And I'm a big fan of Mr. Phillips!"

Outside of festivals, international distribution proved to be a tougher nut to crack.

Some accuse the United States of being the most puritanical nation on the planet. Not true. Even in small, conservative towns, theaters didn't give a rat's ass if the film contained smutty imagery. Just as long as it made money.

But other countries had stricter regulations. Fucking and sucking—even semi hard-ons—were a no-no. In the U.K., there was the notorious "protractor rule." If a cinematic penis was over 45 degrees erect, it was not allowed in cinemas. (Who was measuring penile angles? Nice work if you can get it!)

Believe it or not, Toronto, Canada, and the province of Ontario had some of the toughest anti-pornography laws on the books. To get around them, we shipped the film as *The Outsider*, a documentary about aging. And to be doubly safe, the Bloor Theatre booked a weekend run, while courts were out of session.

In Australia, the release was approved under one condition: All explicit images were to be blacked out. So the distributor spent considerable time applying black tape to the footage. The censors didn't object to erotic sounds, so you could hear heavy breathing, panting, moaning, and cumming—but no picture.

Germany also had censorship laws, but brave Manfred Salzgeber shrugged them off. "Screw them! Let them try to arrest me." I participated in another of his "Berlin and Beyond" tours, screening *Sex Is...* in multiple burgs to hungry audiences. The tour was to be Manfred's last hurrah. It was a big success.

There was something deeply satisfying about our successful DIY operation (which was becoming *the* recurring theme of my career). We were posting numbers real distributors could only envy. Once again I loved living. And my work. The organizing, the interviews, the personal appearances, the countless cities traveled. And when given a focus, a purpose, a strict schedule, this Capricorn was clean. Totally off the sauce and my friend Tina.

By year's end, *Variety* reported that *Sex Is...* placed among the top five highest-grossing documentaries of the year.

Twenty-five years later, *Sex Is...* has been largely forgotten. Still, at the time it was a clarion call to arms, a life-affirming reaction to an era when so many thought sex = death. We helped change that equation and for that *Sex Is...* was really something.

Act 1, Scene 26 – AFTER THE BALL

After the boners of *Sex Is…* my film career went—well, flaccid. Novices will tell you that an artistic and commercial success surely guarantees funding for a new project. But veterans will warn you that with each film you are basically starting from scratch. That proved to be the sad truth.

Also, I was struggling with what exactly I wanted to say. After *Chuck Solomon: Coming of Age* and *Sex Is…*, I was frightened that I had shot my artistic load. I lacked direction.

Still, I tried. I came up with new ideas. Multiple grant applications were written. All were rejected.

A good friend once gave me some sage advice: Filmmaking is a business for the young. You have to have that fire in the belly, the ability to move past the bullshit. I had neither.

And the cheerless fact was that I was turning 40. I felt like Margo Channing braying and bellyaching in *All About Eve*: "I am not twentyish. I am not thirtyish. Three months ago, I was forty years old. FORTY. 4-0!"

Of course, 20 years later, this obsession with turning 40 seems ridiculous. But at the time 40 in "gay years" felt ancient. Never mind I had survived the plague. Ultimately I was still another vain homosexual. I was convinced my looks, my physique, and my attractiveness would all melt away as the clock struck midnight on my 40th birthday. (If my 40-year-old self could have seen my 60-something self, he would have been horrified, and savored the moment.)

Still at 40, I was becoming a cynical and jaded bitch. Not better, bitter.

In the meantime, I had to figure out a way to make a living. As the distribution of *Sex Is…* was petering out, Lawrence Helman asked to relocate our operation from his cramped quarters to an office. We found a funky but functional workplace in the Redstone Building near 16th and Mission, a corner famous for drug dealers and crack hos. Hardly glamorous (at least in a conventional way). But the rent was sure cheap.

With our experience in booking, publicizing, designing, and schmoozing, we thought we could start our own distribution company. We quickly realized that we were failures. Pushing your own product is one thing; pushing others is quite another. The passion was not there.

Idle hands make for idle minds. And idle minds are the devil's workshop. I filled the void with sex and drugs. Upon opening up the crystal door, my proclivities were getting wilder. And I needed to constantly raise the bar.

Word was out, and I was increasingly popular with the hardcore set. At San Francisco play parties that catered to specific fetishes, I was meeting out-of-towners who were interested in getting to know me a bit more. Soon I was being jetted around for salacious weekends, some involving drugs, some not. No bodily fluids or money exchanged, just a few days of out-of-town fun.

One L.A. rendezvous involved a man whose name now escapes me. All I remember was his phone number. 1 800 I TOP MEN. No kidding.

Mr. Top offered an all-expenses-paid weekend pleasure trip. A kinky junket. I arrived on a Friday night. On a dimly lit side street near LAX, I was quickly stripped, collared, blindfolded, and tied up in the back of his pickup. When we reached our destination, I was thrown into a dark closet.

For the next two days, I was periodically taken out for use and abuse, and then thrown back in. Time passed by in this black hole, notated by the amplified sound of a ticking alarm clock strategically positioned close to my ear. Periodically, the door would burst open. My "master" would place two shiny doggy bowls by my shackled feet. One filled with cold Spaghetti-Os, the other with water. He would ask me to first beg, then lap up the vittles and wag my butt, into which he had inserted a rubber puppy tail. Blindfolded, I'd listen to him lubing up and jerking off. After hearing his paltry climax, the door would then slam shut. The whole experience was so romantic.

Another weekend, David XXX—a smoking hot muscle man with a sexy buzz cut—flew me to the Midwest. When we met at a San Francisco S&M play party, I was totally smitten. I thought he might finally be "the one." Before our hookup, I was faxed and had to sign a three-page master/slave contract. Just like *50 Shades of Grey*. But this was 50 Shades of Gay, with a heavy emphasis on black and blue. When I met him in St. Louis, he collared me and perched me on the back of his Harley. I got a quick tour of the city, zooming past the famed arch.

After I smoked some pot, with David XXX, the new man of my dreams, we got down to business. He gave me a full body shave in his basement dungeon. I oiled him up and he posed, lifting weights in his Spandex shorts and funky lace-up combat boots. For the finale, he placed me on his sling and whipped me. We did this for three days straight. Same routine. After a while it became tiring—and tired. By the end of the weekend, we were ready to bid each other adieu. Never to see each other again. Alas, he was not "the one." The contract was canceled.

And on and on this went. For several years. My friends loved hearing about these sordid sexcapades. They laughed and laughed. At me, not with me. Of course, on the surface my exploits all seemed *très amusant*, but underneath they left me feeling empty. And lonely.

My life felt meaningless.

There's that line in Stephen Sondheim's *Sunday in the Park With George* that the two things you leave behind are children and art. I definitely wasn't planning on having children.

That left art. I desperately needed to steer my stagnant ship back in the right direction. Then I got a phone call.

Me in my S&M days.

An enthusiastic female voice explained that she was from the Independent Television Service (ITVS), working in conjunction with PBS. Their mission was to take creative risks, spark public dialogue, and give voice to underserved communities.

Her team was formulating an expansive national series on AIDS, and she said that my work came highly recommended. She asked for a copy of *Sex Is*....

I FedEx'ed a copy the next day.

Why was I so excited?

Back in 1987, PBS had rejected *Chuck Solomon: Coming of Age* for being too gay. Perhaps this new ITVS AIDS series would make amends. And I craved a national television audience for my work.

ITVS also offered a living wage.

So with fingers crossed and candles lit, I waited for her reply. And waited.

Finally the phone call came.

Now, bear with me. I am about to go into tricky territory, fraught with political pitfalls. The issue is minority representation. Even though I had a bad personal experience, it's not my intent to join reactionary elements in bashing the whole concept. By and large, I strongly support it. But it is not without its drawbacks. And I am simply relating my experience, the straw that broke this camel's back and changed the direction of my career. Period.

"Mr. Huestis, we enjoyed your work immensely. Quite impressive. Unfortunately, given the huge scope of our project, we are looking at a diverse cross section of makers, and were not able to find a place for you. I'm sure you understand. But we *were* very impressed with the African American poet Wayne Corbitt in *Sex Is....* You might be happy to note that we have commissioned a segment profiling him to be directed by an award-winning San Francisco filmmaker. She's terrific. And she'll bring the perspective of a Latina lesbian to this piece."

I certainly knew the work of this filmmaker. It was impressive. But she had no history of making AIDS work, nor did she know Wayne. I did. Wayne was the heart and soul of my movie. His courage in publicly coming out as an African American masochist had been partially facilitated by his trust in me. And, of course, I had HIV. Why wouldn't they hire me?

I was furious. I decided to call the filmmaker in question.

OK, it didn't help that I was coming off a speed jag. The meth monster, fueled by resentment, paranoia, and little sleep, was raging to get out.

I started quietly; telling her that I heard that she just got hired by ITVS to do a piece on Wayne Corbitt. I explained that he was in my film. Then I asked how she had been chosen as director. Suddenly, I lost my cool and screamed into the phone, "You might fit a demographic that they're looking for, but what the fuck do you know about being an HIV-positive gay man?"

She let me have it.

"Listen, I don't know why you're calling me, but this conversation is out of line. I don't need to answer to you, or anyone. Besides, this is just a job for me." Click.

Just a job? AIDS was my life, and to her this was just a job.

After I hung up, I remembered Manfred Salzgeber once telling me: "Marc, the bureaucrats are the enemy of the artists." The bureaucratic bean counters for this ITVS project were living proof. And the thought of scrambling to make films in this box-checking funding climate was anathema to me. With such prevailing rules, I wanted no part of that game.

Soon afterwards, Manfred died. His passing was a personal bellwether. An era was ending. I had lost an advocate, and the ITVS incident left a sour taste in my mouth. I was emotionally spent, deeply unhappy. I needed to change direction. To reinvent myself. I had done it before. Could I do it again?

You betcha.

The curtain was falling on the first act of my life. I was now dressing for Act 2.

#

ACT 2
DANCING WITH THE STARS

Act 2, Scene 1 – IMPRESARIO

F. Scott Fitzgerald once famously wrote: "There are no second acts in life." I was determined to prove him wrong. I was leaving filmmaking. Now, all I needed was a second act.

But frankly, I was petrified.

The old cliché is that when one door closes, another opens. But I began thinking of that famous hall of mirrors scene in Orson Welles' *The Lady From Shanghai*, where an open door reflected in a funhouse mirror only leads to another, and another, and yet another. Leading everywhere and nowhere at the same time.

But my philosophy has always been: Don't give up; keep going! Open Door No. 2. And if that door gets stuck, then just kick the fucker open.

And voila! Like sparkling shards exploding from a confetti cannon, out pop thoughts of my Long Island childhood, putting on yearly Halloween fright shows in a suburban basement. Chills and thrills for only a nickel. Since the dawn of time, I always knew how to put on a good show. Christ, I had show business in my blood. So, why not become a full-time producer? But not just any producer; I'd become an impresario. A producer with pizzazz! A sorcerer's apprentice conducting my own gay fantasia.

Lawrence Helman and me in our early years at the new office.

So I picked myself up, dusted myself off, and started all over again. And just like that, I had the idea for a show.

The Sick & Twisted Players were a band of kooky San Francisco thespians, in all shapes, sizes, colors, and persuasions, led by Tony Vaguely, our own local Ed Wood. Tony had just mounted a satire of the camp chestnut, *The Stepford Wives*. Hmmmm. Why not take scenes from Tony's ingenious send-up to the Castro Theatre stage and show the movie afterwards?

I ran the idea by the theater's booker, Anita Monga. In the past, she'd been receptive to my suggestions of adding lowbrow titles to her highbrow programming. *The Stepford Wives*—a guilty pleasure of mine—where husbands turn their suburban housewives into robotic slaves, might be a perfect start. Its mix of crypto-feminism with high camp (and hilariously hideous 70's drag) was perfect for the Castro audience.

Anita was game.

So the stage was set to create a Castro extravaganza with a cheesy live floorshow followed by the film presentation. We could charge a few bucks more, expand the repertory audience by giving them something new, pay the talent, and increase profits for everyone. Win-win-win.

And kismet would (again) have it; Lawrence Helman just happened to have a 16mm copy of *The Stepford Wives* in a secret stash of stockpiled films. But there was a complication; Lawrence's print was a victim of the "vinegar syndrome." All of the print's colors had faded to pink. We convinced ourselves that the cheapo quality of the copy on hand would enhance the lurid kitschiness of the event (because, alas, no good print was available).

The event was booked for July 21, 1995. Tony Vaguely and company would perform the most twisted bits from *Stepford* as well as sick snippets from his other productions, under the rubric title of "Sick & Twisted's Summer Camp." The whole shindig was put together in record speed. It sold out lickety-split.

Though this event certainly would not change the world, it would give folks a carefree frolic. And fun, in itself, could be a radical act. As Emma Goldman once said, "A revolution without dancing is not a revolution worth having." As for me, this show would mark a return to the wild abandon of my *Susan Jane* days and my underground roots.

Night of the show as folks entered, Janice Sukaitis, in ultra-tacky Stepford drag and a syrupy smile, greeted every guest clutching a roll of Charmin bathroom tissue. She'd purr, "Ohhhhhh...it's so squeezably soft," encouraging them to cop a feel. Then a silent switch would be flicked, and she'd robotically repeat, "I'll just die if I don't get this recipe, I'll just die if I don't get this recipe." *Stepford* fans would lap this up; quickly recognizing the references from the film. It was these little touches, I convinced myself, that could make my shows sparkle.

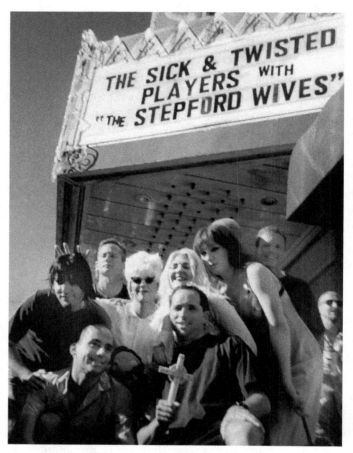

The Sick & Twisted Players at the Castro.

On-stage, the Sick & Twisted served up choice bits of their over-the-top repertoire. Arturo Galster donned a purple wig and hippie skirt for the opening number, belting out Helen Reddy's howler "I Am Woman." The floor show culminated with the whole cast of *Stepford Wives* promenading in 70's flouncy maxi skirts and wide-brimmed hats through the theater aisles, led by a bevy of drag queens pushing shopping carts, blissfully waving to the revved-up crowd.

Then the pink-o-vision film ran. Let me tell you there is nothing like watching a classic movie with a sold-out audience at the Castro. John Waters once called the theater "the Radio City Music Hall for gay people." It is a religious experience. Patrons shout out lines from the films, a la *Rocky Horror Picture Show*. This *Stepford* screening was no exception.

Serendipitously came a trippy, unexpected surprise. During the barbecue scene, just as the characters were roasting wieners, the banged-up print actually burned in the projector, and the celluloid sizzled and bubbled on the Castro's humongous sliver screen. The audience applauded, as if this whole thing had been planned.

ONLY IN SAN FRANCISCO . . . .

EXAMINER/ELIZABETH MANGELSDORF

Members of the performance group *"The Sick and Twisted Players" parade through the aisles of the Castro Theatre dressed as "The Stepford Wives."*

The Friday evening performance, which included skits from movies and TV shows of the '70s, was a benefit for local filmmaker Marc Huestis.

The front page of the San Francisco Examiner, *July 22, 1995.*

The event was so successful, it made the front page of the *San Francisco Examiner* the next day, with the headline: "Only in San Francisco." For me, it was a personal godsend. Besides the artistic gratification of bringing happiness to many, I actually made a small profit. Fuck tired-ass grants. I didn't need to suck the teats of arts councils and foundations. I could do it myself (yet again).

Thus began my twenty-year career as the Castro's schlockmeister. *Bay Area Reporter* columnist Chris Culwell would christen me "Hostess Huestis." TV personality Jan Wahl would dub me "the Flo Ziegfeld of San Francisco." The curtain had officially risen on my second act.

Act 2, Scene 2 – THE SHIP SAILS ON

The morning after our hugely successful Stepford event, Castro booker Anita Monga encouraged us to forge full steam ahead. She had a simple, but life-changing suggestion: invite an actual Hollywood star to attend your next movie extravaganza. But who?

The former manager of the Castro, Richard Rovatti, had begged Anita to book *The Poseidon Adventure* for years. He insisted that kids from the 70s were devoted to those trashy disaster flicks so popular in their wonder years. *Poseidon* was the mother ship of them all. And star-studded!

So taking Anita's advice, Lawrence Helman and I went shopping for *Poseidon* celebs. The male stars—Ernest Borgnine, Red Buttons, Gene Hackman—were dull as dishwater. It was really about the gals. Trashy Stella Stevens in her pink panties and silver shoes. And the biggest star of them all, Shelley Winters, swan-diving into the bowels of the SS Poseidon. So, we contacted Stella, searched for Shelley, and put in calls to Pamela Sue Martin and Carol Lynley.

Stella said no. Pamela Sue Martin never returned our calls. (The bitch, what else did she have going?) No luck in getting through to Shelley. But lo and behold, Carol Lynley took the bait!

Carol, you might remember, played Noni in *Poseidon*, the fragile lounge singer in hot pants who sang "The Morning After" (the song would win an Oscar and was a No. 1 hit for Maureen McGovern). Throughout the picture, Noni endures fire, floods, and a big, fat slap in the face from Stella Stevens to become one of the saga's few survivors.

Carol's career spanned decades. With her long, blond, wispy hair and ethereal beauty, she defined early-60s chic. She made 44 feature films and her marquee name flashed above such titles as *Blue Denim, Bunny Lake Is Missing,* and *The Maltese Bippy,* to name a few.

And little did Lynley know, she played a prominent role in my budding teenage sexuality. Carol was one of the "Carols" in the much-publicized dueling "Harlows" back in 1965. Both were biopics of 1930s film icon Jean Harlow. Carol Lynley starred in a cheapo version shot in black and white "electrovision"; Carroll Baker in the big-budget Paramount release. When Carol L's Harlow had aired on Million Dollar Movie, I watched it repeatedly.

I was obsessed with one particular part: Harlow's disastrous honeymoon with the semi-fictional character "William Mansfield." The couple had everything: fame, money, charm, beauty. Yet, behind the glittering façade, poor tortured William had one secret shortcoming. On his nuptials night, he couldn't ummmmmm... perform. He was *impotent.* His only solution to not getting hard? Blowing his brains out.

As a teen I knew little about such things. I didn't understand what had gone wrong. But I had already realized I couldn't get it up while thinking about girls. So, after watching this movie, I wondered if perhaps, just maybe, oh please, God, please, this thing, this impotence was my problem—not the dreaded homosexuality. I rushed to the library, looked up impotence in the card catalog, grabbed a book, hid in a corner, and read all about it. Then I convinced myself that I was not queer, but impotent. What a relief!

After my erection education from *Harlow,* Carol Lynley was a name forever etched in my memory.

Never mind that other folks might not know who Carol Lynley was. In my mind, she was a big star, and we had snagged her for our *Poseidon* event-ure.

I quickly learned that celebrity, whatever its size, could be exquisitely exciting. Intoxicating, really. Every time Carol would call the office, Lawrence and I were just like giddy schoolgirls!

Our favorite moment was when Carol left this a message on our machine responding to our request to sing "The Morning After" at the Castro gala:

"Hi, this is Carol Lynley. No, I *do not* want to sing 'The Morning After.' I don't mind being parodied, but I don't want to parody myself. And as far as singing the song, you got a big no on that one. I never liked it anyway. (*Carol laughs*) Bye-bye!"

We played that message over and over again. It was music to our ears and the fuel that kept us going.

So, the stage was set. My first trip to the celebrity rodeo. Enter Carol Lynley!

At the baggage claim at San Francisco International, Carol emerged. An aura of light surrounded her. Maybe that sounds corny, but that's how I remember it. At 53, she still looked great. Coiffed with the signature blond hair, now stylishly curled. Her face was a bit weathered, but not cheapened or falsified with Botox or surgery.

With Carol Lynley and Lawrence Helman,
the day before her Castro Theatre appearance.

We all hit it off immediately, gabbing a mile a minute as we drove to the Hotel Triton. We had booked Carol in the "Wyland Room," perfect for a *Poseidon* beauty. It was done up in a marine motif; filled with paintings of dolphins and whales by world-renowned sea life artist Wyland. Plus, a beautiful, bubbly, noisy aquarium abounding with tropical neon fish as a centerpiece.

"Do you like it?" I asked with pride, thinking this was just the touch that would impress her.

Carol Lynley in her famous hot pants
from "The Poseidon Adventure."
Photo courtesy of Twentieth Century Fox.

"My god," she laughed, "It gives me a headache. I don't know if I'll be able to sleep with those fucking fish staring at me and that damn thing bubbling all night."

Later, we wandered the dusky downtown streets, past the gates of Chinatown. We picked a cozy Chinese underground restaurant to dine. There were twinkling stars projected on its ceiling, matching the twinkle in Carol's bright blue Irish eyes. (OK, I'm being corny again.) But really, it was all so idyllic.

Throughout our delightful dinner, Carol was the consummate storyteller. She knew where all the showbiz bodies were buried, though she spoke ill of no one. And La Lynley knew everybody. She was bestest friends with Fred Astaire, dated Frank Sinatra, and had a long-term relationship with David Frost. As we chowed down on our chow fun, Lawrence and I were utterly transfixed. We couldn't wait for dessert!

On the night of the event, November 19, 1995, fired-up people in party hats lined up around the block hours before the doors opened. A group of Poseidon groupies had flown in from across the country. Even my dad came in from New York. Poseidon-mania shifted to high gear when Carol's limo pulled up to the Castro. Fans spontaneously broke into the famous *Poseidon* New Year's countdown and exploded with "Happy New Year!" Party horns blew. Pandemonium ensued. The crowd adored Carol, looking terrific in a white beaded gown dripping in green sequins.

Inside the sold-out house, street performer Susie Sounds, wearing her signature blinking Valkyrie hat, performs a deadpan version of "The Morning After." The Sick & Twisted Players reprise scenes from *Poseidon*.

Then a drum roll...

Carol makes her entrance to a thunderous standing ovation, escorted by porn star Erik George. The energy of the room is scary. Many are in altered states, turned on by a witchs' brew of MDA, meth, pot, and alcohol. Each provided their own unique energy, but not necessarily mixing well together.

San Francisco Chronicle critic Edward Guthmann, who serves as the interviewer, attempts to quell the ruckus.

Edward Guthmann: What's going on out there?

Crowd member screams: Ecstasy!

Crowd chants: Carol! Carol!!

Edward: Show a little respect for the lady. Shut the fuck up.

My dad and I partying. Dad wants you to know it's water in the cup.
Photo by Kent Taylor.

Tony Vaguely, Carol Lynley, Kathy Queer at the reception.
Photo by Kent Taylor.

Loud boos. Carol, back arched into her plush chair, and trying to score points, joins the booing. Then, exhibiting her classic Hollywood training, with a simple sly look subdues the commotion. The interview proceeds.

A few highlights:

Edward: After you saw *The Poseidon Adventure* the first time, was there one scene you liked better than the others?

Carol Lynley: No, I felt wet all over again. It's not easy being that wet!

Audience, sensing a double entendre, erupts in laughter.

Carol: This is a very dangerous room to work!!!

Wild cheers!

Edward: Carol, let's get real here. Shelley Winters, great lady or total pig on the set?

Boos again pepper the crowd.

Carol: Shelley is a great lady! When she would do sad scenes, she would play opera music. Always the same aria. It used to drive poor Jack Albertson bananas. I asked her why. She said that she was in Venice and when her marriage to Vittorio Gassman was over, she heard this aria being played. So, whenever she needed to be sad, she played that to get her in the mood.

On making "Harlow":

Carol: I rehearsed for three weeks with Judy Garland, who played my mother. And the night before we're about to shoot, Judy said: "Carol, I'm quitting. They're gonna say that I'm crazy and I'm drunk and I'm stoned." And she wasn't. Then she said, "I gotta tell you, this is a piece of shit and I'm outta here." And I went home that night and I thought, well maybe she's just testing me. And the next morning Ginger Rogers was there on the set instead!

On her reason for participating in the event, benefiting Ward 5A, which provided care for AIDS patients at San Francisco General Hospital:

Carol: I have friends who are HIV-positive and they've been very brave about it. And I have lost a number of them. I don't know about other people, but I've always resented the big galas on TV where everybody picks up awards and they wear the red ribbons. But then they go home, and they put their ball gowns in the dressing room, and take off the red ribbon, and that's about as far as it goes. And this, for me, was a personal way to raise money for a specific ward, for a specific group of people in a specific city. And that's why I wanted to do it.

When the interview ended, Carol took a long, elegant bow and vanished into the wings. Once and always a star.

The morning after, as we basked in the afterglow of the night before, I asked Carol, "Do you ever watch any of your old movies on TCM?"

Very matter-of-factly, Carol said, "I don't own a TV."

I didn't question why not. Though I had a hunch. Beneath the veneer of celebrity, there was a real person. With real-life problems. I told her that we would send her the money to buy one. And we did.

Over the years, Carol has become a trusted friend and my go-to girl. If I had a celebrity in mind for a tribute, I'd call her for the 411. Her responses were occasionally really dishy but never mean. She taught me to always put your best foot forward, be honest, and *try* to be kind. Quite a feat in the world of showbiz!

After the Castro success, Lawrence and I decided to take *Poseidon* on the road. This time to Hollywood! Carol Lynley, Stella Stevens, and a slew of *Poseidon* participants all agreed to appear. And the most famous Poseidon adventurer of them all, Shelley Winters, was rumored to be coming on-board for a special appearance. She couldn't commit due to health issues; we'd only know the day of the event if she would attend. We were on pins and needles!

At a sun-soaked pre-event celebrity reception at Mani's Bakery in Santa Monica, a shiny limo pulls up. Wow, would a muumuued Shelley Winters emerge? The door opens, and out pops a smallish, slightly pinched woman. Definitely not Shelley.

She hands me a large envelope and dispatches an apology. "Shelley sends her regrets, but would like you to have this original 1972 opening-night program from *The Poseidon Adventure* for your celebration."

It's inscribed: "I wish I could swim with you tonight" and signed and dated 4/25/96 by Shelley. The show goes on without Shelley.

A program for the 1972 premiere of "The Poseidon Adventure,"
signed by Shelley Winters.

Several weeks following the event, the phone rings. The caller
ID indicates "unknown caller" with a Los Angeles area code.

"Hello," harrumphed an elderly, female voice with a distinct
New York accent.

"Hello," I routinely respond.

"Is this Marc?" the mystery guest whines.

"Who is this?" I gamely reply.

"This is Shelley Winters."

Before I can get excited, I'm quickly interrupted. Again the
voice harrumphs, now with an extra umph of agitation.

"Marc, I asked for you to put that Poseidon program up as
part of your silent auction for your charity. It's worth a fortune!"
Winters whinnies.

"Shelley, with all due respect, what silent auction? We had no
silent auction."

"Well, you could have made one."

As if silent auctions are spun from thin air.

"Now I want to know who has this program," Winters
demands.

"I do," I sheepishly answer. "I thought it was a gift. Would
you like it back?"

"I DON'T WANT IT BACK," Winters screeches, "I just want
to be respected! For crying out loud, I've won two Academy
Awards, worked with *everyone* in Hollywood, and just don't want
to be taken advantage of. I'm old, and no one remembers me."

All of a sudden I'm imagining a very sad, lonely lady on the
other end of the line. She's sounding like one of those characters
from a mid-60s psychodrama, an aging actress now starring in her
own horror film: *What's the Matter With Shelley?*

Shell then launches into a ten-minute monologue, kvetching
about how miserable she is, how everyone has forgotten her, how
her daughter hates her, how she can't get no respect. And oy, the
aches, the pains, the misery.

Putting on my faux therapist cap, I try to assuage her ego.
"But Shelley, everyone loves you. You are a big, BIG star—one of

the greatest ever!" She finally melts a bit, and I keep pouring on the old charm, even getting her to laugh. We end the conversation on a better note.

"Just keep the program," Shelley relents.

"Thank you, Shelley. I wish you only the best," I say with great sincerity, almost choking up, "and hope you can see how much we all love you."

Shelley's meltdown aside, Lawrence and I were having the time of our lives. After the *Stepford* and *Poseidon* events, we were on a roll. Our newfound fan base now kept asking, "Who's next?"

We booked Sylvia Miles, best known for her six-minute Academy Award nominated performance as Cass in John Schlesinger's *Midnight Cowboy*. We both were big fans of her work, particularly in the Andy Warhol/Paul Morrissey film *Heat*.

Trouble was not many people shared our enthusiasm for the Paul Morrissey film or Ms. Miles. When we took to the streets of the Castro to hand out flyers promoting the event, the classic responses were: "Who's Sylvia Miles?" or "Sylvia Miles, I thought she was dead." And despite a shitload of press, radio interviews, and TV appearances, tickets were not flying out of the door. Around 600. You might think that is a lot of people. But grand galas cost multiple grands.

On her big night, Sylvia proved to be a great interview— charming, funny, earthy, endearing, and even vulnerable. But...

A cogent quote from Lily Tomlin came to mind. When asked about why box office is so important in determining success, she bluntly replied, "Because it's called show *business!*"

Lawrence and I were lucky to break even on this one. And afterwards, another out-of-town edition of our *Poseidon* event turned into a financial disaster. Our bank account was now upside down. There was no money left to pay ourselves. We were forced to ponder our future together.

It was clear that our company Outsider Productions wasn't big enough for the two of us. One of us had to go. Luckily, Lawrence wanted a life outside show business. To me, show business *was* my life.

We parted amicably. I was now a one-man show. Outsider Productions morphed into "Marc Huestis Presents." In order to survive, I'd have to employ all the skills I had learned throughout the years and do it all myself: publicity, travel, ticket sales, editing clip reels, graphic design. If I could, I would have even sold the popcorn at the shows. I quickly learned that being an impresario was more than just having your name flashing above the title. It was hard work.

Act 2, Scene 3 – STRICTLY FIRST CLASS

John Waters was my idol.

The first time I saw his film *Female Trouble* at the Roxie Theatre in San Francisco in 1974, I thought I had died and gone to heaven. Or more appropriately, to hell. It was a revelation. Waters inspired my early film work, and *Female Trouble* is on my list of 10 all-time favorite films.

Then there was the night in 1984 when a rumor spread that John Waters was coming to *Naked Brunch* at the 181 Club. I had no idea if he actually was there, but just the idea of him in the audience had me flying high.

In 1988, while attending Sundance with *Chuck Solomon: Coming of Age*, I spotted John Waters walking alone down snowy Main Street, the night before the world premiere of *Hairspray*. There was a glow about him. I wanted to congratulate him and tell him what a fan I was, but was so nervous I didn't dare approach him. The next evening, I attended the screening and had lifetime bragging rights that I saw the world premiere of a John Waters film.

I also got to know *Female Trouble* verbatim on its release on home video. At Captain Video, I snatched the first copy off the shelf, before a single customer could get their grubby hands on it. I watched it over and over again. I reveled in memorizing my favorite lines. "Pretty, pretty?" became my mantra.

In the '90s, I *really* got to know the film, verbatim, with the help of the speed freaks who lived in the apartment above me. Every Thursday, long past midnight, they would pop in their VHS copy of *Female Trouble*, and crank up the volume to full blast.

It was literally a rude awakening. And in sketchy abandon, the drug addicts would shout out the dialogue. Close to 2 a.m., when I would hear the character of Dawn Davenport bitching about daughter Taffy's shrieking the same stupid jump-rope chants, I could relate. That same goddamned line, in that same goddamned movie, each week at the same goddamned time, on the same goddamned night, over and over again! It was a nightmare. Still, I didn't dare complain, as some of the noises coming from my bedroom were undoubtedly equally alarming.

So, yes, John Waters and *Female Trouble* were a constant in my life. And to me the world is divided into two camps. When I say "pretty, pretty!?" the ones that perk up and know the reference and those who don't. It's like a password to a worldview and I gravitate instantly to those that get it (for those readers who don't, google it!).

Flash forward to 1996. Lawrence Helman had just left the building, and my fledgling career at the Castro Theatre was in an ebb. I needed an event that would put the "impress" back into "impresario."

In my line of work, gigs need to be planned months in advance. So although it was August, Christmas was just around the corner. I loathed Christmas. I knew that others did as well. Particularly single, bitter gay men. And there were a lot of us in San Francisco. What could be our ultimate (anti) Christmas event?

My all-time favorite Christmas scene was in *Female Trouble*. You know, the one where Dawn Davenport doesn't get her cha-cha heels, then topples the Christmas tree on her mother's head. It reminded me of all those hellacious Christmases at the Huestis home. So, hmmm? Maybe a screening of *Female Trouble* would be a perfect way to celebrate the holidaze.

But what about the traditional floor show before the film? Divine was dead. Should I try to get John Waters? Did I dare?

In Waters' book *Crackpot*, there's a chapter titled "Why I Love Christmas." Since he seemed to be sincerely fond of donning all that gay apparel, why not produce "A John Waters X-Mas"? It had never been done before. And Waters loved the Castro Theatre.

The idea was pitched to John as a benefit for Frameline. To my great surprise, he was interested. But one thing he did make immediately clear: He does not do benefits. Clarification. He doesn't mind if monies go to a beneficiary, but he does not discount his speaking fee for benefits—which was significant.

And there were other complications. At this point in my career, I was beginning to learn the sensitive nature of booking a celebrity's flight. It was often about more than comfort, it was about status. First class, business, or coach. John Waters travels strictly first class and nonstop. Non-negotiable. But the cost of a Baltimore-San Francisco first-class ticket was a huge chunk of change.

I had to make a big decision. Should I put up the money for his fee and flight and risk a loss? Well, why not!

The deal was struck. But my initial dealings with John Waters and his booking agent were frustrating. He could be quite inflexible. A classic Taurus with "no" a popular word in his vocabulary. Okay, John Waters didn't know me from a hole in the wall. But when I made a suggestion he didn't like, he became short-tempered. impatient. I was constantly walking on eggshells.

When he finally arrived for the show, I was nervous meeting him. No, terrified! But Waters couldn't have been more charming. Gregarious, excited, and upbeat on the ride to his hotel. Plus, against type, extremely polite and well-bred.

And quite the recognizable star. Everywhere he went, people were thrilled to see him. Upon checking into the Hotel Triton, the doorman stopped us in our tracks. "Mr. Waters, I have something to show you." He pulled out a huge conch shell, and as if he had been waiting for this moment for weeks, proceeded to blow hard on it. The rafters practically shook. I rolled my eyes. "That's great," John smiled, and we were on our merry way. I apologized. "You must hate it when people do things like that."

"You know what I'd really hate?" he replied. "When they *stop* doing things like that."

After the obligatory stopover at A Clean Well-Lighted Place for Books (John *loves* books), I took him to my low-rent Mission District office, passing the neighborhood drug dealers and crack 'hos plying their trade. Although I had tried to tidy up, there were papers and VHS tapes piled everywhere. Upon his entrance, I reflexively apologized. "Sorry that it's such a dump." His reply: "Why be sorry? It looks like you're busy. I love that!"

That evening I arranged a dinner at Bruno's restaurant between John, myself, and actress Carol Lynley, who was a celebrity judge for the event's Cha-Cha Heels Contest. I had hoped Carol and John would hit it off. Certainly they shared a bond of fallen Christmas trees: John's from *Female Trouble*, Carol hanging upside-down from the huge tree in *The Poseidon Adventure*. I also secretly hoped Carol Lynley would become the next John Waters starlet. Always looking after my girls.

In the car ride to the restaurant, John regaled Carol with tales of recently judging the Adult Video News Awards, the "Oscars of Porn." He went on in lurid detail about Jeff Stryker dildos. I think he was secretly testing Carol's limits, seeing if she was game. She was, and then some. After all, she *was* in show business.

At Bruno's, Carol turned the tables on John. In the course of the meal, the subject of the Manson murders came up. (Doesn't it always in polite dinner conversation?) John had befriended Leslie Van Houten, one of the Manson family members in prison. He started in on a smart-alecky monologue about visiting her. Carol elegantly put down her fork and politely but firmly interrupted. "Stop. I know you're John Waters. But I was a friend of Sharon Tate. She was a beautiful, lovely, loving woman. I don't find any of this funny. So, can we please change the subject?"

God love Carol. John seemed sincerely contrite. The subject was quickly changed.

The show was scheduled for the following day, Friday the 13th of December 1996. The Castro stage was festooned with tacky

Christmas shit: toy soldiers, bargain basement Santas, flickering fairy lights. It's amazing the crap you can buy at the dollar store!

John arrived in the gaudiest white stretch limo this side of Liberace, with Carol in tow. Performer Joan Jett Blakk femceed the Cha-Cha Heels contest, which brought out a Who's Who of local drag. Heklina, who was to later turn into San Francisco's queen of the nightlife, even entered. She lost.

John threw out brilliant bon mots as if they were Brach's holiday bonbons. Lots of double entendres about stuffing turkeys, hanging balls and sitting on Santa's lap. To top it off, I arranged for Mayor Willie Brown to declare "John Waters Day in San Francisco."

After the main event, the zealous devotees lined up at a meet-and-greet with their idol. John would autograph anything. A breast? A pecker? Well, just whip it out. Your ass? Not a problem. What color Sharpie?

Afterwards, John seemed quite pleased with the event. Days after, he sent me a kind Joan Crawford-y thank you note. On the back of an 8x10 of Audrey Hepburn—he remembered I adored her—was inscribed, "Thank you for doing such a dynamic job of producing A J.W. Christmas. Talk to you soon."

We talked about reprising "A John Waters X-Mas." Each August, I'd call. Year after year, he'd say it was too soon to play the Castro again. Finally in 2003, he relented. The timing was good: *Hairspray* was opening on Broadway, and his name was again part of the public zeitgeist (actually, when was it not?).

Dealing again with John, I was reminded that he could be surprisingly conservative. He once told me that his parents were like George and Barbara Bush. I believe it. Also, add these words: Stubborn and unyielding.

These sides emerged as I was booking Waters' flight. When I offered him a donated Baltimore/San Francisco first-class ticket that included a stopover in Pittsburgh, he immediately nipped it in the bud. "I don't want to change planes. I'm too old to do that. And Pittsburgh?" Non-stop meant non-stop. Never mind that this ticket would have saved the production several thousand dollars. I wound up paying full fare.

Still, I was determined to make the new improved edition of "A John Waters X-Mas" bigger, better and brasher. The stage was covered with $1,000 worth of hot pink ultra-punk bristly bunting and a matching tree, topped by a huge rubber rat. Carol Lynley again flew out, this time to do a salty reading of "'Twas the Night Before Christmas." She delivered the line "the stockings were hung" with extra relish.

The highlight of the evening was the second official Cha-Cha Heels Contest. A male porn star named Precious Moments appeared stark naked except for a pair of strappy red pumps. His talent? Jumping rope with his penis tucked between his legs while singing "O Come All Ye Faithful." In Latin. Precious won the grand prize: $150 and dinner for two at the Burger King of his choice.

John's presentation (again) wowed the crowd.

Of the evening, Octavio Roca of the *San Francisco Chronicle* wrote:

"Even for the Castro Theatre, this was almost too much. Then again, 'A John Waters X-Mas' maybe was just right, with everything from Hollywood glamour to Baltimore sleaze, drag-king Santas, a naked performance artist, scary video clips of Karen Carpenter drooling over dessert, a filmed greeting from President Dwight D. Eisenhower, and a lot of Christmas cheer—San Francisco style."

After all that Christmas cheer, John and I said our warm goodbyes. And he kept in touch. There were his yearly Christmas cards, always a treat. Periodically he'd send tastefully tacky postcards making sly John Waters-ey comments on my upcoming celebrity events.

Then in 2004, out of the blue, I got an e-mail from John's personal assistant. Seems John was pitching a CD of quirky Christmas songs to a reputable label. He loved the design for the second X-mas Show, and asked we send it along.

I was over-the-moon flattered. It was like getting a big ol' pat on the back from your dad. I zipped a hi-res jpeg right over to his office.

About six months later, the phone rang. "Hi, this is John. I'm in L.A. calling from the Chateau" (as in Marmont). "Listen, a few things. I'm doing the Christmas show down here in December. I know I mentioned that you should consider booking this, but another producer came forward. I hope you don't mind."

"Why should I mind?" I cheerfully replied.

"Oh, another thing. The CD of Christmas songs is coming out."

"Great!" I responded, happy that my artwork might have helped move the deal forward. "Hey, if there is a special thanks section in the liner notes, could you add my name?" I requested.

Pregnant pause. And then a volcanic eruption. "I can't do that! You had nothing to do with this CD! I can't believe you're even asking!" Before I could get a word in edgewise about the donated art, he was off to the races. I hardly remember the rest of his monologue. John was being John. He saw things as he saw them. You couldn't win. Christ, I thought, you'd think I was asking for a million bucks. All I was asking for was a goddamned credit.

After I hung up, I felt battered, bruised, and belittled. I wanted to crawl into a hole and coil my body into a fetal position. I couldn't even finish out the day. Then came one of those "Aha!" light-bulb moments. I realized that the whole time I was producing the Christmas shows, I had felt that I was working for him, rather than the other way around. Even though *I* was the one footing the bills. Somehow that moment of clarity made me feel a bit better.

The next morning I got a call from the CD producers. To this day, I don't know if this call was a coincidence. "Hi, John Waters gave us your phone number. We'd like to use the image from your Christmas show for the upcoming CD release."

"That's odd," I said, biting my tongue. "I just talked to him yesterday. He didn't mention that." I didn't fill them in on John's outburst. I wondered if John had regretted his tantrum. I never found out, but the label did use the image. I got my credit. In teensy, tiny letters. But it's there. Plus a little extra money.

I doubt that Mr. Waters even remembers that unfortunate phone call from the Chateau. It's now water under the bridge. And in the intervening years, he has bent over backwards to be kind. Once, I was having trouble getting a pitch to Kathleen Turner, star of Waters' *Serial Mom*. In frustration, I e-mailed John, and he opened up the channels to her right away. She didn't do the gig, but I appreciated John's effort.

Every once in a while, I run into John socially; he now owns an apartment in San Francisco. Our exchanges are quite cordial, occasionally warm and engaging. We talk mostly about movies. I know he respects my opinion. He even quoted me in *Artforum* regarding the film *Blue Jasmine*.

As for "A John Waters Christmas," he's gone on to perform it in multiple cities throughout the years. In 2018, he did a 17-city tour, including the Great American Music Hall in San Francisco. It's become his seasonal cottage industry. I will always feel that I gave him the kernel of this lucrative idea, though I'm sure he's stamped his unique genius on these shows and made them his own.

Flaubert once said, "Never touch your idols. The gilding will stick to your fingers." Perhaps that was true with John Waters. I certainly discovered some of his flaws—as he did mine.

Yet, underneath, John Waters is a lovely, bright, and humane man—a real-life hero to the misfits of this world.

I really do appreciate his against-the-grain public pronouncements, whether tart-tongued right-on critiques of gay marriage, gays in the military, or Republican celebrity transgenders (I'm talking about you, Caitlyn Jenner!). And despite the fame and fortune, I know he will always be an outsider at heart.

For that, he will always be one of my idols, gilding and all.

A friend of mine told me that John's trying harder to be nicer to people these days. His reason? He wants people to come to his funeral. I don't think he needs to worry about that.

Act 2, Scene 4 – A LIVING DOLL

You have to climb Mt. Everest to reach the Valley of the Dolls. I took that brutal climb at the tender age of 13, when I purchased my first adult movie ticket to see the tawdry picture at the Hicksville Theatre.

Booze, bitch fights, barracudas, nudies, dope, dolls. As a teen they were all new to me. Well, not completely. My mother pill-popped Miltowns. And my dad downed martinis. But the other things were still a ways off. Yet like every budding queen, they were firmly ingrained in my DNA.

Valley of the Dolls, this sublime celluloid trash, would be the portal to my future—my gateway drug to the wonderfully addictive world of showbiz. And who knew I would eventually work with two of these real-life living dolls? Years apart (in 1997 and 2009).

First came Barbara Parkins, who played protagonist Anne Welles in *Valley of the Dolls* (*VD* for short). Cool as a cucumber and potently pert, Barbara was the quintessential sophisticated, seductive, '60s brunette. She achieved stunning success in the classic TV soap *Peyton Place*. However, her crowning glory came in *Valley of the Dolls* as Anne, the patrician WASP suffering in fur.

I certainly had a soft spot for Barbara. As a kid I was addicted to *Peyton Place*. I was always a sucker for Parkins as cockteasing, conniving, bad girl Betty Anderson, and her raspy-voiced, raven-haired beauty.

So I enthusiastically pitched Babs as well as several other *VD* stars. Lee Grant sharply said no, and Patty Duke had not yet come to the place of embracing *VD*. (She eventually would but it would take many years.) Babs was the only doll kind enough to accept my invitation.

My initial contacts with Barbara were lovely. She promptly sent back her contract in an envelope permeated with the scent of rose perfume. It was a darling touch, although a bit worrying. Was she now an eccentric little old lady, living in a musty antique apartment filled with wilted roses? A modern-day Miss Havisham?

When I finally met her, nothing could have been further from the truth. Waving enthusiastically at the arrival gate, Babs was a vibrant beauty; her signature mane of jet-black hair still absolutely ravishing. And that voice! Tripping off her tongue like a smoky pearl purring. We immediately bonded.

At lunch, I gazed at Barbara and confessed, "My friend Lypsinka (the famous New York female illusionist) is an expert on Hollywood chic. She made me promise I would look at your hands." I took hold of one of them. Indeed, they were long, lean and elegant. I couldn't stop staring. Just as I held them, there was an odd spark between us. All was good.

The timing of my 1997 *VD* event was fortuitous. There was a Grove Press re-issue of the original novel, and two biopics were being shot on the life of author Jacqueline Susann. Crooner k.d. lang had just released a smoldering cover of the film's theme song. A *New York Times* article proclaimed, "Pink Trash: The Return of the Dolls," and mentioned my upcoming show.

But on that warm July weekend in the Castro, *VD* was being upstaged. Everyone was talking about Andrew Cunanan, the gay gigolo turned mass murderer, who had just shot fashion designer Gianni Versace in cold blood.

Cunanan was now on the run. He had once lived in San Francisco, and frequented the local bars. "Wanted" signs with his face were plastered on every corner. Every gay guy in town, including myself, wondered if they had slept with him. (He *was* sorta hot!)

As I took Barbara on a tour of the neighborhood, the streets were crawling with cameras. Newsmen were interviewing lines of men: Cunanan's ex-roommates, ex-tricks, and queens just wanting their 15 minutes of fame. I joked to Barbara that I would wangle my way into an interview with false claims of wild S/M sex with the murderer, and promote *VD* at the same time. Barbara laughed wickedly, and encouraged me to do just that.

On a more serious note, this media frenzy brought back memories of another famous mass killing. It hovered over *Valley of the Dolls* like a lost ghost. Sharon Tate, who played Jennifer in *VD*, was brutally murdered in her Benedict Canyon house in 1969 as part of the Helter Skelter killings orchestrated by cult leader Charles Manson. Barbara had been best friends with co-star Tate.

I wondered if that subject would ever come up. It did. While in the green room of a local radio station, Barbara, joined by her 13-year-old daughter Christina, was autographing an 8x10 of the iconic publicity photo featuring the three Dolls posed seductively on a gold framed bed. As daughter Christina glanced down, I proudly declared, "That's your mom!"

Christina pointed to Tate. "But Mommy, who's the pretty one?" "Darling, that's Sharon," Barbara quietly replied. "Well, whatever happened to her?" Christina inquired. Choosing her words carefully, Barbara whispered, "Something very bad." Just then the studio door opened, and we were ushered into the interview.

The subject was again broached over dinner at Bruno's. This time, Ted Casablanca, pegged to do the gala onstage interview, pressed Barbara for dish on Tate. She haltingly confessed: "I was very close to Sharon. You know I had been invited to her house the night of those awful murders. I could have been killed myself." We all gasped.

In an attempt to alter the feeling of morbidity creeping into our evening together, I quickly changed the subject, feigning interest in her daughter. "Christina, that's an odd name for a child of a movie star," I remarked. I thought I was being cute.

Barbara appeared puzzled. "Why?"

"You know, Christina Crawford."

"Who's she?" Barbara queried with a blank stare.

"Joan Crawford's adopted daughter. She wrote *Mommie Dearest*." I couldn't believe a Hollywood showbiz parent didn't know the legend of Joan and Christina. I realized I had stepped in it, so I slumped into the shiny red Naugahyde-cushioned booth and turned the conversation over to Ted.

Barbara Parkins, Sharon Tate and Patty Duke
in the iconic publicity photo for "Valley of the Dolls."
Photo courtesy of Twentieth Century Fox.

Ted Casablanca was a tall, strappingly handsome man, a much-in-demand online gossip columnist and entertainment reporter for E! Entertainment News. Born Bruce Bibby, Ted actually named himself after Neely O'Hara's unsavory lover in *Valley of the Dolls*. The film's fans go nuts when Neely screeches, "Ted Casablanca is not a fag! And I'm just the dame to prove it!"

Since a good portion of the event's revenue would benefit Project Inform—apropos, since they were on the cutting edge of advancing HIV drugs, which were our "dolls"—Ted offered his services gratis. His only request was a massage before the event.

Let me tell you, arranging such perks can be harder than simply paying a talent fee. Particularly with a subject as touchy as a massage. Who knows what the expectations are? So I just came out and asked: "With or without release?"

Ted was mortified. "How can you ask such a question?"

My quick retort: "Honey, this is San Francisco. We ask those sorts of questions."

So I hired a suitable young man for Mr. Casablanca. I'll never know what went on in that massage. Well, maybe I do, and I ain't telling. But who doesn't love a happy ending?

July 18, 1997, the day of the sold-out *VD* event, was a spectacularly sunny San Francisco day. The Castro Theatre had the air of a rock concert. There were queens with hand-painted signs, begging, "I Need 2 Tickets." When a tall guy in Jackie Susann drag flashed two extras, there was practically a riot. Lots of pushing and grabbing. She wound up giving them to a black homeless woman, for free.

Barbara's limo arrived and the star emerged, hair in a chic chignon and her gorgeous body decked out in a beautiful lace-and-taffeta gown with a fine mesh bustle. She had designed it herself and was showing it off, shaking her frou-froued derrière in front of the flashing cameras.

Inside the Castro, the stage was set. The preshow music blared the *VD* theme. Its lyrics described my mindset: "Is this a dream, am I here, is it real?" I breathed in the moment. Ever since I was a teen, I had fantasized about this film. Now I was actually doing a show with one of its stars!

Flynn DeMarco emceed as Anne Welles, and perfectly mimicked every clipped syllable and cultured vowel of Barbara's speaking voice. Two other performers who would become the backbone of my Castro company, made their debuts that night.

Connie Champagne played Neely O'Hara, the out-of-control lush and dope addict. Connie was an RG—drag slang for real girl, "a drag queen trapped in a woman's body." And Connie had, to coin one of Neely's lines, "talent. Big talent!" As an extra bonus Connie, umm, shared some of Neely's infamous habits and quirks—earning the nickname "Connie Cham-pain-in-the ass" in certain theatrical circles. Still, the moment the spotlight was fired up and she channeled Neely, she was flawless!

Matthew Martin played Helen Lawson, the tart-tongued showbiz barracuda, archly played in the film by Susan Hayward. I had known Matthew since the late '80s, when he was a bubbly tap-dancing busboy at the Café Flore, known for his spot-on interpretation of Hayward as Barbara Graham in *I Want to Live*. He was destined to play Helen Lawson. When Matthew sneered, "The Castro doesn't go for booze and dope," the audience went bonkers. Many, after all, were fucked up on one thing or another. And the infamous wig-snatching scene between Neely and Helen brought the house down.

Finally, it was Barbara's turn, gliding down the aisle and soaking up the applause. After she had adequately milked the moment, she squinted into the spotlight and exclaimed, "Who *are* you people? And where have you been all my life?!" She was happy to become the belle of the ball at the Castro with 1,400 queens raging.

In the Ted Casablanca interview, Barbara proved to be smart and devilishly naughty.

A sampling of her interview:

On Judy Garland, who played Helen Lawson until Susan Hayward replaced her:
Barbara: My first scenes were done with Judy. She grabbed me by the arm and said, "Let's go burn up the screen." I think she felt it was a parallel to her life, and the story freaked her out. She locked herself in the dressing room for a week and then she said, "I quit." They gave her a half a million-dollar wardrobe, and she

went home. After filming, all we got was a basket of flowers. We should have been bad!

On Susan Hayward:
Barbara: Should I say it? (*Audience screams "yes!"*) She was spastic! I mean she was a great actress and all, but I watched her do the song, it was frightening.

On Sharon Tate:
Barbara: Sharon, I loved. She was magic. I was the maid of honor at her wedding. It was such a loss; she was about to come into her own and never had the chance.

On her romantic co-star Paul Burke (who played Lyon Burke):
Barbara: I couldn't get into falling in love with Paul. It was depressing. At the time, like every other woman, I was in love with Cat Stevens. I covered my mirror with his photos. So when I kissed Paul Burke, his face vanished and I thought of Cat Stevens. Eventually, I went to London and met Cat. We dated for a while and he was great.

When someone in the audience asked why *Valley of the Dolls* had become such a cult classic, Parkins struggled a bit. "Maybe because it's...uhhh...so bad?"

One man offered a perfect explanation: "As a gay man, you go through hell and come back. You're a survivor and never compromise your integrity. That's why all of us want to be you."

Barbara graciously bowed to his interpretation, and as the theme music swelled, made a grand exit, still taking in this unexpected adulation.

In the days following, my Castro event garnered raves. Liz Smith wrote in her nationally syndicated column: "Barbara Parkins was a smash last week in San Francisco... Parkins, still a soft-spoken dark-haired beauty, actually wiped away a few tears as her ovation went on and on."

Variety reporter Dennis Harvey enthusiastically wrote: "You might well expect San Franciscans to have a particular affinity—and talent—for camp spectacle.... But it took entrepreneur Marc Huestis to perfect a meld of screen and live ultra-kitsch."

I also got a hand-written card from Barbara Parkins. Addressed to Mark Usteus [sic]:

> *"Dear Mark— Valley of the Dolls!! Well, well, well. I knew it had a following—but our nite was spectacular. Truly."*

After our magical Castro evening together, Barbara and I talked regularly on the phone. On a visit to Los Angeles, we had dinner at the Formosa, a classic spot for old-school Hollywood wheeling and dealing, and discussed bringing *VD* to Chicago and New York. We left excited.

Afterwards, to negotiate a deal, Barbara brought in her agent. After several back and forths on the phone, he demanded twice the fee that I paid in San Francisco. I explained my expenses and said that while it was probably undoable, I would think about it. "Call me back on Monday," I tersely replied.

That weekend I had one of my meth-infused party-and-play sex marathons. It started Friday night and lasted until Sunday afternoon. I barely got any sleep.

Monday morning, Barbara's agent called. My teeth were clenched and clattering and I was drooling—side effects of the drug. I really was in no shape to talk turkey, but regardless plowed forward. I asked if he would consider a smaller fee for Chicago and New York, which were smaller houses.

The agent barked, "Absolutely not. You know, Marc, you wouldn't have a show without my client."

Suddenly, my green-eyed crystal demon reared its ugly hydra head. I screamed into the phone: "And you know, mister whatever your name is, your fucking client would not have a show without me!!" I launched into a two-minute tirade, then abruptly hung up.

As they say, all good things must come to an end. I didn't hear a peep back from Barbara afterwards. And I couldn't blame her. Who wants to deal with a tweeked-out crazy person?

OK, a step back. I obviously overreacted to her agent, but I still think what he said was wrong. In show business, we are all in this together: talent, producer, director, agent, house manager, publicist, theater staff, and so on. When one person is denigrated, everyone suffers.

But... I was a monster. Drugs make you do really shitty things. And crystal is the worst. I wish I could take back that moment in time.

Ironic, huh? Doing a campy event about drugs, and then getting high afterward. Life imitating art.

I was beginning to realize that Tina had dug her filthy claws deep into my life and her grip was insidious. To paraphrase the lyric from *Valley of the Dolls*, somehow I had to get off of this merry-go-round.

Act 2, Scene 5 – THE HEIRESS

Part 1 – Tina, Darling

I never crossed paths with screen legend Joan Crawford, but I got the consolation prize: I worked with her daughter, Christina Crawford.

If you don't recognize that name, you should turn in your Gay Card.

Ms. Crawford, the adopted daughter of Miss Crawford, wrote about her mother's questionable child-raising skills in the controversial mega-bestseller *Mommie Dearest*. It sold some 700,000 copies in hardcover, over 3 million in paperback. In turn, it spawned the mother of all camp films, *Mommie Dearest*.

I was a *Mommie Dearest* groupie since the book's publication in 1978. I was not alone. On the 8 Castro bus line, in cafes, and on park benches, you'd see groups of gay men devouring the distinctive red-covered paperback.

That sunny day in 1981 when *Mommie Dearest (MD)* hit the screen, I was first in line for the bargain matinee at the Regency Two Theatre. At the first image of Faye/Joan icing her face, the gay men in the audience all collectively oohed and ahhed. But as the picture progressed, we went from suppressed titters to giggles, then guffaws and out-and-out howls, as Faye's performance went increasingly off the rails. When we left the theater, we realized what we had witnessed was a beautiful thing—the birth of a camp classic.

Over the next 20 years, the cult of *Mommie Dearest* flourished, inspiring countless drag homages, and cold-creamed man-hags shrieking, "No wire hangers, EVERRRRRRR!"

I was pondering just the right vehicle to top my highly successful "John Waters X-Mas" and *Valley of the Dolls* events.

Suddenly the image of Faye as Joan bellowing, "Tina! Bring me the ax!" popped into my head. That was it: a *Mommie Dearest* film event.

But how? Joan Crawford was dead. Faye Dunaway was notorious for not talking about the picture, even abruptly halting interviews if that title was uttered. Diana Scarwid who played the adult Christina was not a draw.

But what about the tortured daughter herself? I wondered where Christina Crawford was hiding. She had escaped the public eye after the release of the book. She was a great mystery. And mystery sells! I was determined to find her.

I scoured every Hollywood directory. I hunted for clues in every article on *MD*. In one interview, I stumbled upon key information: Crawford owned a bed & breakfast in the middle of Idaho. Through intense sleuthing, I was able to track down the place and the phone number.

One day, I got up my courage to make the call. After several nerve-wracking rings, a woman's voice answered.

"Hello, is Christina Crawford there?"

"Who's calling?" a voice calmly inquired.

Trying to exude confidence, but actually scared shitless, I continued: "My name is Marc Huestis, I'm a producer at the Castro Theatre in San Francisco, a 1,400-seat movie palace and..."

The officious voice suddenly brightened. "This is she."

"Christina Crawford? *The* Christina Crawford?" I nearly pooped in my pants.

Let me tell you, when I want something, I can be very persuasive. So I breathlessly told Christina how much the movie means to the LGBT fan base, how I know she hates it, but how she could discuss the serious issues raised in her book, and how Castro audiences are like no other.

My nose was so brown it stank.

When I finished my uninterrupted spiel, there was silence on her end. And then the writer revealed...

"You know, I *have* been working on a new expanded 20th anniversary version of *Mommie Dearest*..."

I jumped on the information. "Well there is no such thing as a coincidence. Maybe this phone call is providence. Kismet!"

"You may be right," she murmured. "Let me call you tomorrow."

The next morning, bright and early, I get a prompt answer. "It's Christina, I'll do it. Under one condition. I can sell my book at the event. It should be ready by Christmas."

Without missing a beat, I countered, "Perfect. I'll call it *Christmas With Christina Crawford!*"

Never in my life had I been so thrilled about an event. And I'd make it the best dysfunctional holiday event ever!

Although it was still months away, I sprung into action. After a blurb appeared in the *Bay Area Reporter*, bedlam erupted. In two days, I fielded 150 frantic phone calls. Castro booker Anita Monga gladly extended the one-night-only engagement to two (Dec. 19 and 20, 1997). They both sold out.

The show came together magically. The local drag troupe performing the satire *Christmas with the Crawfords* agreed to open my show. I traveled to New York City to record video greetings from both actress Mara Hobel, who plays young Christina in the film, and the legendary Lypsinka, then playing Joan Crawford in a staged version of her melodrama *Harriet Craig*. I engaged Erik Lee Preminger, son of Hollywood royalty Otto Preminger and Gypsy Rose Lee, to lead the onstage interview with Christina. (His dad was rumored to be romantically linked with Joan.)

Event poster by Rex Ray.

I communicated with Christina frequently. She was game, laughing heartily at the idea of a theater full of Joan Crawford-ey drag queens. Everything was developing perfectly.

Well, almost. A month before *Christmas With Christina Crawford*, Christina asked how many copies of *Mommie Dearest* should be shipped to San Francisco for the post-event book signing. (Selling her self-published revised edition, after all, was her incentive to appear.) I estimated that 300 books (six boxes) should be plenty.

When the UPS truck arrived a week later, the driver looked peeved.

"I have a large delivery to unload. Where do you want it?"

"Right here in my office."

"I doubt it'll fit," he grunted. When his work was finished, my small cramped office was filled with almost 50 boxes of books. Ms. Crawford had a mind of her own.

While climbing over boxes of *Mommie Dearest*, I was frenetically faxing, phoning and e-mailing press releases. The local advance publicity was glowing.

Yet the national press was less kind. Veteran gossip writer Liz Smith wrote in her syndicated column about the 20th anniversary edition of *Mommie Dearest*:

"Joan may have been a lousy mother and a deeply disturbed human being, but she really didn't deserve to have 40 years of stardom and hard work wiped away by Christina's literary 'catharsis'."

Well, any publicity is good publicity, and I was honored Liz Smith even mentioned the event. Besides, I had a show to put on.

The surprises continued. A few days before the show, I got a call from a woman named Keri Berkwitz.

"I know you're not going to believe this, but I was the baby Christina in *Mommie Dearest*."

"Huh?" I said.

"You know, the baby Faye is holding as she walks down the staircase in that silver lamé dress. *That was me!* I'd like to come to the show with my friend."

I thought for a second whether I was being hoaxed, then shrugged. Even if it was a scam to get free tickets, it was a great story. So I offered Baby Christina free admission to appear onstage and tell her tale.

The next day, I met Christina Crawford at San Francisco Airport for the first time. Out of the arrival gate walked a professional-looking middle-aged woman with a toothy smile. Slightly butch, handsome, blond hair carefully coiffed in a modified shag. Exuding no aura of Hollywood royalty, she wore an outfit suggesting businesswoman instead of diva.

Crawford was particularly interested in taking a tour of the charity I had designated as the show's beneficiary. So, we drove to Project Open Hand, providing home-delivered meals for people with HIV/AIDS. Suddenly, Christina was radiating a Joan Crawford celebrity vibe, gliding through the Open Hand kitchen with an air of elegance recalling movie stars of the Golden Age. She carefully inspected huge pots and pans, commented on their cleanliness, reviewed the menu, and showered volunteers with praise.

For a moment, I imagined Joan visiting the Pepsi plants, diplomatically addressing her husband's fleet of workers. (Joan was known for treating fans and workers kindly, as she had come from a dirt-poor family.)

For the event, the Castro had been magically turned into a twisted Yuletide wonderland. Cardboard coat hangers were strung across the stage. A spotlight highlighted a huge blood red painted ax and a chopped down Christmas tree. As carolers cheerfully belted out "O Come, All Ye Faithful," the electrified *Mommie Dearest* faithful flooded through the theater doors. Young, old, straight, gay, male, female, non-binary. The whole shebang was the perfect antidote to the usual anxiety and depression of the season.

The show was a roaring success. From the pre-show mash-up of Crawford film clips to the Joan Crawford look-alike contest.

The bonus? Baby Christina showed up—and turned out to be a real-life baby dyke!

Christina Crawford's interview with Erik Preminger was the star on top of the tree. Dressed in "Don't fuck with me fellas" red, accented by pearls, CC was funny, tough, and even vulnerable, confessing: "I was always hungry for normal love and affection, the type of a thing that kids take for granted. A hug, a kiss, a pat of encouragement, a kiss on the forehead. I was literally starved."

Regarding her notorious memoir, Christina said, "If the book helped in changing laws to protect children and get people help that suffered from various forms of family violence, that is the true lasting legacy."

When asked by Erik of her motives for participating in this event, she rose to the occasion. "I have never done anything like this before, yet I have heard the stories, heard the jokes, and thought that with the 20th anniversary edition of the book, it was time that we all met!"

Then she pulls a bit of Christmas magic out of a hat. For the winner of a raffle prize, Christina had a special gift: a Yuletide clothes hanger—yes, made of wire—that she had personally wrapped in tinsel and a large glittered checkerboard bow.

Take that, Mommie Dearest!

After the show, Christina got down to business, selling and signing books. She sold a lot. Wads of green were shoveled into her shiny black bag. Christina's eagle eye darted back and forth, supervising the process. On stage, the guest of honor was happy. Now, she was *really* happy.

Merry Christmas, Tina Darling!

A week later, I received a thank-you note from Christina on personalized stationery, her name in huge, embossed gold Gothic letters on white glossy paper. It read: "To the best producer ever! Christina Crawford." My celebrity handler, Kathy Nelsen, got a card too. Apropos, since Kathy was right next to Crawford, making sure all those books could be sold and signed as quickly as possible. Christina recognized that Kathy is the smartest, best-dressed, most well organized celebrity-handling lipstick lesbian ever.

Like a victorious quarterback after the Super Bowl, I celebrated the event's success with a trip to Disneyland. On the rollercoaster at Space Mountain, I hatched a new plan: a four-city tour of the *Mommie Dearest* show, starring Christina. This kitschmeister was itching to take his hit Castro show on the road.

But like a rollercoaster ride, I would eventually learn, what goes up, must...

Part 2 – Daughter Dearest

I had big plans for the *Mommie Dearest* tour. "April Fools with Christina Crawford" in Los Angeles and Seattle in April 1998; and "Mother's Day with Christina Crawford," in New York and Chicago in May.

The New York City event at Town Hall would have historic significance; back in the spring of 1973, 25 years previously, Joan Crawford had made her last public appearance in that same theater, as part of the "Legendary Ladies" conversations produced by famous publicist John Springer.

Admittedly, I was taking a huge financial risk with such an ambitious tour. The budget for theater and film rentals, plane tickets and accommodations, as well as Christina's fee, would run in the tens of thousands. But who cared? The Town Hall event would be my Broadway debut!

In retrospect, I was in over my head. But the devil on my left shoulder kept whispering, "You're finally on Broadway, baby." That helped me ignore the devil on my right shoulder, warning me, "Flop, flop, FLOP!!!"

At first, Christina was excited about the tour. Why wouldn't she be? She got paid an appearance fee and got to hawk her book. She sounded just like Joan as she gushed to *The Los Angeles Times*: "I spent 14 years as an actress and love the profession with all my heart and soul. So, to come back into a theater situation, it was really like coming home."

She was equally happy that Erik Lee Preminger would again be her interviewer in L.A. and Seattle. For New York City, I had engaged noted celebrity scribe and critic Rex Reed to do the honors. All was well.

Then we hit the road.

In Los Angeles, Christina was staying with friends. I, along with my trusted production assistants Lawrence Helman and Hrappa Gunnarsdottir, camped out in a small room at the Hollywood Roosevelt Hotel. To me, it had historic significance. The Blossom Ballroom hosted the first Academy Awards in 1929, and I'm sure Joan had roamed the hotel halls and slept in a few of the beds.

We were scheduled to meet Christina in the hotel's elegant dining room for a production powwow. At 1 p.m. sharp, Christina rolled up in a black Mercedes.

"Wow, fancy car!" I remarked, trying to sound casual.

"It's a loaner from my friends," Christina icily replied, imperiously handing the keys to the valet.

As we settled into our lunch, Christina seemed cold and distant. When asked whether the Roosevelt Hotel had brought back memories, she curtly replied, "Too many." Perhaps the ghost of her mother was haunting her while she picked at her Caesar salad.

The meeting soon grew confrontational. I showed her the "Joan on a Stick" paper-mask cutouts of her mother, glue-gunned on a chopstick. I suggested selling them to accelerate audience fun—and increase the bottom line.

"Absolutely not!" Christina exclaimed. "I will not have them staring at me throughout my interview."

"Well my dear, you have no choice," I coolly replied. "This tour is costing me a fortune, ticket sales are not great, and I need to do what I can to recoup my expenses."

She huffed. Then relented. The luncheon broke up on a bad note.

That was not the only thing that was sour. The L.A. Weekly was harsh:

"It's all a bit of a mystery how Christina can cheerfully participate in a shameless send-up of what was, in reality, her sobering hellish life."

Day of the show, rehearsal did not go well. When shown the short staircase that leads to the main stage, Christina flipped out.

"I can't do it. I won't!"

Only after a good amount of hand-holding, plus assurances that Lawrence would walk her up the stairs, flashlight in hand, Christina's fears were somewhat allayed. I remember her having no problems with the stairs at the Castro, but whatever. It was becoming obvious that we were dealing with a very different Christina this time. Daughter Dearest.

Before leaving, she barked out, "Have the books arrived yet?"

"Yes, Christina," I answered in a singsong voice, subtly rolling my eyes. It took all my willpower not to say, "Yes, Tina Dearest."

Showtime. The theater was only half full. Why? Maybe Los Angelenos are used to seeing all kinds of semi-celebrities in the Stop & Shop. Maybe they tend to be skeptical of anything that originates in San Francisco.

Unexpectedly, Christina's interview with Erik didn't match the Castro lovefest. And when I got the box office report, I realized the April Fools joke was on me.

Another problem: Lawrence had little patience for Christina's constant need for control. The next morning, as he steered the rented SUV for the drive to LAX, she took issue with his selected route.

"This is not the best way to go!" Christina bellowed from the back seat.

"It might not be the best way to go, but it's the way I'm going," Lawrence shot back with his signature snark. Christina scowled the rest of the way.

The Seattle event was not much better. Bad attendance, low box-office. And Missy Crawford continued to be a bitter pill, complaining in the preshow limo ride about how poorly her bed and breakfast business in Idaho was doing.

"I have an idea," I volunteered, trying to elevate the mood. "Why don't you rename it the 'Wire Hanger Inn' and advertise in all the gay rags? I'm sure that would be a big hit."

If looks could kill, I'd have been dead on the spot.

I was quickly getting to know the darker side of Crawford. But despite it all, there *was* one thing I did like about Christina. She ignored her critics. For example, when someone mentioned Myrna Loy in an interview—a celebrity who publicly questioned the book's veracity and slammed the authoress as "vicious, ungrateful and jealous"—Christina would get a sarcastic grin on her face and drolly counter, "She's wonderful!"

Those words became a running joke between Lawrence, Hrappa, and myself. Every time there was someone we didn't like, we'd smile and say, "She's wonderful!" A nasty situation? "It's wonderful!" Let me tell you, there were a lot of "wonderful" times on this tour.

There was a break between the April and May events, so we all retreated to our corners before the second round. Back at the office, there was a fax awaiting me. Christina's invoice not only listed her fee, but an itemized addendum, charging *me* for promotional copies of the new edition of *Mommie Dearest* I sent to the press.

I was furious.

Not only had I publicized her goddamned book through the tour, I had also set up signings in Seattle and Los Angeles at A Different Light Bookstore. Their West Hollywood front window was full of stacks of *Mommie Dearest*, its bright red covers visible a block away! Yet she had the nerve to charge *me* for copies I had sent to the press to further *her* book sales.

I wanted to eviscerate Christina in writing, but we had two more cities to get through. So I sent back a diplomatic fax saying I would not pay for these copies, ending with: "If you please, in the future I will forward all press requests for the book your way, and you can do with them what you will. Let's move forward. Warmest regards."

On to New York. The first order of business was a luncheon with Rex Reed and Christina to get acquainted before the Town Hall event. I chose Joe Allen's, a Midtown restaurant famous for its theatrical clientele. I'm sure Joan frequented this joint. Maybe with Christina in tow.

Rex and I were early, so we sat down for a chat. Well, he chatted. Nonstop.

When Christina arrived, we both stood up. Rex reached to shake her hand.

The first thing out of his mouth: "Who was your copy editor for the new edition of your book? My god, there are tons of typos!"

Christina scowled.

Hoping to save the situation, Rex quickly changed the subject, dishing Joan's Upper East Side apartment, where he had been a guest. He recalled the plastic-covered furniture and the fear of being stuck to the sofa when they sat down. Then how, whenever people got up, Joan would quickly grab a can of disinfectant and meticulously spray the area where her visitors sat. Christina let out a forced belly laugh. I finally began breathing again.

Returning to Brooklyn, where I was staying with a friend, I got a surprise phone call. It was John Springer, the press agent behind the 1973 Town Hall interview with Joan. He had caught wind of Christina's Town Hall appearance and was furious. Springer was *not* one of Christina's fans. He threatened to stand up in the middle of her interview and expose her "lies." Oh goody, goody. Drama! I happily acceded to his demand for two tickets: Center orchestra, aisle seats. One for him, the other for Janet Leigh.

The show received a goodly amount of advance press: an extensive *New York Times* puff piece on Christina, a full-page photo of Lypsinka (one of the evening's performers) dolled up as Joan in *The Village Voice*, and a cartoon in *The New Yorker*. But others offered a hefty dose of snark. *The Daily News*, acknowledging the event's sold-out crowd in San Francisco, added, "Then again nights can be slow out West." Christina did a frosty TV interview with Liz Smith, who remained a fierce defender of Joan's legacy.

Despite the big build-up, sales sucked. I, along with event beneficiary GMHC, agreed to comp much of the house.

Day of the show was ultra-stressful. John Epperson, aka Lypsinka, was lip-synching a recreation of the Joan Crawford-John Springer 1973 Town Hall interview. The primary concern was getting the multiple tech cues right. In the middle of an intensive run-through, a box-office assistant whispered in my ear. Christina had arrived unexpectedly in a limo stuffed with boxes of books. And she demanded my crew unload them.

I was truly annoyed. I went out to confront her. All diplomacy had vanished.

"We are in a middle of rehearsal, and I am paying the crew union wages. You should have thought of this before. I'm not responsible for your goddamn book sales."

Christina refused to back down.

So, rehearsal was interrupted while the non-union members of my production team unloaded the goddamned boxes of her goddamned book.

The big night arrived. There was a modest turnout, largely comped. Totally unplanned, Christina and Lypsinka wore dresses featuring elaborate frontal beadwork resembling armor. There was a small gaggle of paparazzi outside, taking photos of them together. I weaseled my way into a few preshow photos. We all had our best game faces on and smiled bravely.

A smattering of celebrities arrived: Lady Bunny, Michael Musto, Sylvia Miles. John Springer didn't attend after all, but my dad Hank came in from Long Island.

I introduced him to Christina.

"I saw your interview with Liz Smith on TV. Boy, that must have been difficult!" my father remarked.

Christina responded frostily, "Mr. Huestis, after working with your son, *nothing* is difficult."

Bitch.

On with the show. Lypsinka brought the house down; reviews afterwards used words like "awesome," "brilliant," and "flawless." (John went on to do a version of this performance for years.) Also appearing on the bill was Mara Hobel, who played young Christina, all grown up, looking fab in a black crushed velvet pantsuit, and thrilled to be remembered. And Rutanya Alda, who played Joan's dowdy maid Carol Ann in the film. She read entries from a dishy diary kept while on the set, mostly reporting on Faye Dunaway's diva behavior. It was hysterical stuff and she had the audience enraptured. (Rutanya went on to finish and publish *The Mommie Dearest Diaries*.)

Christina and Rex took the stage. It was the first time she ever seemed nervous, and she overcompensated by stirring up the audience with provocative tidbits. One, in particular, got their attention. Discussing the death of Alfred Steele, Joan's third husband and head of PepsiCo, she voiced suspicions about the circumstances. Was she openly implicating Joan in her husband's death?

At intermission, journalistic snoop Michael Musto attempted to get to the bottom of this. But when he cut in line during the book signing, Christina affected a haughty Joan attitude and waved him off. (Her rude brush-off appeared in his post-event *Village Voice* column.)

When the evening wrapped, promoter Chip Duckett threw an after-party at popular nightclub Life. Mara and Rutanya showed up. Christina did not, despite saying she would. Duckett was furious.

Next Magazine sniped: "The damaged daughter of the Queen Bee was nowhere to be found. It seems that in spite of her well-disciplined upbringing, Ms. Crawford is still a very naughty girl."

The box office report arrived the next day. It was worse than I thought. The New York engagement had put me $15,000 in the hole, on top of the $5,000 lost in L.A. and Seattle.

Thank God for credit cards.

Next and final stop, Chicago. My friend Alan Williams had arranged four gratis rooms at the luxurious Four Seasons Hotel for Christina, Lawrence, Hrappa, and me. I plopped my head on the lush mattress and just stared up at the heavenly ceiling. But it was hard to really enjoy the 4 star amenities; I was obsessed with the thought of losing $20,000. My mind was swirling with ledgers bathed in red. And all because of that... that *ingrate*.

Just then, the ingrate called. She had a diva demand that was *not* in our agreement: final payment for New York and Chicago before she went on.

Is she fucking kidding me?

That evening, our host Alan threw us a dinner party in a private room at a ritzy Chicago eatery. The last thing I wanted to do was to have din-din with daughter dearest. So, I got smashed. In my deeply inebriated state, the whole thing seemed like a surreal dream sequence from a Buñuel movie. The only thing I remember is Christina's irritating guffaws echoing loudly—and me being awful to everyone.

The next day, I was hung over, woozy and withdrawn. No one talked to me. They ignored my apologies in the limo ride to the theater.

Chicago's Music Box is a historic movie palace, a miniature version of the Castro. Christina was given the royal tour by the excited owners. As she inspected the spotless interior, all of a sudden Christina noticed popcorn on the floor. She pointed her finger, turned to me and ordered, "Marc, can you please take care of that!"

"What?" I snapped.

"There in the aisle break. There's popcorn on the floor!"

So, believe it or not, I got on my hands and knees to pick up the kernels. Despite my ignominy, I had to laugh. Life was imitating art. I flashed back to that scene in *Mommie Dearest* where Joan has beaten her daughter with a can of Bon Ami. "Christina, clean up this mess," Joan barks. "But how?" little Christina tearfully asks. "You figure it out!!!!"

We called a truce that night and got through the final show. There was a big after-party in a cavernous gay nightclub, again organized by Chip Duckett. This time Christina showed up, allegedly soothed by an extra appearance fee. She stood in a corner drinking a large glass of milk as a huge drag queen in a mint green pinafore swung on a giant wire hanger.

The next day, Christina and I met in the lobby to check out. We barely said goodbye. The tour was finally over and I couldn't wait to be rid of her.

Afterwards, I received no thank you letter from Christina. The debts I incurred on this tour almost closed the doors of my business. It would take years to pay back.

Retribution came a few months later, at of all places, the Safeway checkout counter. While perusing the pages of the *National Enquirer*, out popped a huge picture of Christina with Lypsinka from the Town Hall event. The caption screamed: *"IT'S BA-A-A-ACK! Christina Crawford hired a drag queen to play her mother at a book signing for the release of 'Mommie Dearest.'"*

The lengthy story detailed a vicious family feud. Christina's adopted sister Cathy, one of the twins, was suing Christina for statements she made on tour.

As I read every juicy morsel, I let out a huge shriek of joy. The customers behind me thought I was crazy.

I bought every copy on the shelf. I went home, reread the story and laughed. And laughed. As Olivia de Havilland's character says in *The Heiress*: "I can be cruel. I have been taught by masters."

When I talk about my years as an impresario, people usually are dying to know about Christina Crawford. My first impulse is to say: "Now I understand what Joan went through."

But there are always two sides to every coin. Certainly Christina is a piece of work, and damaged goods. Yet despite everything she put me through, I feel sorry for her. Joan must have been a terror. To deal with her mother, Christina had to be willful, stubborn, and damned difficult. Mommie Dearest must have met her match with Daughter Dearest.

So why dwell bitterly on the past? When asked about Christina, I don't take the bait. I borrow a page from her playbook, smile broadly and say, "She's wonderful!"

Act 2, Scene 6 – LOOK AT ME

In the late '50s and early '60s, Sandra Dee was the reigning all-American princess of Hollywood. She was blonde, doe-eyed, perky, totally adorable and supremely lovable.

Dee was also the saddest star I ever met.

She fell into my lap on the rebound from my disastrous tour with Daughter Dearest, Christina Crawford.

The timing couldn't have been more perfect. Local TV entertainment reporter Jan Wahl was an avid fan of my shows and itching to get involved. Affectionately known as "Our Lady of the Hats" for her endless collection of large and colorful chapeaux, Jan was also an expert on old Hollywood and had just been on a celebrity cruise with Troy Donahue. "I would love to interview him at the Castro," she said. "Should I ask him?"

"Please do!" I enthused. After that Crawford woman, I was desperate for something, *anything* to get back on track.

A few hours later, Jan called me to say Troy was in. Troy had offered to contact Sandra Dee, his *Summer Place* co-star, to come along for the ride. She, too, quickly agreed. I was thrilled!

For my generation, our first introduction to Sandra Dee was through the song "Look at Me, I'm Sandra Dee!" belted out by the Pink Ladies in *Grease*. But other film folk remember Sandra Dee as the lead in such frivolous froth as *Gidget* (the original beach flick), *Tammy Tell Me True*, and *Come September* (where she met crooner Bobby Darin, her future husband). She also had meatier roles as the troubled good girl gone bad in *A Summer Place* and as Lana Turner's tortured daughter in my personal favorite, Douglas Sirk's classic melodrama, *Imitation of Life*.

Sandra Dee and Troy Donahue in "A Summer Place."
Photo courtesy of Warner Bros.

Troy Donahue, also a teen idol, was best known as Sandra's idyllic lover in *A Summer Place*. He was also blond, blue-eyed, lanky and corn-fed. A real white-bread looker.

Dee and Donahue graced the covers of every fan magazine during the Eisenhower and Kennedy eras, and Sandra was box-office gold. Youngsters flocked to her films. Both boys and girls worshipped her.

The one person who didn't adore Sandra Dee was Sandra Dee. Her trajectory from belle of the ball to woman on the verge had been well documented by supermarket tabloids. Fortuitously, several weeks before the Castro event, *The National Enquirer* featured Ms. Dee on its cover with the caption; "Anorexia and alcohol drove me to the brink of death."

The article detailed Sandra's journey down the rabbit hole of multiple addictions and her courageous road to recovery. According to the *Enquirer*, her weight had stabilized and she insisted she was off the sauce. "I still have a glass of wine with a meal now and then. But I can control it" (famous last words). "My goal in life is quite simple now, I want to be happy!"

I was rooting for her. Truth was, I adored Sandra in the movies. Beneath that façade of virginal purity was an actress with a natural vulnerability not seen in typical teen ingénues. And brittleness. If you touched her, she might fall apart. You just wanted to pull her off the screen, give her a big hug, and tell her everything was going to be all right.

Maybe this gig was just what Sandra needed to boost her confidence. And seeing her old friend Troy might also lift her spirits. The famed screen couple hadn't seen each other in years.

"Summer Beach Party with Sandra Dee & Troy Donahue" was set for Friday, July 17, 1998. Its tagline: "Grab Your Beach Balls, Throw on Your Summer Muumuu and Ride the Wave to The Castro Theatre." The emcee was drag queen entertainer Lady Bunny, co-founder of Wigstock, and no stranger to a good muumuu. Since we met in New York in 1989, I loved Bunny. Out of drag, little Jon was a shy diminutive thing with a wisp of a voice. In drag and super-duper high hair, Lady Bunny was a lioness. Throughout the years I was thrilled to watch her climb up the ladder of drag celebrity.

Troy was familiar with Lady Bunny, as well as the wild goings-on at the Castro. His good friend opera composer Jake Heggie lived in San Francisco, and filled Troy in with the 411 on the hood. Troy had also been in the John Waters film *Cry Baby*, so he was no stranger to campy good fun.

Sandra, on the other hand, had no idea what was in store. Meanwhile, more tabloid red flags were being raised. Closer to the event, another fortuitous *Enquirer* headline declared: "Sandra Dee 'very ill' as she wobbles off airplane." In the article, her spokesmen spun: "She wasn't intoxicated. She was suffering from a virus and the effects were just compounded by the flight."

Soon afterwards, the phone rang. It was the "spokesman," who also acted as her agent and manager. "Sandy's been having problems flying lately," she informed me. "We're going to have to cancel the flights. She can take Amtrak."

So I canceled the three non-refundable flights (for Sandra plus the husband and wife spokespeople/managers) and booked a reserved berth on the California Zephyr train. I even sent my travel Scrabble set to occupy the time (after reading that Sandra devours "almost a book a day").

A few days later, another phone call. The train ride would be too long for Sandy; rebook the flights. Well, at least they didn't ask for first class!

Troy, in contrast, was easy-peasy, lemon-squeezy. He arrived several days before the tribute. Right away, he gripped my hand, looked me straight in the eye, and expressed how happy he was to do the event. His eyes were still that trademark aquamarine blue. By his side was his paramour, a famed Chinese opera singer named Zheng Cao. Despite their age difference—Zheng was born in 1966, Troy in 1936—they acted like sweethearts on their first date. They even held hands! Their puppy love was infectious.

Lulu played our tour guide, yakking a mile a minute as we drove past San Francisco landmarks. As we rolled by the Legion of Honor, Zheng—for no reason except sheer happiness—

spontaneously broke out into the famous "Flower Song" from *Madama Butterfly*, singing Suzuki's mezzo at the top of her lungs.

A day later, Sandy was set to arrive. I rented a fancy limo, and Lulu and I met Sandra, flowers in hand, at the gate. I was not ready for the scene that followed. Sandra stumbled off the plane, unescorted, her managers lagging far behind. The star looked totally lost in space.

I had never seen somebody so plastered in my life. And the flight was only an hour long! Sandra was taking tiny, teetering steps, grabbing hold of an imaginary railing as she weaved and wobbled forward.

Sandra was rail-thin, a sleeveless blouse exposing her bony arms. On one of them, I spied a large, pus-oozing burn. Big as a silver dollar, and exposed to the elements. Even in her stupor, Dee saw me staring. She slurred, "Oh *that*! I fell the other day on my heater." A heater? It was the middle of the summer, and she lived in Malibu.

We escorted Dee, her managers, and her yapping toy Pomeranian, Theo, to the waiting limo. Sandra babbled loudly and continuously throughout the ride. Her voice no longer had that squeaky-clean girlish timbre. It was now boozy, and several octaves lower, like a 78 rpm record playing at 33 1/3.

Although it was night and the limo windows were tinted, she kept saying over and over again how beautiful San Francisco was. Repeating how she wanted desperately to get out of L.A., and that San Francisco would be the perfect place to move to. Then she went on a disjointed monologue about her granddaughter Alexa, and how she was going to convince her son Dodd Darin (her only child with Bobby Darin) to move the family up here. "I love it here soooooooooo much. They'd love it toooo. What do you think, Theo? Oh my babyyyyyyy!" Smooching with her dog as he licked her face.

Dee was deposited at the Hotel del Sol. Back in the limo, Lulu and I looked at each other in stunned silence, eyes wide open. Then we both mouthed the words "Oh my god!" We laughed, but the whole thing was just so damn sad. Sandra was so sweet, yet so damaged, exposed, defenseless.

That night, I had nightmares about Sandra Dee. We were together in the green room and I couldn't open the door. It was bolted shut, and everyone kept screaming that the star was on. She was sobbing in fear. The next day, I woke up nervous and disturbed. Sandra was one of the most lovable drunks I had ever met. But she was still a drunk. How could she appear onstage?

I called Troy for advice. He had visited her adjoining room the night before, and was in shock at her current condition. Donahue had been clean and sober for quite some time; he knew all the telltale signs of serious disease.

We wondered aloud if there should be some sort of flash intervention. But there was simply not the time, place, nor personnel for such a life-changing event. Troy ended the conversation with the familiar words "God grant us the serenity to accept the things we cannot change."

So, on with the show. During the afternoon, reports had leaked out from hair and makeup that Sandra was already on her way to becoming pickled.

Meanwhile at the Castro, guys were lounging on lawn chairs while waiting in line, spritzing their faces to cool off. Boom boxes were blasting the famous theme song from *A Summer Place*. There were Hawaiian shirts, vintage sunglasses, and fake leis aplenty.

Unlike my usual Castro events, which attracted stone-cold freaks, "Summer Beach Party with Sandra Dee & Troy Donahue" attracted an even weirder crowd: suburban white heterosexuals, who grew up worshipping Dee and Donahue. There was even a contingent from the Troy Donahue Fan Club, flying in from all parts of the country. It was nice to see these folk mixing with the Castro's regular patrons: Friends of Dorothy. This night, we were all friends of Sandy. And Troy.

The famed screen couple arrived in a shining vintage black-and-red Olds 88. The stars emerged, big smiles on their faces, and the crowd roared. Both wore elegant tailored black suits, Sandra sporting humongous Jackie O sunglasses. Hair and makeup had done their job; Sandy looked terrific. Outwardly at least. She didn't seem too tanked.

At the pre-show reception in the Castro mezzanine, saronged boys served drinks and edibles from the '50s. Lots of Ritz crackers, Velvetta cheese chunks, and pigs in a blanket. Troy partied and posed with the drag queens. But at 6-foot-3, he towered over the crowd and was keeping an eagle eye on Sandy.

Troy Donahue (r) celebrates with Lady Bunny (center) and the winners
of the "How to Stuff a Wild Bikini" Contest.
Photo by Kent Taylor.

Sandra was more introverted. She let yappy pooch Theo do the talking. Celebrity handler Kathy Nelsen carted the dog around in a stylish mesh carrier. I secretly instructed Kathy to keep Sandra far away from the rum punch. As a substitute, I bought a bottle of white wine, and had Kathy sneak into the green room and pour ice shavings in the glass. It seemed to work; Sandra didn't notice her drink was being watered down. She began to loosen up and mingle with the adoring crowd.

There was a gap of 90 minutes between the reception and onstage interview. I arranged for Sandra and company to get a quick bite at 2223 Market Street, a stylish neighborhood restaurant with a secret backroom for VIPs. After the short, brisk walk from the theater, Sandra complained that her feet were killing her. Ever the experienced hospitality hostess, Kathy volunteered to find Sandy comfortable slippers while she ate.

Kathy hustled out the door, ran four blocks to Walgreen's in record speed, and hotfooted it back to the restaurant. Mission accomplished. Or so she thought.

The VIP room was empty. Sandra and her managers had left. Panicked, Kathy snagged the maître d'. "What happened? Where are they?"

"There's no smoking allowed in the restaurant, and Miss Dee desperately needed a cigarette."

"Oh my god, Marc is going to kill me," Kathy nervously uttered. "I've lost his star!"

She bolted out to Market Street, desperately scanning the area. Finally, she spotted Sandra a few doors down, perched on a bench in front of the Baghdad Café. Smiling, smoking, drinking a glass of wine. Barefoot and fancy-free. And there, kneeling before Sandra's feet, was not a fan, but a homeless woman. Massaging Sandra's teensy-tiny toes.

Sandra was in heaven. "I loooove San Fraaaancisco soooo much! Oh, honey that feels so goooood! Hey, do you have a card? I'd love to get you to come to my hotel after the show and finish the job!" Sandra didn't seem to mind that an indigent lady was taking care of her; or, she might not have even understood what was going on. She simply rejoiced that her feet were feeling a lot better.

Kathy diplomatically reminded the star of her big interview, and they journeyed back to the Castro.

*Sandra Dee and Troy Donahue, together once more
with the help of Lulu, myself, and Kathy Nelsen.*

Celebrity interviewer Jan Wahl introduced the stars to
tumultuous applause. Troy, again the protector, held Sandra's
hand as they mounted the stairs.

Then "the star thing" happened. It's the miracle I've seen over
and over again. That magical moment. No matter what state the
star is in, once the spotlight hits, they come to life, turn it on, and
sparkle for their fans. Drunks appear sober; the wheelchair-bound
start walking. Sandra was no exception. She became radiant,
charming, even erudite. Sure, there was a slur to some sentences,
but she was still a star, silently affirming: "Look at me, I'm Sandra
Dee!"

Then some revealing exchanges.

On watching her movies:

Sandra: I never saw my pictures. I never saw *Summer Place*, I never saw *Gidget*. I can't stand to watch myself. Some people go, and look at the entire scene, and they learn. I go and just look at what I've done wrong. And get depressed.

Jan Wahl: So you don't see the Sandra Dee we all love?
Sandra: No!
Jan: I wish you could see yourself as we see you. I wish that for you.

On being married to famous singer Bobby Darin:

Sandra Dee: He was terrific; I loved him till the day he died. I love him today. And he was the best father. And a good husband. I just wasn't a very good wife.

Then the spotlight turned to Troy.

Troy Donahue: I became disenchanted with a lot of things that were happening to me. My career started to dwindle. I began to become more and more involved with drugs and alcohol. Granted, I had a lot of fun doing it! I remember living in a bush in Central Park and saying, "Oh man, this is what I always wanted! This is really cool!" And I lived on the streeets twice in my life. I really don't know what happened, but 16 years ago, I got sober. It's called saving your own life with the help of a lot of people. I didn't know I was living a nightmare. Until I found there was a dream at the other side. I am just so grateful for the life that I now have.

Jan: Congratulations on your sobriety, one day at a time.
Troy: One day at a time!

Sandra looked stunned. Troy's soul-baring truth had opened up her own inner turmoil. She then spoke in staccato, tears forming in her eyes.

Sandra: Wait a minute; I have to say something... That was beautifully said. And I am so proud of you. Really I am.

They embraced. Our collective hearts swelled. And broke. It was a raw, unmasked moment.

This was to be Sandra & Troy's last public appearance together. In 2001, Troy died of a sudden heart attack at an L.A. gym. He was 65. Sandra died in 2005, age 62, of complications from kidney disease. I think all that hard living had just caught up with her.

I could only imagine her final days: A Malibu shut-in, alone except for visits from her loving son Dodd. And presumably the bottle. Once and always, little girl lost. But I'll always have a picture in my mind of Sandy's face as she received a foot massage from a homeless lady at the Baghdad Cafe. For that one moment, I'll bet she was happy.

Act 2, Scene 7 – BAD SEEDS & BLACK EYES

Patty McCormack

A pair of bloody shoes, a penmanship medal, a stash of excelsior, and a few sticks of matches. Iconic objects that play prominently in the film *The Bad Seed*.

This 1956 cult classic boasts one of the baddest girl ever to hit the silver screen. Little Rhoda Penmark, played to pint-size perfection by 11-year-old Patty McCormack, who was nominated for a Best Supporting Actress Oscar. She's a penurious little sweetheart dressed in pert petticoats, long blond pigtails, and possessing a perfect curtsy that cloaks her secret life as a cold-blooded killer.

The Bad Seed may not be among Gay 101 films, like *Mommie Dearest*, but it's definitely Gay 102. During the halcyon days of *Naked Brunch* in the '80s, it was required Betamax viewing at the House of Fish. Thus, when I started my Castro extravaganzas, Patty McCormack was on my list of "gets." But by the late '90s, I wondered if the '50s melodrama *The Bad Seed* had become merely a faded flower.

Unsure, I called up my old pal Lawrence Helman for advice. "Patty McCormack. What do you think?" Lawrence immediately shot back: "No one remembers who she is. You'd get maybe ten people in the audience!"

Still, my instinct was telling me differently. For me, little Rhoda was the reigning evil princess in the land of vicious queens.

Patty McCormack as Rhoda Penmark in "The Bad Seed."
Photo courtesy of Warner Bros.

So I was willing to take the risk. Through agent Greg Mayo, I snagged actress Patty McCormack. And when I announced "The Bad Seed with Patty McCormack Live!" to the public, my phone started ringing. Relentlessly. So Missy Lawrence had been wrong. And cardinal rule in showbiz: Trust your instincts!

The Castro event was slated for July 16, 1999. My promotional tagline was "What does Patty McCormack look like now?" Many seemed eager to find out, ordering whole blocks of tickets. I think these jaded queens hoped she'd be a washed up overweight drug addicted ex-child star.

For McCormack's interviewer, I rang up New York's guru of gossip Michael Musto. I had met Musto during the Christina Crawford debacle at Town Hall. I always adored his column "La Dolce Musto"; he had a gift for being dishy without being mean-spirited. But Michael, a good boy who still lived with his aging Italian mother, barely ventured from New York City. He needed some coaxing. Michael agreed, but only if friend Lynn Yaeger, a notorious fixture and fashion muse in the New York scene, could come along.

Patty and moi the day before the "big shoe."

Patty McCormack arrived shortly thereafter. Never in a thousand years would you know that the woman standing before me once was little Rhoda Penmark. Patty was now an attractive fiftyish woman with a full mane of blond hair (with brown roots), a megawatt smile and a Brooklyn Italian accent that made her sound like Carmela Soprano. (Patty would later have a recurring role on *The Sopranos*). She was down-to-earth and wickedly funny.

As Michael, Patty, and I dined at Piaf's the night before the show, I wondered what it must be like to be an ex-child star. Were those long gone days of glory, when she was the toast of Broadway and Hollywood, the ripest time of life? The David Hare play *Plenty* came to mind: the protagonist haunted by the contrast between a thrilling past and a banal present, filled with bitterness and disillusion. But as I got to know the real Patty, there was no need to project any pity. She was effusive, vital, and forward thinking.

The day of the extravaganza, many came festooned in Rhoda Penmark drag: blond braids and bright yellow slickers. A phalanx of loud motorcycles escorted the star to the Castro, with the Donna Summer song "Bad Girls" blasting. As she got off the Harley, she whispered in my ear, "All these gorgeous men, and I can't get a date." I assured her she was not alone. Dressed in simple black and a tailored white blazer, she waved to the crowd like an excited schoolgirl.

Michael Musto followed behind on the back of a miniature motorcycle. The jaded New Yorker was holding on for dear life. He looked petrified, but stylish, in a Vivienne Westwood sample-sale jacket.

When Michael began the interview, Patty was a bundle of nerves. But she soon relaxed into Michael's questions, offering hysterical anecdotes about *The Bad Seed,* sharp-witted observations on being a child star, and words of wisdom about her life as a survivor.

A few highlights:

Michael Musto: What was it like to work with Nancy Kelly, who played your mother? Because I understand that she made a little remark about you being overweight.

Patty McCormack: At the curtain call, Nancy had to reach over the couch and scoop me up to spank me. And after awhile, she began to complain that I was gaining too much weight. Also

I ate a lot of Italian food, and she requested that I didn't eat garlic anymore. Ummm… *(Pauses)* Oh, this is so bad, I can't say it.

Michael: Oh please do!

Patty: OK, she might not have liked the odor of the garlic, but I never complained about the hint of the smell of gin on her breath. *(Audience laughter.)* The truth was I loved her very much. She was good with me.

Michael: How did you survive? Because so many child stars, once they have the fame rug pulled from under them, they just fall into despair and drugs.

Patty: The truth is that you and other people called me a child star—but I was a child actor.

Michael: So you're saying on *Different Strokes* they weren't really actors?

Patty: I think on *Different Strokes* they weren't really stars! *(Loud laughter and applause.)* I'm being so bad! Seriously, I went through my period of being lost and it came out differently. I was very insecure and ate a lot. Because it was available, and I was Catholic. And thank god, I did continue to work. Nothing on the level of this film. No more Academy Award nominations, but I was a working actor. And still am. For whatever reason, I didn't get stuck in time.

Michael: Did you play Rhoda as evil or was she cursed? Was she afflicted or really mean?

Patty: I played Rhoda as being right. *(Audience applauds.)* It's true. She was surrounded by inept people. It wasn't easy to be Rhoda.

Michael: What did you do to convince people that you were not like the character of Rhoda?

Patty: The truth is all my life I didn't want to be Rhoda. I just wanted to be Sandra Dee! So I did work hard at being a nice person, because people did suspect that I had a darker side. And it's only lately that I'm embracing it!

Michael: How did you feel watching *The Bad Seed* tonight, for what must have been like the 200th time?

Patty: I thought I couldn't bear to see this again! But sitting there and hearing you all react to it, I kept sitting there. And I can't tell you how surprising it is to me that, first of all, you-all are here. *(Audience applauds.)* I wish you-all were casting a film. I'm old now, so it means a lot—gee, I sound like Sally Field, don't I? *(Audience howls.)* Really. I came from a time when it was not cool to have big work in the past because has-been was a dirty word, and I was constantly fighting to be in present time with my work. So I didn't have *The Bad Seed* on my resume and just pretended it didn't happen.

Michael: Have you come around to embracing it and realizing what it means to people?

Patty: Because of age, and life, and the love that people have for it, and that you honor it so, you make me honor it. And I'm very grateful for that. No kidding!

Michael: And are you at peace with yourself, Patty McCormack?

Patty: *(After a pause)* You'll never know! *(Winks at the crowd.)*

And with that, Patty McCormack curtsied and left the stage

Karen Black

I first fell for Karen Black in 1969, when she tore up the screen as a cockeyed, acid-tripping hooker in *Easy Rider*. In the 1970s, Black was the Queen of the Bargain Matinees at San Francisco's Regency Theatre, appearing in *The Day of the Locust, Nashville, Airport 1975, Family Plot,* and *Burnt Offerings*. During that period, she seemed to be in *everything!*

Then in 1982, she did an extraordinary Robert Altman film, *Come Back to the Five & Dime, Jimmy Dean, Jimmy Dean.* Set in a deserted Texas town, it's the haunting story of the 20th anniversary reunion of "The Disciples of Jimmy Dean," and the deep, dark secrets revealed by its devotees. It had a wet dream cast of queer icons: Cher, Sandy Dennis, Kathy Bates and Karen Black.

It was also one of the first films that dealt seriously with being transgender. For Karen Black, who plays JoAnne the MTF transsexual, it was yet another brave career choice. Over the decades, Black was not afraid to take on offbeat roles in no-budget films. Her eclectic, eccentric performances championed society's outsiders and outcasts. So Karen Black was a perfect choice for a Castro tribute.

Karen had just done a film with local director Lynn Hershman Leeson, produced by my friend Henry Rosenthal. So I called Henry to get the number for Karen's agent. "Call her directly," Henry advised. "She loves to work. And she always needs the money."

So, while the iron was hot, I cold-called Karen.

"Hello," the slightly distracted but familiar voice answered.

"Hello, my name is Marc Huestis and—"

"Marc who?"

"Huestis"

"What?"

"Huestis."

"Pronounce your name for me again, dear!"

"Huestis. Hue, like a bright and brilliant hue in the sky."

"Oh, Hue-stis! What can I do for you, bright and brilliant Marc Huestis?"

I laughed and pitched the gig. She was immediately interested. Okay, the money helped.

Inspired by Karen's classic film *Nashville*, I quickly came up with the concept. A kickass country evening at the Castro, "Ho-Down with Karen Black," to occur July 21, 2000. The Castro would become "The Grand (Gay) Ole Opry" climaxed by a rare screening of *Jimmy Dean*.

Although I am a Yankee through and through—never set foot in the Deep South, never wanted to—and generally hate country music, I got *really* excited about this theme. It would give one of my faves, Arturo Galster, a chance to shine. Arturo was internationally known for the group Patsy Cline and the Memphis

G-Spots, playing Patsy to perfection. Her tagline: "I put the cunt back into country." So Artie would host a program that included Matthew Martin and his sister Mary doing The Juggs (a takeoff on The Judds) and Connie Champagne doing Country Connie (a takeoff on Ronee Blakley's tragic Barbara Jean in *Nashville*). When I told Karen about the floorshow, she was itching to sing a few herself!

In my conversations with Karen, I learned that she immersed herself in everything she did. And given that she had a certifiable genius IQ, you never knew what would come out of her mouth. Lots of questions and concerns, chock-full of ideas. Sometimes way too many, but at least she cared. I think she was expecting 20 or 30 attendees to show up for, as she put it, "this puny film festival sort of a thing." I told her that I don't do puny. I do big.

A week before the show she called and asked exactly how many people were expected to show up. "Oh, about one thousand, four hundred." "ONE THOUSAND FOUR HUNDRED?" she screeched. "I think I'm about to throw up!"

"Well, honey, do it now, not the day of the show. I'll see you soon!"

Karen arrived solo from her Glendale home. Lulu and I picked her up in a great big pink Cadillac. It was such a thrill to see those Black eyes alive and in person! And that face! A work of art in itself, made up to perfection—big magenta lips, exquisitely drawn brows, smokey eye make-up, a white cashmere beret framing her idiosyncratic features. The whole look was artfully composed; the entire effect resembled a prized Picasso portrait from his Marie-Therese period. Angular shapes, brilliant contrasting colors with eyes askew.

Karen Black, Lulu, and a pink limousine.

That night we dined at the Foreign Cinema, a very fashionable restaurant in the middle of the Mission. O.K., I'd like to press the pause button here and backtrack a bit. I know, I know. I've been talking quite a lot about these damned dinners. Dinner with Carol, dinner with John Waters, dinner with Christina. Well, really, I'm not showing off, just giving you the inside track on an important element of this weird job. By this point in my career, I was realizing that it's vital to build up a level of trust between me and my guests, and it's best to break the ice over cocktails and break bread with fine food. And often the restaurant picks up the tab, so everyone gets a free meal! It's a win-win-win for everyone.

Now back to the restaurant. There, Karen gave us a heaping helping of her singular personality. After the appetizers, when the conversation veered toward her eyes, she let out a deep sigh. Like she had been forced to discuss the matter *so many* times before. She unfolded one of the cloth napkins, took out a Sharpie (please note: every star should have one in their purse), put on her reading glasses, and began to draw.

"OK, here's the speech about my eyes. I have very small, close, deep-set Czechoslovakian eyes. And what you've been looking at, if you have been watching Karen Black at all, are drawings!" She then began to madly map out her distinguishing feature on the napkin, demonstrating the whooshes and swooshes of makeup and mascara she regularly employed to bring forth those famous Black eyes.

For 15 minutes I was a captive audience to this madcap, bizarrely entertaining lecture. After she finished, she burst into a spontaneous, scary laugh. At that point, I realized that Karen Black was nuts. Lovable, but nuts. Eccentric with a capital E!

Black's neuroses were in high gear at the rehearsal; she had both the attention span of a five-year-old and the concentration of a consummate artist. Some of her questions were loony-tunes, some were astutely on point. She was endlessly curious, almost to a fault. And thirty minutes went by like three hours as I attempted to mollify her neediness.

Karen arrives to a throng of fans and photographers.

Before the event, Karen dressed at Lulu's apartment, conveniently located down the street from the theater. She was a nervous wreck. Babbling non-stop, fidgeting, fussing, while putting on her red-checkered shirt, cowboy hat, and crisp blue jeans. Already late, she was shoved into the pink limo for her big Castro entrance. When the stretch pulled up in front of the theater, it was like a scene out of her film *The Day of the Locust*! Lots of screaming and shoving by overzealous fans trying to get the star's attention for that perfect photo. I was surprised no one was trampled to death!

Arturo Galster as Patsy opened the show: "I'm sure y'all know Karen did a movie called *Five Easy Pieces*. What I wouldn't give right now for *one* easy piece!"

Celebrity handler Kathy Nelsen held Karen's hand throughout each performance. Karen would frantically whisper in Kathy's ear: "I can't sing now. These people are so *good*!" Kathy repeatedly reassured Karen that everybody would love her.

And just like that, Karen was nudged down the aisle and bounded up the stairs. The ovation was deafening. Feeding off the crowd, Karen clicked into "the star thing."

She sang the jazz classic "Lazy Afternoon," accompanied by just a simple acoustic guitar. When she closed her eyes and softly purred the lyric "If you hold my hand and sit real still, you can hear the grass as it grows," you really could *hear* the grass grow. After she finished, the overstuffed balcony started stomping. Forcefully, rhythmically, repeatedly. It was like a cross between an elephant stampede and the Loma Prieta earthquake.

"I have never heard that sound before," Karen declared. Nor had I. The tumult lasted a full two minutes. It was the greatest ovation I had ever experienced in my twenty years at the Castro.

Her Q&A was a master class of childlike playfulness, inspired improvisation, and on-the-fly genius.

On making "Five & Dime":

Karen Black: First we did it on Broadway. It took me months and months to prepare for this role. I would visit gay bars and do research. And there was a lot of suicide with transsexualism. A lot of no gold at the end of the rainbow. A lot of disappointment. It was very sad. I was crying a lot. I had such empathy, and it was very rewarding, hard work.

On "Five & Dime" co-star Cher:

Karen: What can I say about Cher? *(Pregnant pause)* Well, Cher was rich. Whenever she'd get depressed, she'd buy herself some great outfits. And model them and brag, "I just bought this!" After the show, she'd go out and she'd be photographed in them and dance. That was her life.

On Jack Nicholson and "Five Easy Pieces":

Karen: He's a really wonderful spirit. I said to him once, "You know, Jack, sometimes I really try and access a human being, and I just can't get anyone. No one's home." And he said to me, "Blacky, there's always someone there. Just keep trying." He really has a lot of respect and feeling for his fellow man. I had a crush on him too! I tried kissing him once. It didn't work. He likes really thin girls. He didn't like me.

On "The Day of the Locust" and "Airport 1975":

Marc Huestis: What was it like to work with Donald Sutherland?

Karen: Awful. He didn't speak to me. He had planned how his character would be, and if I didn't do things how he had decided, he would be upset. He would have me constantly change so it would be in service of what *he* wanted. So it was a really rough time for me. He was mean. Mean!

Marc: Speaking of mean, I think you should have gotten an Oscar nomination for *Airport 1975* just for pretending that you loved Charlton Heston. Now that's acting!

Karen: Well, I didn't like him until I saw his gun! *(Winks at the crowd as the audience roars.)*

Final thoughts:

Marc: If anyone could make a movie of your life, who would direct it, when would you want it set, who would you want to star in it, and what would the title be?

Karen: Hmmmm. Well, Dennis Hopper would play me, Marlon Brando would be my mother, and you would direct it.

I loved that answer!

Karen Black and myself, cooking up some country-themed fun.

The morning after Karen flew home. And Lulu called. "Girl, guess what? Last night, Karen Black left her panties in my apartment!" I inquired what they looked like. "They're size large. Cotton. Like old ladies wear." I joked that we could sell them on eBay. Or better yet, have a geneticist capture the DNA and create a Karen Black clone.

In the years to follow, Karen and I became friends on Facebook. It was there that something remarkable happened. In 2012, the film *Amour*, Michael Haneke's masterpiece on death and dying, was released. I had a deep, visceral response to the picture—it brought back memories of tending bedsides during the AIDS crisis. So there I was on Facebook singing its praises to my five thousand friends. And lobbying Academy voters on my page to vote for Emmanuelle Riva, who as the stroke-stricken wife gave one of the greatest performances ever on film.

All of a sudden, out of nowhere, Karen Black popped up in my topic thread. She insisted that Riva *must* win, and then wrote with great eloquence about how much the film meant to her. How death comes to us all. How we should face it head-on. How it can bring out pure love. It was deep, brilliant writing.

What I didn't know at the time was that Karen was battling ampullary cancer, affecting the ducts from the liver and pancreas. The news became public in 2013 when Stephen Eckelberry, her husband of twenty-six years, organized a GoFundMe campaign to raise monies for an alternative treatment to save his ailing wife.

The news was shocking. But upon reflection, I understood Karen's love for *Amour*. Art was imitating life. Karen was dying.

I was one of the first to donate to her crowdfunding, and the campaign went viral, raising almost $70,000 (from an original goal of $14,000). And on the site, Karen was able to experience the love and affection from her fans, as well as how much her work meant to them. No doubt she took spiritual solace from hundreds of heartfelt testimonials.

As Karen became sicker, she posted a final video on social media. In it friends and family surround her. She's skeletal, frail, but giving her all as she belts out a song—reminding me of something she said during her Castro interview: "I want to perform until I drop!"

Karen Black died August 8, 2013, in Los Angeles. She was 74.

And Lulu still has her panties. We decided not to sell them for DNA cloning. Because there never will, nor should there be another Karen Black.

Act 2, Scene 8 – INTERMEZZO / REQUIEM

Throughout my long career, my showgirl mother was never far from my thoughts. She was a true original, who once gave me the wisest piece of professional advice: "Whatever you do, Marc, make it sparkle!"

Mom was the first to teach me the razzmatazz of showbiz. A Lithuanian émigré, born as Matilda Bluvaite, she followed her star to become Marija, the Continental Gypsy, exotic dancer. For years it was a dream come true.

But dreams can only last so long. Like so many in the business, when mother Marija hit middle age and was unable to get work, she morphed from entertainer to eccentric—secluded and miserable in her Long Island home.

Misery might want company, but I wanted little part of hers. During my twenties and thirties, she and I had maintained a distant relationship. Truth was, I had moved to San Francisco to be as far away from her as possible.

But family ties do bind. In the '70s and early '80s, I would periodically visit with her while in New York. On those occasions, Marija would get dolled up and we'd see a Broadway show. She'd slap on her theatrical makeup, put on her rhinestone sunglasses and Mata Hari trench, comb her go-go red hair to one side, and douse her body in Tabu, the (cheap) perfume of her choice. Goodbye, Hicksville...hello, Manhattan! These visits made her happy.

MARIJA the Continental Gypsy

Marija in her salad days. As her exterior beauty faded,
we both found new aspects of ourselves.

Not wanting to be alone with her for very long, I'd bring friends along to meet my wacky mother. To my mom, they were a captive audience for whom she would perform her old routines: sing her favorite songs, show off a few dance moves, and lie about her age (on the A train, she told Tommy Pace she had my brother when she was eleven!). They all thought she was a hoot, humoring the many myths and delusional stories she shared.

In 1982, as part of the divorce settlement with my dad, Mom was mandated to sell our Bethpage home—which she always hated—and relocate. So, she considered moving to the West Coast and came to visit. I took pity on her, but the last thing I wanted was for her to live with me. Since *The Sound of Music* was her favorite movie, I pointed her in the direction of the Sierras and Lake Tahoe. It was about as "Climb Every Mountain" von Trappy as you could get in America. She was intrigued and boarded the Greyhound to check out the area. She loved it, and quickly snapped up a small cabin in the mountains.

But after six months, she hated the High Sierras as well. The same complaints I heard when she lived in Long Island were now transferred to beautiful, blue Lake Tahoe. "All people here care about is the almighty dollar!" I finally realized if you are miserable inside, it doesn't matter where you live.

After I moved to San Francisco in the '70s, I had come out to my mom. She wasn't thrilled, and the subject was rarely revisited. After she moved to Tahoe, I decided to share my HIV diagnosis. She was less than sympathetic.

"If you didn't have all that sex, you vouldn't be dying."

"Mom, I'm not dying, I'm living with HIV."

"Vhatever. I don't vant to hear about it. It's your problem."

I would like to say I was crushed by her reaction, but I wasn't. It just reminded me how cold and self-centered she was, and why our mother and child reunions would be infrequent. So, visits to Lake Tahoe were restricted to Thanksgiving or Christmas. And not every year.

Naturally, I would tell her about my Castro shows. Despite the fact that many of my guests were the stars that we both loved on the Million Dollar Movie years before, she now had little interest in them. Or my career.

I think she was jealous. The stage wasn't big enough for the two of us.

And there is nothing sadder than a stripper after the spotlight had faded. My mother was no longer "Marija, the Continental Gypsy." In Lake Tahoe, Mom held jobs as a hostess at several casino restaurants. But due to her fiery temperament, they never lasted long. Thus, she was now jobless, friendless and semi-destitute, dependent on Social Security and regular checks from my brother Henry, who had relocated about as far away as *he* could get—to Saudi Arabia. She constantly complained that the money he sent was chump change. "That bastard is a cheapskate, just like his father!"

She turned into a recluse, her sole company being her dog White Cloud. I did check in via phone occasionally, but I dreaded calling. She always answered in the same depressed tone, happy to recount the litany of her imagined miseries.

But in the mid '90s reality intruded. She actually had a genuine illness. Mom had been diagnosed with renal failure, and was put on home dialysis.

By this time, I was preoccupied in producing show after show, with little downtime, and had good excuses about why I couldn't see her more regularly. Honestly, I think she really didn't care. She liked to see me about as much as I liked seeing her. Which was not much at all.

But eventually my excuses dried up, so up to Tahoe I went. It was Christmas of 1998. The snow at her cabin was piled up high, unshoveled, and the door was partially open. When I knocked, White Cloud barked loudly.

"Halt, *schweinhund!*" I heard her shout, then telling me, "Come in, I'm here."

When I entered, I came upon a vision that will haunt me the rest of my life. My mother, half-naked, hair grayed, was sitting on a red pail in the middle of the room, with a cob of corn in her mouth. You can guess what she was doing on the pail. All across the frayed carpet were piles of feces—both the dog's and hers. The stench overwhelmed the filthy, cluttered room.

"How long have you been living like this?" I demanded to know.

She just shrugged and gave an embarrassed half-smile. Partially chewed yellow corn niblets stuck to her face.

I walked her to the toilet. The bathroom tub was piled high with used plastic dialysis bags.

After I put her to bed, I cried myself to sleep.

The next day, something miraculous happened: I turned into her parent. I cleaned up the mess. Excrement was everywhere. And let me tell you, it is the ultimate in humbling experiences to clean up your own mother's stale shit. But the caregiver instinct takes over; you don't have time to be disgusted or puke. You go into autopilot and do what you have to do.

The rest of my visit was spent trying to facilitate home care for Mom, with little success. At Christmastime, everything basically shuts down. Yet another reason I fucking hate Christmas.

I arranged a few rides to doctor's appointments for Mom, but then professional obligations took precedence and I had to return to San Francisco. I convinced myself that things would be OK. (Delusion runs deep in my family, and the apple doesn't fall far...)

A few days later, I got a call from social services. My mom had been rushed to a Reno hospital. Harmful bacteria infected her home dialysis needles, and she was suffering from a severe case of sepsis.

I took the first train there. Upon entering her hospital room, I found her in uncontrollable spasms—the result of septic shock. Several nurses were holding her down. It was like a scene from *The Exorcist,* and seeing her in this condition was absolutely heartbreaking.

I stayed by her bed through this crisis, only leaving at the end of visiting hours. I brought a book to read, but could barely concentrate. Throughout two long, long days, Mom became verbally abusive, the invasive bacteria flooding her brain. Literally foaming at the mouth, she would call me a filthy faggot, hoping I died of AIDS.

I didn't take any of it personally. I had tended many friends with AIDS-related dementia, which results in a similar spewing of venom. When it got really rough, I buried my head deeper into my book and pretended I wasn't listening. The important thing for me was just to be there for her. "Keep calm, keep calm," I chanted to myself. "This is not about you. Be a mother for her."

After two days of madness, spiking fevers, and explosions of greenish mucus, the sepsis was under control. I was able to sit by my mother's bedside without fear. Hurricane Huestis had moved offshore.

I held her trembling hand. And for the first time, I could see her vulnerability. She was scared.

Mom stayed in the hospital for months. My older brother Henry was summoned from Saudi Arabia, my younger sister Michele from New Jersey. It was determined that Mom needed 24/7 care, and should be placed in a nursing home. Since none of us said we had the means (or desire) to pay for a top-notch facility, she became a ward of the state.

She was moved to Hilltop Manor Nursing Home in Auburn, California. Though it was nestled in California's scenic Gold Country, it was anything but a manor. It was a depressing blend of the asylums in *The Snake Pit* and *One Flew Over the Cuckoo's Nest*.

When we were younger, my mother warned us: "If you kids ever put me in an old age home, I'll kill you. I'd rather die than live there." And here she was, living in the place she most feared. And dying.

The Manor hallways were crowded with lethargic patients. Many looked lost in a fog. Many had just given up. As I entered one day, a haggard woman in a wheelchair greeted me. She lifted her ossified hand to say hello. When she flashed a toothless grin, I almost lost it.

Unlikely as it may seem, illness changed my mean, anti-Semitic, gloomy mom into a nice person. Lovely, really. Her prejudices left her, and she was often very funny. And Marija would always be happy to see me. Of course, her escalating dementia helped.

Since I didn't know how to drive a car, I found myself compelled to hop on the Greyhound to Auburn for the three-hour journey. I would visit Mom at least twice a month, usually on weekends.

At first it was dutiful. But after a while I actually looked forward to seeing her. I'd bring her goofy, childish toys, like a battery-operated singing sunflower. Press the button, its eyes would open wide, its jerky mouth would move with the lyrics: "You are my sunshine, my only sunshine, you make me happy when skies are gray!" She would crack up laughing whenever I turned it on. I would sing along, making funny faces, smiling on the outside.

Occasionally I'd give Mom a makeover, gathering her colorless, thinning hair in the Pebbles Flintstone topknot she now favored. Sometimes I'd paint her nails—always with glittery, sparkling polish. (Make it sparkle!)

Sometimes I love being with the demented. They say the darndest things. Now and then, out of the blue, she'd say something that made absolutely no sense. Then she'd turn it around and quiz me about my life. Once I was shocked when she asked if I had a boyfriend. Another time she complimented me on my newly bleached out hair. "You look good as a blond," she enthused. I blushed, embarrassed. But it warmed my heart; after all, I always was a mama's boy.

Once, when I said I was waiting for an e-mail, she looked at me with a puzzled expression. It was the late '90s and she had no idea what I was talking about. When I explained personal computers and electronic mail, she shrugged. "E-mail, she-mail, what's the difference?"

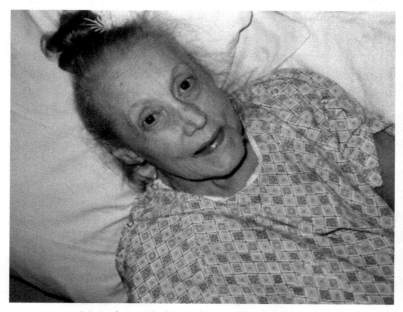

Mom, happy in her Pebbles Flintstone hairdo.

I'd also bring her musicals on video, and we'd sit and watch. It felt just like when I was a kid and we bonded over the Million Dollar Movie. *Calamity Jane* with Doris Day became one of her Hillside Manor favorites. She'd make me play Doris crooning "Secret Love" over and over. That was a song she used to sing to us at bedtime when I was a child. Now as adults we would both sing along. As a gay man, the song's theme of a secret love not secret anymore took on a deeper meaning.

One time I found my mother with a shaved head. She had a big grin on her face. She hated that her once beautiful full head of hair had gone limp and gray, so she decided she'd rather be bald.

What touched me most was that she thanked me for coming after each visit. My mother was not known for her gratitude, yet she had discovered it late in life. That meant a lot.

But all was not well in Mudville. Her kidneys were failing. Encroaching death was visible in Mom's skin tone. Actually it was quite beautiful—veiny, clear, translucent and pearlescent. And it was there in the smell of her room. Musty and diseased. I had smelt that many times before. I knew the end was near.

Mom was now hospitalized in Sacramento. Against doctors' advice, she decided to continue dialysis. Until now, she had always insisted that if things got rough, there was no need to prolong the inevitable. But I learned that you'll never know the choices you will make until death is at your door.

My last weekend visit with Mom was grueling. There she was with a frightened look in her eyes, hooked up to the lumbering dialysis machine, a primitive plastic pail with huge black rubber gloves hanging limply off its brim. As the machine began churning, my mother shrieked. I held her hand tight for the hours-long ordeal. Afterwards, utterly exhausted, she fell into a deep sleep.

I left the hospital exhausted myself, but a personal catharsis had just occurred. As the sliding electronic doors opened, I took a deep breath and was overcome with a sense of overwhelming gratitude. I was so happy just to be able to walk. And hear the birds singing.

Matilda Marija Huestis died the following Thursday, August 10, 2000, at age 67. I was glad I was not there. Despite years of physical, spiritual, and psychological abuse from her, Mom and I had made our peace with each other. In her last days, we had grown closer and learned to enjoy each other's company. And at long last, I had seen the moody Lithuanian gypsy princess laugh. I felt blessed.

Mom's funeral was a lonely affair. She was buried at the Happy Homestead Cemetery—who comes up with these names?—her plot overlooking the piney Sierras and beautiful Lake Tahoe. My brother and sister attended. None of us bonded at the gravesite. I was sad that they had not experienced the reconciliation with Mom that I had. Particularly my brother. He had always pined for her love and acceptance, only for Mom to tell him he was the reason her life was so miserable, and then cast him aside. Still, he was kind enough to pay for the funeral. Which was made apparent when the officiating priest took him aside before the service began, and asked for the check.

The only other mourners were my friends Hrappa and Erica Marcus, who drove me to Tahoe, my mom's neighbor Penny, and her beloved dog White Cloud, which Penny adopted during my mother's illness. Penny told me she would bring the dog to my mom's bedside in her last days. White Cloud instantly recognized Mom, slobbered all over her, tail wagging a mile a minute. It was a joyous moment for my mother.

I placed the singing sunflower on Mom's grave. I turned it on and sang along to "You Are My Sunshine" loudly and cheerfully, to the bewilderment of the others. I was the only family member to offer a eulogy. Actually, I read a letter from my father, who attempted to make peace with his ex-wife at her interment. As I read his words, I started to sob. However, my tears were nothing compared to my brother's uncontrollable wailing; it was guttural and primal. I felt so bad for him; Henry had no one in his life to guide him through his grief. He was utterly alone. After Mom's death, he was never the same.

After her body was lowered into the ground, we all went our separate ways. Quickly. I returned to my hotel, and later that night watched the final episode of the first season of *Survivor*. The one with the famous final tribal council where Susan Hawk said to Wigglesworth: "If I was ever to pass you in life again, and you were laying there, dying of thirst, I would not give you a drink of water. I would let the vultures take you." I know it sounds odd, but it made me happy. Its forced drama made me forget about my real one. Hrappa and Erica couldn't believe I was so heartless as to be interested in a reality TV show afterwards. And that our family didn't at least have dinner together. They didn't know my family.

As a final gesture, my brother and sister allowed me to choose the epitaph for Mom's gravestone. I knew exactly what it should say:

"Blossom of snow may you bloom and grow forever."

Rest in peace, Marija. Continental Gypsy. Unforgettable showbiz mom. Your blood runs deep through my veins.

Mom's gravestone.

Act 2, Scene 9 – WHAT BECOMES A LEGEND MOST?

W hen I was a teen queen, one of my favorite things was the famous ads for Blackglama furs—featuring ultra-glamorous stars dolled up and dripping in mink. The tagline: "What becomes a legend most?"

In the aughts of the 21st century, I discovered some surprising answers to that question, when I honored three legends of the Golden Age of Hollywood: Ann Miller, Jane Russell, and Debbie Reynolds.

Ann Miller

Golly, I always loved Ann Miller in the movies. The tap-dancing, wisecracking, "star lady" who shook the blues away in such films as *Easter Parade, On the Town, Kiss Me Kate, Stage Door,* and (my favorite title) *Reveille with Beverly.*

Ann was famous for her gorgeous gams and high hair. Raven-black, larger than life, and (over)done to perfection. Of course Ann Miller was never one for subtlety; through the years, her hair got bigger, her makeup heavier, her lips more crimson. Her motto became "Have eyelashes, will travel." So why not invite her to San Francisco? After all, Ann Miller got her big break here, circa 1936, having been discovered by Lucille Ball while dancing at the Bal Tabarin Ballroom in North Beach.

When I got the gumption to pitch the star in 2002, there were several challenges. After eight years in business and the post 9/11 economic downturn, my audiences were getting smaller.

And cheaper. And Ann Miller's asking fee was hefty—and non-negotiable. But I realized the old gal might not be around much longer. So, I agreed to her terms. I did get one concession: Ann plus an entourage of two would travel coach.

Ann Miller's Blackglama ad- 1980.

"Too Darn Hot with Legend Ann Miller Live!" was set for July 26, 2002. Ann arrived, from Burbank, with several sizable suitcases, stuffed to the gills with all the accoutrements of glamour.

At the time of the gig, she was about 80, and I had been warned that she could barely walk. In fact, she had to turn down the penthouse suite I had procured because there was a small staircase. So I wondered, what would she look like? My heart was pounding as the elevator door at the Hotel Bijou opened. She emerged on the arms of her two aides-de-camp, shaky but exquisitely dressed for dinner, her jet-black hair slicked back in a tight bun, accented by large Spanish spit curls. And jewels for days.

She looked up at me and the first words out of her mouth were "Honey, I shrunk. I used to be five-foot-seven; now I'm five-foot-three!" Once a long-legged thoroughbred, she was now a petite old lady with a jittery gait. Yet still lovely to look at!

Ann's on-stage interviewer Jan Wahl joined us for dinner at Grand Café. Ann was obviously worn out by the flight, but sharp as a tack. Once she got her second wind, she regaled us with tales of MGM in its heyday. "Annie" yakked up a storm in her homespun Texan vernacular, dripping with "honey" and seasoned with phrases such as "Well I'll be darned!" and "Bull-pucky!"

Dinner was served, and Jan commented on Ann's solid gold ring, encrusted with sparklers. Those were some big rocks on her little hands. Ann was famous for her couture costume jewelry. "This one's Balenciaga!" she crowed. Her assistant Pat took her ring off and passed it around the table. We all ogled her prized possession.

Pat slipped the oversized bauble back on Ann's bony finger. A ring once snug as a bug in a rug now dangled loosely. Ann lifted her fork, and lo and behold the ring slipped off her hand and dropped right into her mashed potatoes! There it was, glistening radiantly in a sea of brown gravy.

We pretended not to notice. I don't think Ann even realized it was gone. Pat slid it back on Ann's finger, then gave us a knowing wink.

As we exited the Grand Café, an excited gay couple recognized Ann Miller and was beside themselves. One whispered, "There goes a true star."

There was great buzz surrounding the July 26th Castro event. Even Turner Classics Movie host Robert Osborne promoted the event in his *Hollywood Reporter* column, declaring, "It's Miller Time!"

Glamour queen Ann Miller enthroned for her meet-and-greet.
Photo by Rikki Ercoli.

Queen Ann came out of the limo dressed in a ravishing red St. John evening jacket and white tailored pants, holding a matching rhinestone clutch. Enveloped in sequins and jewelry, she posed for photos like it was a big old Hollywood premiere in which she was the one and only star.

Given Ann's limited mobility, the night's big challenge was to walk the ten feet from the wings to her plush chair on stage. But she was determined to do it unaided. Once again, that miraculous "star thing" kicked in. Ann Miller conjured every bit of her strength; waving to the crowd, her costume jewelry sparkled in the spotlight. She made it look effortless. "Listen, I was injured in a car accident a couple of weeks ago. But I would have *crawled* to get here tonight!" Ann declared, then dove into her interview.

Jan Wahl and Ann Miller.
Photo by Rikki Ercoli.

Some highlights:

Jan Wahl: Here you were, a young girl in Hollywood. Wasn't there a problem with lecherous producers?

Ann Miller: No, there wasn't, because I had a mother that would have hit them with a baseball bat. And that would have taken care of that!

Jan: They said Clark Gable once said to somebody when they were looking at the group picture from MGM, and you were in it: "Look at those gorgeous girls, and I had all of them."

Ann: Well he's just crazier than hell! *(pauses)* Although he was called "The King," and I'm told with good reason. *(Ann winks, the crowd erupts!)*

On filming "Small Town Girl" with Busby Berkeley:

Ann: You know, we didn't have air conditioning in those days; all they had were these big huge fans. It was so hot! And I had developed a blister on the back of my heel that started running blood. So, I called up to Busby Berkeley. I said, "Mr. Berkeley can we stop, I've got to put a Band-Aid on this blister." And he said, "Hell no lady, we can't stop. We got a whole company here." About an hour later, I said, "I'm telling you, my shoe is full of blood." And he said, "We're almost done. Let's just get this over with." And we did. And when I came home, those shoes were just brimming with blood. I could never use them again. He was sadistic, but he was a genius. There'll never be another Busby Berkeley ever.

On being in David Lynch's "Mulholland Drive":

Ann: Everybody stops me on the street and asks me, "What the hell was that movie about?" And I'm here to tell you I didn't know for a long time. Still don't. But it's called grab the money and run.

Ann's final remarks:

Ann: I gave my tap shoes to the Smithsonian, and I started to get tears in my eyes, because I thought, here I am, a little nobody from Texas, and I've come so far that they're keeping my tap shoes, what a great honor! And let me tell you, what goes around comes around. Here I am, at my age, back in the town that gave me my break. So, I love you, San Francisco. Thank you!

Then words that irked the hell out of me.

Ann: Finally, I want to thank the producers for doing this occasion.

"Producers?" I thought. "Producers? There is only one—*me*! And I have a name."

But there was no time to mope. After the star made her stage exit, I burst into the green room ready to sing her praises. Ann Miller had a sour look on her face. She was tired, cranky, and wanted to leave *tout suite*. When Lulu explained that the limo driver was 15 minutes away, Ann erupted into a firestorm. In the glory days, a car was on standby at *all* times, just waiting for the star to snap her fingers. Alas, those days were long gone.

"We're starved, and my favorite restaurant in Chinatown is closing in an hour," she railed. Then, Lulu offered to hail a cab.

Ann screeched in disbelief. "A cab? A CAB!? Listen, mister. You take a broad to the theater in a limo, you bring her back in a limo!"

And so, I found out one answer to the question "What becomes this legend most?" A limousine.

Still, Ann settled on a cab. Cussing, huffing and puffing, she dispensed with goodbyes, slamming the door in my face as her final word.

Two weeks later, Ann Miller did call to tell me what a great time she had in San Francisco. No mention of the limo incident! All was forgiven.

That was to be Ann Miller's last public engagement. She passed away peacefully of lung cancer on January 22, 2004. No one knew her exact age, but the broad was ageless. And in the afterlife, wherever she went, I pray it was in a limousine!

A Tussle with Jane Russell

Truth be told, I never really cared much for Jane Russell in the movies.

Okay, she had her moments. Like many gay men, I adored Jane's camp number "Ain't There Anyone Here for Love?" from *Gentlemen Prefer Blondes*, where as Dorothy Shaw, she comes on to the entire U.S. Olympic Team. But the boys are too busy looking at each other's bulbous butts in flesh-colored Speedos. What's not to love?

"Ain't There Anyone Here for Love?"
from "Gentlemen Prefer Blondes."
Photo courtesy of Twentieth Century Fox.

Still she was a legend. So I weighed my options. On the plus side, Russell had worked with Marilyn Monroe, and for the Castro Theatre, that could be box-office gold.

On the minus side, Russell was notoriously Republican. And a devout born-again Christian. As she said in an interview, "I'm to the right of Attila the Hun." Gulp.

I decided to take a risk.

The gatekeeper to Jane Russell was a man named Marvin Paige. Marvin's claim to fame was as a casting director during the heyday of Hollywood, working on such classics as *Breakfast at Tiffany's*. Within film circles, he was an institution, and I was told (jokingly) that he belonged in one. My trusted showbiz mole Carol Lynley gave me the full 411 on Marvin. "Christ, he was ancient even when I was a teenager" (and Carol was in her sixties). "The main thing to know is there's the good Marvin and the bad Marvin," she warned. "When he's good, he's great; when he's bad, he's horrible."

"Do you know if he's gay?" I asked, thinking that was a way to get to the heart of the "good Marvin."

"Marvin comes from a generation when such things were not asked. You'll see."

So, Carol helped set up a phone meeting.

"Hello, Marvin Paige Casting," answered an officious, slightly irritated voice. But before I could get a word in edgewise, "Could you please hold?"

Five minutes later: "This is Marvin."

I quickly respond, "Marvin, this is Mar—"

"Can you please hold?"

Again, minutes pass. Next time, I actually got my name out before another "Can you please hold?" Damn, this guy is either the busiest man in Hollywood, or has serious problems. I chose to think the former.

Finally, a conversation ensued. I put on my flirtiest voice. It helped. But what really sealed the deal is when I offered him a $500 agent's fee, plus hotel and airfare. His tone immediately changed. He started calling me "kiddo." We had a delightful conversation about classic films and stars. My gaydar detected a sister, but just a hunch.

"OK, kiddo, fax me a proposal, and I'll get it to Jane."

In subsequent conversations, I grew to love Marvin. He was one of those unsung behind-the-scenes people who actually knew showbiz inside and out. And he knew *everybody* (at least from a certain era).

A deal was struck, and a good one. None of the Ann Miller "non-negotiable" shenanigans, and the price was right. Plus, Jane had a fear of flying, and would drive with her daughter from Washington State. No first-class air for her! There was one big caveat. "Do not," Marvin emphatically insisted, "I repeat, *do not* tell her if there are drag queens in the show."

When word of the event appeared on the pages of Roberto Friedman's popular "Out There" column in our local gay weekly, the *Bay Area Reporter*, I got a flurry of calls. One bitter old queen hollered, "Fuck Jane Russell! How dare you have that homophobic Christian right-winger at the Castro." To which I could only answer, "Well, I guess you won't be coming!" Click.

Honestly, I was not thrilled to be showcasing a self-described "teetotaling, mean-spirited, right-wing, narrow-minded, conservative Christian bigot." Yet in my research on Jane, I could find not one homophobic comment. And let's be real. Even the right-wing gals of the Golden Age had their gay hairdressers, makeup people, costume designers, etc. If they wanted to look good in front of the camera, they knew whom to treat right.

As I started prepping the career clip presentation, I began to really *like* her in the movies. Not *The Outlaw*, which was just silly. But the noir films with Robert Mitchum, the *Paleface* comedies with Bob Hope, the camp potboilers like *The Revolt of Mamie Stover* and silly musicals like *The French Line*.

She was a talented jazz singer, with understated phrasing and a magnetic, muscular, "just try to get me" delivery. Her rendition of the classic "One for My Baby" in *Macao* positively oozes sex. Although not a particularly gifted actress, you could not take your eyes off of her. Curvaceously gorgeous, very Jessica Rabbit.

So, with newfound appreciation for Jane Russell's work, I continued planning her celebration. And yes, there would be drag queens, and damned good ones. Matthew Martin would play Jane, recreating "Two Little Girls from Little Rock" with Jordan L'Moore as Marilyn, and reprising "Ain't There Anyone Here for Love?" with a bevy of beefy boys in skimpy shorts.

This prompted persistent calls from Marvin. "Do the drag queens really need to be part of the show?" Finally, I had enough, responding, "Listen, Marvin, this is my show. And it is the fucking Castro Theatre, not the 700 Club!" He backed off. "OK, kiddo. Just don't tell Jane."

Marvin arrived several days before the gig. He was a pip; dressed in a loud shirt, a louder tie, solid polyester pants, and a fitted blazer that smelled of mothballs. His thinning, dyed hair pomaded back on the sides, framed by oversized black glasses. Straight out of '70s central casting.

And as I greeted him at baggage claim, what were his first words? You guessed it. "Just don't tell Jane about the drag queens."

A day later, after a 14-hour non-stop drive from northwest Washington, Jane Russell arrived with her daughter and granddaughter. The star certainly showed the wear of a long road trip. But when she arrived for dinner at Moose's, she looked newly refreshed and elegant. Quite a handsome woman. As we walked into the dining room, heads turned. The soft tinkly notes of her signature song, "Buttons and Bows," from the grand piano by the bar, was accompanied by the sound of champagne flutes clinking as the room collectively toasted the honored guest. Jane took a quick bow.

Over oysters, Jane looked me straight in the eye. "So, I'm curious. What's the floorshow you have planned?"

Marvin kicked me under the table. "Ummm," I stammered, "I have some local talent doing a few of your numbers from *Gentlemen Prefer Blondes*." When she queried, "Are they men?" Marvin broke out in a sweat. I couldn't lie.

"Yes, Jane. But not to worry, we will put you in the green room until you have to go on."

"If you put me in that darned green room, I'll knock your block off. I want to see the floorshow. It sounds terrific!"

I shot Marvin a big smile. Case closed.

Dinner at Moose's with Jane Russell, Jan Wahl, and Marvin Paige.

The next afternoon, Jane had a run-through at the Castro. For the show, she had agreed to perform three songs accompanied by David Hegarty on the Wurlitzer. It was a coup; Jane rarely sang in public anymore. She arrived on time and beat out the song tempos like an old pro.

Jane confided in me that her 11-year-old granddaughter had never seen her on the big screen. So, after rehearsal, I suggested that the family watch a little of the preshow clip reel I had put together.

I planned to show just five minutes. Jane sat down, hand in hand with her granddaughter, her daughter on her other side. Ten minutes later, the trio still sat transfixed. Fifteen minutes turned to twenty, then finally the full forty-five minutes. As the lights came back up, Jane had tears streaming down her face. Slowly, majestically, she rose and grasped my hand tightly. "That was so beautiful, Marc."

"Ladies and Gentlemen Prefer Jane Russell" was held on July 23, 2004. Political affiliations aside, it was sold out. The evening helped benefit Breast Cancer Action, a wink and a nod to the star's famous anatomy.

Jane arrived in a midnight blue St. John sequined jacket, black pants—and comfortable tennis shoes. She held court, got along swell with the gay boys, and relished having her picture taken with "the girls"—Matthew and Jordan in the red sequined gowns from "Two Little Girls from Little Rock." While Marvin looked like he was about to have a coronary, Jane thought they were adorable. And after the reception she watched their floorshow with a big ol' smile on her face.

Despite her conservative credentials, Jane Russell enjoyed drag performers Matthew Martin and Jordan L'Moore.

Russell made her grand stage entrance through the aisles, overcome with emotion. Pointing to her gray hair, she mused,

"I'm sorry you all don't recognize me. I spent the first half of my life as a brunette, but honey, now I'm a blonde."

The interview got off to a slightly rocky start as Jane adjusted to the spotlight (advanced macular degeneration) and the acoustics (deafness). But she faced the problems head-on, wisecracking, "I have trouble hearing and seeing, but I can still sing and dance."

In her conversation with Jan, Jane credited her career to a series of "the Lord's accidents." The Lord stuff had the Castro audience squirming. After Jane had name-dropped the Lord for the thirtieth time, Wahl broke the tension by quipping, "So then, the Lord brought you to Bob Hope in *The Paleface*." The audience roared.

Interview highlights:

On the notorious buxom publicity shots for Howard Hughes' "The Outlaw":

Jane Russell: The photographers stood above me on a high-rise and would say, "Janie, come along and pick up these two pails." I knew what they wanted. I went to Howard Hawks, who was the director at the time, crying. And he said: "Now listen, you're a big girl. So, learn how to say no, loud and clear!" So, from then on, I would stand with my hands upon my hips when they were up on the balcony, trying to get me to walk under it, and I'd just say "No!" And they would pack up their gear and go home.

On Howard Hughes:

Jane: He was very polite, he was very nice, he didn't like to fight people, and I did. So, the poor darling ended up with me hollering at him half the time. Most of the things that have been written about Howard Hughes don't sound like him at all. He was just a gentleman.

Jan Wahl: Why was he so obsessed with breasts?

Jane: (*shrugs*) I don't know. That's his bag, I guess.

On Marilyn Monroe and "Gentlemen Prefer Blondes":

Jane: Of course, I had been working a lot longer than Marilyn. That was only her second big picture. She was like a little sister. She would work with the coach every night, and in the morning instead of looking to Howard Hawks, the director, she'd look to the coach. Well, Hawks took the coach off the set, and Marilyn would run to her dressing room and cry. She was a very sweet girl, but I think she had a very tough life.

Jan: How about the "Anyone Here for Love" number. Were you aware of the homoerotic nature of it? *(Audience howls.)* Hey, I had to ask!

Jane: No, it didn't occur to me. I was married to a football player for a long time. I knew that guys, when they're doing what they're doing, they don't want any part of a female!

Then, we had a surprise for Jane, but not another one of "the Lord's accidents." It had been engineered by me. The Producer.

Out from behind the curtain came a paunchy, mustached man. It was the former child actor George 'Foghorn' Winslow who co-starred in *Gentlemen Prefer Blondes*, playing the rich kid Henry Spofford the Third. Winslow—now a postal worker in Sonoma County—paraphrased his famous line from *Blondes*: "Jane, you know I'm 58 years old now, and I'm *definitely* old enough to know a good-looking woman when I see one."

As quickly as George was on, he was off, leaving Jane to do her final three numbers: "Buttons and Bows," the Oscar-winning song from *The Paleface*, a version of "Big Bad John," rejiggered by Peggy Lee and retitled "Big Bad Jane." And finally, "Bye, Bye Baby" from *Gentlemen Prefer Blondes*. The audience, composed largely of older gay guys, gaily sang along. For a moment the roused Castro Theatre had the feeling of an old English music hall.

At the end, Jane blew the boys a huge kiss and waved goodbye.

The morning after, I heard this message on my answering machine from my favorite "teetotaling, mean-spirited, right-wing, narrow-minded, conservative Christian bigot":

"Marc, I just wanted to say goodbye and thank you very much for everything. You've been wonderful, and your show was great, and I'm glad I did it. Bye, bye darling...Jane."

The last time I saw Jane was in Burbank at the Hollywood Collectors Autograph show in February 2005. Many of my Castro girls were in attendance at the show: Carol Lynley, Karen Black, and Lorna Luft. The star attraction was Jane Russell, who sat in a throne-like chair separate from the others. Her fan line was huge.

Jan and Jane basking in the love of a highly appreciative audience.
Photo by Rikki Ercoli

Also attending was my friend Margaret Pellegrini, one of the last surviving Munchkins. I had produced a sing-along *Wizard of Oz* in 2004 where Margaret was the featured guest. Known as the "Flower Pot Lady" because of her original Oz costume, she was four-foot-tall, frizzy-haired, and adorable. At the autograph show, Margaret kept peering over Jane's way, star-struck. When I queried if she wanted to meet Jane, she chirped, "Would I ever! Do you think she would sign a picture?"

I asked ever-grouchy Marvin Paige for a special favor—to make this happen. Surprisingly, he acceded to my request.

Margaret got to jump the huge line. "Oh, Miss Russell, I'm such a fan. What an honor to meet you," my Munchkin pal squealed. Jane cooed back, "The honor is all mine! Come here, darling, and sit by me." Suddenly, teensy-weensy Margaret the Munchkin was sitting in the lap of Big Bad Jane.

It's times like this I love my crazy job.

The Munchkin & I.

The Unsinkable Debbie Reynolds

Debbie Reynolds had a special place in my heart. The first movie I ever saw on the big screen was *The Unsinkable Molly Brown* with Debbie as a singing, dancing Titanic survivor. Ever since, I'd dreamed of growing up and getting to know someone just like her.

Since then, I have savored Debbie in *Singing in the Rain, How the West Was Won, Mother, Tammy and the Bachelor, Will & Grace,* and on and on. Sometimes people throw around the word "legend" lightly, but in the case of Debbie Reynolds, it was utterly apropos.

Debbie was always at the top of my to-get list. After Ann Miller and Jane Russell, it was time to do it Debbie's way.

Fate again interceded. From out of the blue, talent rep Greg Mayo rang me up. "Hey, listen, I ran into Debbie Reynolds in Palm Springs last week at a benefit for the Thalians. I mentioned the Castro to her, and she seemed interested. Do you want her?"

Is the Pope Catholic?

Greg hooked me up with Marge Duncan at Debbie Reynolds Studios, who took care of many of Debbie's bookings. I liked Marge immediately. No muss, no fuss, no drama. A deal was quickly struck for more than I had ever paid for a celebrity appearance. But I didn't care; after all it was Debbie Reynolds. Still I was a bit nervous about all the extras. I sheepishly asked Marge, "Does Debbie need to fly first-class?"

"From L.A. to San Francisco? Of course not. That's a waste of money. Debbie flies Southwest all the time!" Debbie's attitude was: Fuck the frills; just give me the damn money. Or, as she said as Molly Brown: "It's not money I love. It's not having it I hate."

"The Unsinkable Debbie Reynolds" was slated for July 22, 2005. I wracked my brain trying to come up with a good interviewer. Then an unconventional thought: Why not ask my pal Carol Lynley? Debbie had once invited Carol for a private Palm Springs weekend. They had a gazillion mutual friends. Plus, they both had survived Shelley Winters; Carol in *The Poseidon Adventure* and Debbie in *What's the Matter with Helen?* Carol came on board immediately.

Debbie's assistant Jen Powers handled the arrangements, and relayed how excited her boss was about this particular gala event. Debbie was used to playing to straight seniors in threadbare casinos. So a majestic movie palace full of diva-worshiping gay guys was a dream come true. "Is Debbie okay with drag queens?" I inquired." Are you kidding?" Jen shot back. "Bring 'em on. The more, the merrier!"

On the day that Debbie was to arrive in San Fran, her greeter frantically searched for the star at the Southwest gate. Looking for the 5'2" glamorous made-up woman with strawberry blond hair, he finally realized the Hollywood legend was the little old lady in a motorized wheelchair, hidden behind huge sunglasses, her gray hair peeking out of a simple cap. The only dash of showbiz glitz: her cane was wrapped with hot-pink fun fur.

Debbie Reynolds cheerfully put her best face on and her best foot forward for the big show. She sprung out of the limo dressed in a cobalt blue St. John knit ensemble (these legends *love* their St. Johns), highlighted by a sequined lapel and beefed-up with shoulder pads. She was every bit the sparkly Debbie Reynolds we all know and love.

When I opened the door of her stretch, what was her opening line? "Thank you for all this, Marc Huestis!" saying my name with enthusiastic familiarity and treating me like a long-lost friend.

At the meet-and-greet in the dolled up Castro lobby, petite Debbie filled the room with her mega-watt energy. She took time with everyone, holding many of the elderly patrons' hands. When an octogenarian female fan presented her with a box of Girl Scout cookies, Debbie proudly exclaimed, "I'm the oldest living

Girl Scout!" and took a bite of one of the Thin Mints. (Debbie is famously proud of her time as a Girl Scout.)

But after the joyous reception, inside the theater things quickly went south. Something went awry in the projection booth. The sound on clips I had painstakingly edited was garbled beyond recognition. I was absolutely crestfallen.

Debbie came to the rescue. As she made her splashy entrance, everyone instantly forgot the technical difficulties. Surveying the crowd of gays, she exclaimed, "I have never been with so many men that didn't want me. But you love me, right?" The queens went crazy.

Debbie Reynolds meets her fans at the Castro Theatre.
Photo by Steven Underhill.

Then Debbie gave The. Best. Interview. Ever.

For 90 minutes, she had this audience utterly captivated and begging for more.

Highlights of her interview:

On her relationship with Elizabeth Taylor and ex-husband Eddie Fisher:

Debbie: Well, Elizabeth and I have known each other since we were 17. And what the hell, I gave her my husband—how close can you get? Of course, she regrets that particular decision, because at the time she needed comforting. Actually, Elizabeth is a great girl. I was at the first AIDS benefit in San Francisco, and Elizabeth followed. It's the first time she hasn't stolen one of my husbands! I'm just kidding. I'm very proud of her.

On Gene Kelly and "Singing in the Rain":

Debbie: The first thing Gene Kelly asked was "Do you dance?" And I said, "I can dance. I can do the time step." And he said, "Can you do a Maxie Ford?" and I said, "What kind of car is that?" I wasn't a big hit. I was just a kid. I had six months to learn how to dance. And I was scared to death of Gene Kelly. He was a tough, wonderful guy. He was a taskmaster, and that's very good for me to have had that. I'm still here because of great teachers like that.

On Shelley Winters and filming "What's the Matter With Helen?":

Debbie: In between scenes, Shelley Winters played Nazi war records from the '30s so she can get in the mood. She is brilliant but she is cuckoo! When we did the picture I used to pick her up every morning in my Rolls-Royce, just to get her to work on time. She owned the whole block. Let me tell you a secret. Shelley is rich as shit! She didn't like to work; she liked to sleep because, well, she stayed up a little late. She used to put marijuana in the cookies *(imitates Shelley chomping on the cookies)*. And there was always a different guy visiting. She liked visitors. She told me she had insomnia. I said, "I didn't catch his last name."

On her career and men:

Debbie: I have never stopped working, I'm afraid I might want sex again. (*Looks down at her crotch*) When I closed the store I said just zip it up. Mostly I stay on the road. I can't stay home too often, because I'll meet somebody and then I'll marry another idiot... But I do now have many men in my life. All gay. They won't steal from me. And they like my costumes!

Debbie Reynolds marvels at Jason Mecier's portrait of her.
Photo by Steven Underhill.

On stars, past and present:

Debbie: I have never worked with a star I didn't like. Everyone I worked with—Jimmy Stewart, James Cagney, Jack Lemmon, Fred Astaire, Donald O'Connor—we always had great fun. There's a reason that people become a star, because there's a talent and individuality. That's what makes a star; they have that certain "it." That's just like Marc; he has "it."

Wow. Debbie Reynolds, living legend, just said I had "it." Debbie Reynolds sure *knew* how to treat a producer. And even remember his name!

Debbie ended the event with the sweetest *a cappella* version of her hit song "Tammy." You could hear a pin drop. It was a fitting finish to a very special evening.

Debbie Reynolds yukking it up with Carol Lynley.
Photo by Steven Underhill.

After the show Debbie, Jen and I dined at 2223 Market Street, in the same private dining room that had briefly hosted Sandra Dee. I apologized for the show's technical snafus. "Don't worry, dear. That stuff happens all the time at benefits," Debbie assured me. "Just relax and have a good time. You're among friends."

We had a magnificent dinner. Debbie had basked in the love from her gay fans, and had worked up quite a thirst. As our private waiter brought us a fancy bottle of California chardonnay, there was a magical metamorphosis. Right before my eyes, Debbie turned into Molly Brown, straight from the scene where she entertains continental royalty. I could almost imagine her sitting there in her famous feathered dress—charming, captivating, and cajoling us to have just a little wine.

As I listened to Debbie's stories, I thought of that little boy in the darkened theater watching my first movie and falling in love with the star. And now I was all grown up, and sitting right next to her. It was almost too much. Tears welled up. I excused myself and retreated to the men's room briefly to regain my composure.

When I returned, the first bottle of wine was completely empty. Debbie wasn't lying when she said she liked to party! When the waiter asked if we would like another, Debbie simply smiled.

The waiter brought another, and another, and still more. Debbie kept slowly refilling all our glasses, as she briskly downed hers. Yet she never lost her grace. She left the restaurant quite pixilated, merrily waving to a few lucky passing fans as she got into her taxi and disappeared gently into the night.

Act 2, Scene 10 – THE PHANTOM CLOUD
or THE OPPOSITE OF SEX IS...

In the storm of activity that was now my life as an impresario, there was a dark phantom cloud that followed me. Like magic, it rose from a small translucent rock placed in the bowl of a glass pipe. It was lit up by the flame of my discontent. It was my new, now-frequent friend Tina. Crystal meth.

I visited with Tina (darling) only periodically. I told myself that I had her under control. But Tina is a deceptive, seductive bitch. And again Newton's Law prevailed. What goes up must come down. Tina's hangovers were fierce. So I'd only partake every three months or so.

I've said previously that I never let my usage impede my professional life. The most important thing was that the show must go on; everything else was secondary. And while I was in production, I *was* clean as a whistle. Thus, I convinced myself that I was a functional speed freak.

I'm sure others picked up that I did drugs. There were the periodic hangover rampages that undoubtedly scarred my reputation. A few memories stand out.

In 1998, after my whirlwind tour with Christina Crawford, I reunited with Erik Lee Preminger. Together we produced an event titled, "Gypsy Rose Lee's Home Movies," which featured a stockpile of film chestnuts from his mom's private collection.

It was a lovely presentation and well attended, with almost 1,000 paid. When I initially reported these figures to Erik, I could hear his distrust on the other line. He was convinced it was a sellout of 1,400. Maybe all those years of traveling with his mother and dealing with scheming producers had taken their toll.

Several days after, while I was in the throes of a crystal meth hangover, Erik again called. He outright accused me of fudging the numbers. Okay, I have many faults both as a person and a producer. But one thing you must know: I am honest to a fault. Cheating a colleague is something that I would *never* do. Never. Ever.

I told Erik that. Then I lashed out with a fury that only someone on a speed rollercoaster could summon. It wasn't pretty. At the end of my monstrous monologue, Erik said to me, "Buddy, you make my father look nice." (His dad Otto Preminger was notorious for being mean as shit.)

Some years later, a competitor told me of a dinner conversation he'd had with John Waters. John asked him if perchance he was a friend of mine. The competitor responded, "I wouldn't call him a friend, but I do know him." After an awkward silence, John purportedly confessed, "Well, I have to say, I'm scared of him." While that might be taken as a badge of honor—John Waters was actually afraid of *someone*—it was also revealing. Perhaps he, as well as others, was onto my sketchy behavior.

And here I thought I was able to compartmentalize my secret, to hide my periodic drug usage from colleagues and friends. But you know what happens to your nostrils when you snort crystal meth? They buuurrrn. And they bleed. Those clever enough could spy the crusty scabs on the tip of my nose after a wild weekend. However, I convinced myself that most people hadn't a clue. I was, after all, good at hiding the evidence with makeup.

And as I entered my 50s, another monkey was on my back. I was becoming an aging faggot. I know some of you might be taken aback by that pejorative. But its connotations are apropos to the man I saw in the mirror: grayed, damaged, infected, useless, and self-loathing. Oozing with ugliness. Oh, sure, I was dancing with the stars as fast as I could, but WTF. I would always have to come face to face with my so-called life.

I also became apathetic towards my health. I had lived with HIV so long, I didn't give a fuck whether meth might wreck my immune system. I felt like Roz Russell, the washed-up old maid in *Picnic*, desperately shouting to the universe, "I want to have a good time! I want to have a good time!" *That* was getting harder.

Year by year, the parade of anonymous men who came to my door via Craigslist to party n' play began to diminish. And the few who did make it walked away when I opened the door and they saw me in the flesh. "This isn't going to work" was the common refrain. Jeez, I might as well have hung a sign with those words by the entrance. The only ones who would enter the black hole of my bedroom were the hardcore speed freaks. They didn't care what I looked like, just as long as we would party. So I would party n' pay. Paying sometimes for the drugs, sometimes for the company.

Sometimes I smoked iT, though I preferred snorting. I did draw the line at shooting up. I was petrified of needles, and had to turn away when partners tied themselves off and ran it up their veins. It was a little too junkie-real.

It became a dangerous gambit, climaxing in one fateful night. Sick of trolling Craigslist, I decided to prowl the Powerhouse, a Folsom Street bar where sex was free and easy.

The bartender, an avid fan of mine, kept plying me with free drinks. So I got blotto. No one in the bar was interested in tricking with an aging drunk. So somehow I made it to the place of last resort, Ringold Alley, well known for after-hours cruising. It had once crawled with men on the prowl. But after AIDS hit, it was largely a dead zone. On this particular night, there were only a few sloshed sleazebags like me, and men looking to cop drugs or sell their bodies.

I vaguely remember meeting a man who promised he had some crystal. Magic words. Off we went in a cab. As we pulled up to my place, I realized I didn't have enough in my pocket to pay for the taxi fare. In I rushed to my apartment, my trick waiting in the car as collateral. The only money I had was in a hiding place. It was several bundles of $1,000 in various bills, bound by rubber bands and stuffed in a coffee can at the bottom of my squalid kitchen closet. I peeled off a twenty, paid for the cab, and my trick came in.

The moment he walked through the door, I felt sick. All those free vodka gimlets had taken their toll. I rushed to the toilet, retching uncontrollably. Then I passed out. I have no idea how long I was unconscious, but when I came to and crawled to the kitchen, I noticed my trick had fled. And the coffee can, which I had forgotten to return to its hiding place, was empty. Over five grand, my lifetime cash savings, gone in one fell swoop.

The next day, I ransacked the place to see if maybe I had placed the cash somewhere else. No such luck. I called the police. They came and asked a few questions. Honestly, I was so fucked up the night before I had no idea what the thief looked like. They took one look at the disheveled apartment and said they could not be responsible for the guys that I had brought home. "Next time, buddy, you should be careful." It sounded as if they had made this speech a gazillion times before. It was, after all, San Francisco.

I was severely depressed. Several days later, on an impulse, I left my office early. Upon entering my apartment, I noticed a brand-new bicycle in the front room. It was not mine. I ventured into my bedroom and someone was rummaging through my things. It was the guy who ripped me off. He had been clever enough to grab my spare keys as I was passed out in my puke. It wasn't enough that he stole all that money; he wanted more.

My first thought was at least now I knew what he looked like. Then my adrenaline rushed. I became a banshee, screaming at the thief to get the fuck out. "How dare you rip me off, and then come back, you piece of shit." I grabbed the shiny mountain bike and chased him out of the apartment and down the street. I begged the patrons of the upscale neighborhood bakery Tartine to call the cops, but the chichi clientele would have no involvement with the crazy queen interrupting their croissant and cappuccino. I spotted a neighbor named Doug and asked him to call the cops. He did. And became my hero.

In a flash, the police were there. I could provide no clues that this man had robbed me a few nights prior, but upon searching him, they found a small baggie of shiny white rock. He was immediately put under arrest. The cops then asked to whom the bicycle belonged. Though I was certain I had inadvertently paid for it, I told them it belonged to the man they had arrested. I wanted no tangible reminder of him, not one iota of his energy.

One would think that after I had lost all my cash, and what was left of my dignity, I had hit bottom. But I hadn't. After a few months, I was back to my old tricks. They say you have to hit rock bottom to get clean. But I was discovering a bottomless pit of mini-bottoms.

I now had a new pattern. I found myself tricking with destitute semi-homeless men, meeting through PnP listings on Craigslist, or in late-night street encounters. Rough trade, often tattooed. Not fashion tats, but ones probably inked in prison. And often these temporary lovers were dressed in dirty, smelly clothes, and schlepping a knapsack with all their worldly possessions.

These men could pick up on my vulnerability and need of company. I would make no judgments on their current condition. Actually, many were hot, and I found I could strike up interesting conversations with them. Their life stories of desperation were compelling. Of course, the endgame would always be getting high. And we did. We'd lie on the bed for hours, watching porn (often straight; they preferred it), flogging our fantasies, desperately stroking for that moment of release. Since we both were so fucked up on crystal, we couldn't get it up. The drug does that to you. So there was no fear of exchanging bodily fluids.

By five in the morning, we'd take a break from our bowl-smoking and pud-pulling. Stroking non-stop can make you hungry, so I'd play the Good Samaritan and cook up a bowl of pasta. We were usually stinking like pigs from all that sweat, so I'd let them shower. Some of these guys had not had a decent shower in days.

Honestly, I liked many of them. I felt sorry for them. Of course, they probably felt sorry for me. Somehow we bonded. Although I always identified as an outsider, these guys were the true outcasts from society. They had nothing to lose. But I still did. I often became the victim of their petty theft. At least now I had learned my lesson, and tried to remember to hide anything of value.

After the umpteenth hangover and rip-off, I thought maybe it was time for Narcotics Anonymous. I did not come to that decision lightly. My dad became heavily involved in a 12-step program when he became sober in 1968. It saved his life. Still, I had a strong aversion to these things. Oftentimes, when I'd come to my dad with a problem, he'd proselytize, "Oh, that's step number five." Or announce, "We have a saying in the program..." I'd always think, "Dammit, I'm not a fucking robot; I am a unique human being." Still, my life was a mess. Maybe I should give NA a shot. What did I have to lose?

A friend brought me to a meeting inside a church in the heart of the gay ghetto. I sat silently. I couldn't bring myself to stand up and say, "Hi, my name is Marc, and I am an addict," followed by the rousing choral response of "Hi, Marc!" It felt way too Susan Hayward from *I'll Cry Tomorrow*. But I would be respectful of the men and listen to their stories. Some beautiful, some heart-wrenching. I was happy they had found their place. Their recoveries were now everything. I understood, but I wasn't ready to make my recovery my life. And after this one meeting, I ran to the nearest bar to slug down a few vodka gimlets. I never attended another.

Ultimately though, I was tiring of the endless cycle of partying, playing and paying (in one way or another). Despair set in. "There's gotta be something better than this," I kept telling myself.

One night in 2007, I produced an event titled "The Bad Boys of Project Runway" with Santino Rice and Jeffrey Sebelia (the guy with the tattooed neck who won Season Four). When the event ended, I was ready to party hardy. And I did, with a vengeance.

Up all night. Hunting on Craigslist. A constant stream of meth and men, coming and going. Then back to the Powerhouse. Another lost weekend.

Monday morning, through the pea-green haze that was now my brain, I received a phone call. My backpack and wallet had been retrieved near Ringold Alley. I was so out of it I hadn't even noticed that they were missing. Before hanging up, the kind caller mentioned that he was a big fan of my Castro extravaganzas. A compliment, yes, but this time the words stung. Is this to be my legacy? The fucked-up out-of-control guy who does faaaabulooous shows at the Castro?

Suddenly the moment of change had arrived.

After 17 years on the crystal merry-go-round, I was ready to quit. Cold turkey. At first I didn't know whether I could do it, but as the hours, days, then months went by, my confidence grew. One day at a time. Honestly, it wasn't that hard once my mind was made up. And after half a lifetime of being a part-time boozehound, I knew I had to stop drinking too. Alcohol was the trigger for sex, which was the trigger to getting high. Bing, bang, boom.

I wish I had a sage piece of advice for those who are in a similar situation and wanting, needing to quit whatever is their poison. I really don't. No head trips, no change of diet, no exercise routine, no substitutions, no meetings, nothing. Me, I just quit. Period.

Now it's been over ten years without crystal. I realized I couldn't have sex without getting high. And I wasn't going to get high to have sex. So I stopped having sex. Mr. Sex Is… became Mr. Sex Isn't…

I had screwed around with hundreds, maybe thousands of men, in an effort to quell my loneliness—only to find I was lonelier than ever. Believe it or not, life without sex was actually liberating. Sniffing around for dick was just Too. Much. Work. Now I'd rather watch TCM. Or eat.

And let's face it, at a certain age, you become invisible. Poof. But there *is* a saving grace to being inconspicuous. You can see people more clearly when they can't see you. And what I saw didn't really interest me.

So I have been totally celibate (except for my own private happy endings). I've embraced it. I wish I could also say life was so much better sober and sexless. It is and it isn't. It's still the same life, warts and all. But at least now I know I can be clean.

Again, I come back to the constant in my story: That magic wand waved over Dorothy by Glinda, followed by the wisest words ever spoken on film: "You've always had the power my dear. You just had to learn it yourself."

Well, I *have* learned a new way of living, and learned it myself. I certainly don't miss the rollercoaster of highs and lows. I feel healthier, I can think more clearly, and I'm not as much of a monster.

I do look at life differently. Okay, it's cornball stuff, but bright, white cumulus clouds high atop mountain vistas are replacing the phantom clouds floating off the bowl of a glass pipe. (More on that later.)

For now, the fog has lifted, and there's a little clarity. And even a little is fine with me.

Act 2, Scene 11 – CLASS ACTS

There are so many class acts that I have invited to tread the boards at the Castro Theatre. Among them: Academy Award nominees Lesley Ann Warren from *Victor/Victoria*, Ali McGraw from *Love Story*, Piper Laurie from *Carrie*, Margaret Avery, who played Shug in *The Color Purple*, and superstar Ann-Margret from *Tommy*. Plus in a class all by herself, Rita Moreno, the amazing EGOT (Emmy, Grammy, Oscar, Tony) winner. Each woman was wonderful and offered her own style of smarts, dignity, humor, and grace.

If I wrote about them all, this book would turn into *Gone With the Wind*—and it's already long-winded. But there are three class acts that deserve special recognition. Olivia Hussey, Ann Blyth, and JoBeth Williams.

Olivia Hussey

Franco Zeffirelli's *Romeo and Juliet* played a huge part my big, gay teenage life. But I never would have guessed that Olivia Hussey, the film's transcendent Juliet, would become my career salvation, some 40 years later.

Flashback: 1968. At 14, my hormones were raging; my body was a molten mass of testosterone.

At that time, high school field trips were my chance to see culture—to be swept away briefly from the conformity of suburbia. Without a doubt, the outing to see *Romeo and Juliet*, arranged by my mentor, Mr. Yesselman, ignited my budding teenage sexuality.

For this particular adventure, each kid had to get a permission slip signed by our parents. *Romeo and Juliet*, we were told, included nudity and was *très risqué*. I couldn't wait!

R&J had its exclusive Long Island engagement at a plush theater in Mineola. This was my first taste of a real movie palace. There were sprays of floral bouquets and shimmering chandeliers; even the carpeting had an upscale smell about it. It was the perfect environment to be enraptured by the poetry of cinema. The lights slowly dimmed, an image flickered onto the big screen, the music swelled. A narrator solemnly intoned: "Two families, both alike in dignity, in fair Verona, where we lay our scene."

Enter Romeo. Gorgeous Leonard Whiting, super-hot in his striped tights and bulging codpiece. I was immediately smitten. Then the big moment. The nude scene, with the morning light accenting Whiting's beatific butt, and showcasing mounds of perfectly molded flesh. It excited me in ways that I had never been excited.

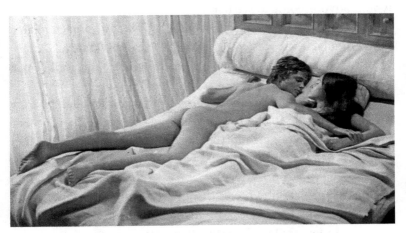

Leonard Whiting's backside rocked my world.
Photo courtesy of MGM.

Ah, me. I desperately wanted to be Olivia Hussey, with her honeyed voice and mane of long and shiny black hair, lying close to Leonard Whiting and all that firm flesh.

Inspired by the Bard's beautiful boy, I begged my dad to buy the complete works of Shakespeare. With my allowance, I bought the *R&J* record, bought the poster, bought anything with Whiting in it. My fantasy life was in full bloom! I wore myself out with obsessive longing for my first-ever serious screen heartthrob.

Flash-forward to 40 years later, the year 2008.

My life was anything but idyllic, and my business had taken a turn for the worse. In these pages, I have gone on and on and on, mostly about the star-studded Castro successes. But, darling, there were lots of failures. Lots. Most not even interesting enough to write about. After a series of bad bookings, I was broke, I was depressed, and I was convinced that the curtain was falling on the second act of my life.

I needed desperately for something to work. Then Greg Mayo called. "What about Olivia Hussey?" Throughout the years he periodically pitched her. My standard response: "I love her but would anyone come to see her?"

Greg reminded me that Valentine's Day was approaching and the Zeffirelli classic was celebrating its 40th anniversary.

I was desperate. So I gave the green light to Greg. Still, I was nervous as fuck.

To sell tickets, I pulled out every last promotional angle from my bag of tricks. I called every middle and high school in San Francisco. The conversation usually went something like this: "Hello, may I speak to the head of your drama department?" The response: "What drama department?" As someone who lived for drama in high school, I found this utterly depressing.

Undaunted, I leaned on friends to buy blocks of ten tickets to sponsor underprivileged youth. I sent out a personal letter to my most loyal customers explaining that, if this event were to fail, I would no longer be producing my Castro extravaganzas.

At first, all signs pointed to another depressing turnout. But just as I was about to give up, I received a check for $1,000 from a loyal fan, with words of encouragement that brought me to tears. It gave me the strength to persevere. To this day, I think of dear Linda Larrabee as my guardian angel.

After that, the tide turned. First, film historian Jenni Olson had gotten the San Francisco Board of Supervisors to honor my work at a special ceremony in City Hall. Many of my friends and co-workers came to shower me with a little love. Even San Francisco's grand doyenne of society, Denise Hale—the former Mrs. Vincente Minnelli and Liza's stepmom—journeyed all the way from her plush Northern California ranch to pay tribute to me and my work.

City Hall celebration.
Photo by Daniel Nicoletta

Afterwards, Mick LaSalle wrote a front-page article in the San Francisco Chronicle focusing on my plight. "Huestis is preparing for his *Romeo and Juliet* show, putting everything he's got into it.

This one's make or break." In 2008, newspapers still had huge influence. So the phone started ringing. Non-stop.

Best of all, folks weren't interested in my saving my business, but were *really* excited about this upcoming event. *Romeo and Juliet*, it seemed, had been a sexual milestone for scores of boomers. I was not alone! I had hit a collective nerve.

When people ordered tickets, they reminisced in great detail about the first time seeing *Romeo and Juliet*—where they saw the picture, who they were with, what they wore.

If they were straight men or lesbians, they fell madly in love with Olivia and her bountiful breasts. If they were straight women or gay guys, they were hot for Leonard and his magnificent buns. If they were bi, hell, they had hit the jackpot and were turned on by both of them! Some of the ticket buyers wanted to talk for hours. I had to make all sorts of excuses to get them off...the phone, that is. I knew this would be an audience unlike any other I had drawn together.

And for my gay core, there was a special wink and a nod, an acknowledgement that Zeffirelli, then closeted, now an openly gay man, knew *exactly* what we wanted to see. Even in 1968.

The show sold out a week in advance. And the phone kept ringing. I could have sold out two shows. Olivia Hussey—who knew? She turned out to be my biggest celebrity draw. Ever.

Excitement filled the air when the curtain rose on "*Romeo and Juliet* with Olivia Hussey Live!" on February 14, 2008. It was particularly gratifying to see over 100 sponsored high school students attending. There was little chance that Romeo's butt and Juliet's boobs would have the same effect on them as they did on my generation. They see way more on the internet. But if even a few could be exposed to Shakespeare in a way that might inspire their young minds toward a love of the classics, it would be worth it.

Due to her busy scheduling, Olivia arrived at the theater straight from the airport just a half-hour before the film ended. Forty years after the making of the classic, Olivia was still stunning. Her body was in perfect shape, her face barely touched by time, her voice still tinged by that soft raspy purr.

There was no time to bond with Olivia. Her only words to me were how scared she was and that she had to pee. Then she was swept down the aisle to a rapt standing O, single red rose in hand. After she took the stage, she offered a ladylike bow and apologized to the audience for her shyness. She then proceeded to give a most charming, funny, and effervescent interview.

Beautiful Olivia Hussey, the personification of
tragic love for children of the 60s.
Photo by billwilsonphotos.com.

Highlights:

Olivia Hussey: I think *Romeo and Juliet* captured a perfect moment in time. Franco said, "I want young people to feel the passion and feel the love." And nobody was prepared for the response. It was a "happening"—it told us what the '60s were about.

Marc Huestis: And how did you get the role? I understand they auditioned over eight hundred girls.

Olivia: Eight hundred girls in London alone! But Franco said the moment I walked in, he thought, "That's my Juliet. Now let's see if she can act." He asked, "How do you see Juliet?" and I said, "Long blond hair and blue eyes, very romantic." And he said, "Oh you bitch, you know nothing!" And that was the beginning of our relationship. It's funny because everyone thought I was so madly in love with Leonard when we shot that film, and actually I had a big crush on Franco!

Marc: And whom did Franco have a crush on, pray tell?

Olivia: Not me! (*Audience roars, getting the gay drift.*)

Marc: I understand the picture was all dubbed in post-production.

Olivia: Yes. And in fact when we were dubbing *Romeo and Juliet*, Fellini was in the room next door dubbing *Satyricon*. And I didn't know who he was. But I used to visit him every day. Franco was such a bully. I said, "Franco, I don't like you, I'm going to talk to my friend next door." I'd sit on Fellini's lap, and watch him dub his film while he did drawings of me. One day, in walks Franco and he said, "What are you doing here?" And I said, "This is my friend!" And he said, "You fool. This is Federico Fellini!" And I said, "Is it really?"

Marc: Okay. Let's talk about the nude scene.

Olivia: That was the first time that the nude scene had been done with people as young as we were. Up until the end I'd say, "Franco, do I really have to be naked?" I was very shy. Of course Leonard was an exhibitionist, so he just walked around naked.

Marc: Well, he had a lot to exhibit! (*Audience howls.*) And you got to meet Prince Charles!

Olivia: I did, yes. Prince Charles had asked to be seated next to me at the Royal Command Performance of *Romeo and Juliet*. Of course, Franco was beside himself. "Oh my god, you've got to go to Capucci and they'll make your gown." They made these beautiful satin slippers and they were too tight. I said to Prince

Charles, "My feet hurt so bad!" and he said, "Take your shoes off, put your feet up." So I had my feet up across his leg. Then he invited me to go to Buckingham Palace, but I wasn't interested."

Olivia Hussey and moi.
Photo by billwilsonphotos.com

Marc: You could have been the queen, honey!

Olivia: That's what Franco said. And I said, "I'll leave that to you, Franco!"

(Another audience eruption.)

Marc: Final thoughts?

Olivia: Most actresses can do maybe one hundred projects, and they're lucky if they ever get to do a classic, something that, long after they're gone, will touch people's hearts still. So I really have been honored and privileged to be a part of it.

And just like that, Olivia was gone. Parting was such sweet sorrow. But Olivia's Castro Theatre interview still lives on via YouTube. And it is a testament to her enormous popularity that almost 1 million fans from around the world have viewed it; commenting in a multitude of languages how stunning Olivia still is and how much this film means to them.

Ann Blyth

Ann Blyth made film history when she gave Joan Crawford the slap that was heard around the world as the most venomous daughter ever: ungrateful Veda Pierce in the Joan Crawford classic *Mildred Pierce*. Her portrayal as the spawn from hell earned her a Supporting Actress Oscar nomination in 1944.

But in the '60s Huestis household, another Ann Blyth picture made a deeper impression: *The Helen Morgan Story*. Every time it played on the Million Dollar Movie, I was glued to the TV set—obsessed with the story of the suffering alcoholic chanteuse madly in love with a very young, unbearably handsome Paul Newman. In my solitude, I'd turn off the bedroom lights and belt Helen Morgan's signature song, "The Man I Love," with all the torchiness I could muster.

Blyth's character had such an indelible impact on me that the show-stopping character I played in the Angels' cabaret—the one where I threw the bottle and beaned a guy in the audience—was named after her: Ellen Organ.

As for *Mildred Pierce*, although I was not a super fan, it was another one of those films that was required viewing for gays. Joan Crawford was a camp goddess; as Mildred, the mother of all mothers, she kicked ass. Besides, let's face it, we gay guys all have a thing for our mothers.

Joan Crawford and Ann Blyth in "Mildred Pierce."
Photo courtesy of Warner Bros.

So when Greg Mayo pitched Ann Blyth at the Castro, I took the bait.

My initial research revealed that Ann, a devout Roman Catholic, had basically given up acting in the mid-60s to become a mother of five and devoted wife of a prominent L.A. obstetrician, James McNulty. It must have been tough for her to give up such a distinguished career to live a life of domesticity. How, I nervously thought, would she take to the Castro audiences?

My fears were allayed in our first telephone conversation. She was so kind, punctuating our conversation with carefully chosen words, spoken with a graceful lilt. I got up the courage to ask her how she felt about a bunch of six-foot-tall Mildred Pierce-y men in drag. She laughed. But she did emphasize one point; beyond the fun and frivolity, she was bound and determined to present herself as a lady.

In constructing her career clip reel, I discovered Ann Blyth was a damn good actress with amazing range. Whether showing her musical talents in the Technicolor classic *Kismet*; her dramatic chops in Lillian Hellman's *Another Part of the Forest*; or her ethereal charms as the mermaid in *Mr. Peabody and the Mermaid*, Blyth could do anything. Oddly, *Mildred Pierce* was an outlier—a rare time she played pure, unadulterated evil.

However, I was reminded that her family life took precedence over her career. A few days before the event, Ann called. Her husband Jimmy had fallen ill, and she feared she would have to cancel. When we spoke, she was distraught, her voice shaking with emotion. Mustering every ounce of my power of persuasion, I was able to convince her the show must go on.

When she arrived in San Francisco, she was every bit the classy lady she was on the phone. And she looked marvelous. We had a delightful dinner with Eddie Muller, the "Czar of Noir," (now a host of "Noir Alley" on TCM) who would conduct the onstage interview. They got on immediately. We soon discovered that Ann got on with *everyone*. Ann's M.O. was obvious. She would speak ill of no one. Sometimes that could be a dreadful bore, but Ann's memories were retold with such warmth, kindness, and clarity, they were simply irresistible.

"*Mildred Pierce* with Ann Blyth Live!" occurred July 21, 2006. The patron saint of the event might have been St. Joan, but the guiding light would be St. Ann.

And the evening of the gala, Ann's star shone bright. Chicly dressed in a red ruffled blouse and pleated black knee-length silk skirt, she embraced the gay ambiance that surrounded her, happily taking pictures with every star-struck drag queen.

After *Mildred Pierce* screened, Ann took the stage and opened with a barbed question: "Who was that character, Veda? I had forgotten how evil she was!" The audience roared. Eddie and Ann proved to be the ideal pair: The hardboiled film noir expert and the dignified lady of the silver screen.

Ann Blyth arrives accompanied by Jeff Valentine.
Photo by Rick Gerharter.

Highlights:

Eddie Muller: San Francisco has a special place in your heart. It was in the touring company of *Watch on the Rhine* where you actually were discovered.

Ann Blyth: Yes, really around the corner from where I am staying. We played the Curran, and it was here that I learned that I was going to be signed to a seven-year contract at Universal. Of course, being so young it was really a dream come true. And certainly for my mother it was! *(Audience laughs.)* My mother, not Mildred Pierce. I know you're sharp. I can be just as sharp!

Eddie: Enough of this niceness. Let's talk about Joan!

Ann: Well, I remember the day I met her for the first time because she tested with me. I think she felt that perhaps there might be some chemistry between the two of us. *(Deepens voice.)* And obviously there was. I only have good memories of working with her and being around her.

Ann Blyth in a lighter moment with Eddie Muller.
Photo by Rick Gerharter.

Eddie: How many times did you actually get to slap her?

Ann: I'd rather not think about it! Actually we worked ourselves into such a state of agitation and fury, that if you didn't do it right the first time, you'd probably go home and do it the next day.

Eddie: And all these years later, that is one of the great scenes in movies! Let's talk about that year's Academy Awards. For those of you who may not be familiar with the story, on Oscar night Joan took to her bed ill, and did not show up.

Ann: I thought everybody knew that!

Eddie: In this crowd I guarantee you 99.9 percent know.

Ann: Well, I think maybe she might have been afraid. Afraid she wouldn't win, afraid of the people's reaction were she at the theater, who knows.

Eddie: Hollywood legend has it, of course, that she was faking her illness, for whatever reason. And boy, did it make for a good photo op when everybody had to go to Joan's house to take the pictures of her in bed with the Oscar.

Ann: Cynical, aren't you?

Eddie: You worked with many of the great leading men in movies. Burt Lancaster, who was—

Ann: *(interrupts)* I know you're trying to say that everybody I worked with was either terrible or they did drugs. Well, if they did, I didn't know about it!

Eddie: We'll see!

Ann: Keep talking!

Eddie: Okay. You're on the boat and the boat is capsized and you're headed to the desert island. Your pick. Burt Lancaster, Robert Mitchum, Paul Newman. Who goes to the desert island with you?

Ann: Why can't I take all three! *(Audience applauds; someone shouts, "Go, diva!")*

Eddie: Great answer. I think you'd wear them out!

Before the interview was over, there were a few surprises in store. Ann's daughter Eileen came out from the wings, and waxed rhapsodically about how special her mom was. Then a woman from the audience took the mike. She revealed that Blyth's husband, Dr. McNulty, had brought her into the world. Ann was sincerely touched, her eyes moistening, since she also missed her ailing husband on this special night. When Eddie asked if there were others who were birthed by Dr. McNulty, a slew of hands rose up, including that of my friend, Jim Van Buskirk (small world, isn't it!). Ann placed her hand on her heart and thanked the crowd. She ended the evening by singing a few bars from *Kismet's* "Baubles, Bangles and Beads."

Ann and I remain dear friends. Every August 16th, I call her for her birthday, and every December 26th, she'd call me on mine. One year, she even did me the kind favor of calling my dad to wish him a Merry Christmas. Imagine my father's girlfriend's surprise when the "other woman" on the phone turned out to be Ann Blyth!

JoBeth Williams

The Castro guest that gets the extra gold star for pure class is JoBeth Williams.

Many know JoBeth as the dark-haired beauty from the boomer classic *The Big Chill*. Others know her as the fierce and frantic mother in the horror classic *Poltergeist*, screaming that now-famous line "Run to the light, Carol Anne!"

Oddly, my association with JoBeth began with neither of these films. I had organized a 2006 benefit for the ACLU celebrating *To Kill a Mockingbird* with "Scout," actress Mary Badham. Having met Miss Mary at a Hollywood autograph signing, I realized that, however sweet, a simple sit-down with her might not be all that revealing or entertaining. I needed an added attraction to augment this extravaganza.

I wanted Harper Lee's classic prose to be an integral part of this tribute. In rereading the book, I fell in love with a portion that was left out of the film. The chapter about the cantankerous old neighbor, Mrs. Henry Lafayette Dubose, who constantly refers to Atticus as a "nigger lover." After her death, it is revealed that she was a morphine addict, and her ill temper was due to withdrawal from the drug. The chapter is filled with the forgiveness and humanity that made *Mockingbird* a moral compass to many. Complex, compassionate, and so well-loved.

I originally asked my friend Mimi Kennedy to read this piece. Since her schedule did not permit, she passed my information onto JoBeth Williams. Despite not knowing of me, given the cause, she most graciously agreed.

The night before the show, I met JoBeth at her suite at the Hilton. It was love at first sight. She was not only gorgeous, but also warm and open, with a sly sense of humor. Before we rehearsed, we sat down for tea (and a little dish). She confided to me that years ago, when she was a student at Brown University, she had had a steamy no holds barred affair with a very well-known transsexual activist (before her transition), then named Stanley. Having known the person discussed, I complimented her on her good taste.

The night of the *Mockingbird* event, JoBeth was luminescent as she read Harper Lee's words, the spotlight hitting the diamond pendant around her neck just right. JoBeth had certainly stepped into the light.

But the most memorable experience with Williams occurred when she was in town in 2008 performing in the play *Quality of Life* co-starring Laurie Metcalf. JoBeth invited me to the opening at the Geary Theatre and the after-party. Since she was the center of attention, I barely got face time with her. But as I was walking out the door, she told me she was in town for the duration of the run and suggested we "do lunch."

A few weeks later, we met at Max's, a comfort food oasis in the heart of San Francisco's theater district. She, being an actress, ordered light modest fare. I, being a producer, ordered the big, fat calorie-infused chicken pot pie, which looked large enough to contain a flock of blackbirds.

All of a sudden there was a thunderous thud, followed by a piercing alarm. Everyone looked around. A spray of water came from above, and large chunks of drywall ceiling began dropping everywhere. Screaming customers fled.

But we just sat there. JoBeth merely shrugged, rolled her eyes and pronounced with great understatement: "That damn *Poltergeist* movie follows me everywhere." We both howled with laughter. We continued to enjoy our lunch, ignoring the frenzy surrounding us.

JoBeth and me at Max's. She's modeling my big old chicken pot pie.

Act 2, Scene 12 – I AM SPARTACUS

In my salad days, people told me that I looked like Tony Curtis. I did have his signature slicked-back hair, accented by a curly cowlick in front. And a naturally tight physique. But bad acne had pockmarked my face, and even after it cleared, my self-esteem remained scarred. So, I would always brush off the compliment.

Tony Curtis is the one on the right, in case you can't tell us apart.

Regardless, I did play Tony Curtis in 1983 at a kooky benefit at Club 181. It was called "The Night of the Falling Stars." I came out in a skimpy gold lamé toga with matching gloves and booties. And an oiled-up bod. My one line, delivered in Curtis' distinctive Bronx accent: "Spahtacus, I luves yuse."

From that day on, I felt an affinity with Tony. So it was kismet (again) that I actually got to work with Curtis (twice).

My first date with Tony occurred in 2008. Zoe Elton and Mark Fishkin at the Mill Valley Film Festival had long expressed interest in working together on a big Castro Theatre tribute. The festival was a local treasure. I was honored that somebody, *anybody*, would want to collaborate with me. (Self-esteem issues followed me throughout my whole life.)

Tony Curtis was the first name to be floated. But festival director Fishkin made it clear that they did not pay for in-person appearances. The enticement, he suggested, could be a Lifetime Achievement Award from the fest. Since I was accustomed to paying (often large) fees, I was skeptical that would fly. Awards are a dime a dozen, and no money, no honey.

But as fate would have it, Curtis was about to embark on a national book tour promoting his second memoir, *Tony Curtis: American Prince*. That made things a lot easier. Tony could reap the rewards of a major publicity push for his new book in the lucrative Bay Area market. That's money, honey! Through Tony's publisher, the deal was set.

"A Tribute to Tony Curtis," a co-presentation with Mill Valley, would occur November 8, 2008. I quickly went into high gear. I watched over 50 of his films, starting with campy sword and sandal fantasies like *Son of Ali Baba* ("yondah lies da castle of my fadda"), and arriving at his classics *Spartacus*, *The Defiant Ones* (Best Actor Oscar nomination), and *The Boston Strangler* (his favorite). I burned the midnight oil to make a memorable 15-minute clip presentation.

The featured film for the Curtis tribute would be *Some Like It Hot*, recently named the American Film Institute's number one screen comedy of all time. It was an obvious choice. It's the most brilliant piece ever made about gender identity, an issue near and dear to the LGBT community. So with this iconic film's famous star appearing in person, bringing with him that Marilyn Monroe Midas touch, it was a natural for a sold-out house at the Castro. No?

Well, there was only one problem.

Now, I'm going to press pause to be brutally honest.

People ask me why I mostly did tributes to legendary *women* from Hollywood's Golden Age. After all, a huge percentage of my audience are gay *men*. Gay guys like men, right?

Wrong.

Gays worship their divas—as in female. And to quote my favorite line in *Valley of the Dolls*, "You know how bitchy fags can be." Yep. And bitchy fags *love* dishing aging starlets, especially their appearance. If a famous gal has had work done (i.e., a facelift), they can either crow, "Oh, doesn't she look amazing, she hasn't aged a bit," or cackle, "Ewww, that face. Fire her doctor, *now!*" If no work has been done, the boys can complain, "That girl's a mess! Why doesn't she have some work done, *now!?*" Then they can break out in catty titters.

But an aging male star is a different story. For older gay men (my audience's demographic), it's like looking in a mirror. It's an affront to their vanity. They just don't want to see it. They want male beauty frozen in time and sealed in amber—with a decaying picture hidden in the attic. It's super depressing to see screen legends like the once beautiful Tony Curtis now bald and bloated, no longer the object of dreams and desires. Falling off the pedestal. Merely human. *That* doesn't sell tickets.

You may dispute this as mere poppycock. But I have box office receipts to back it up. Tony's tribute, with a screening of one of the gayest pictures of all time, barely sold 800 tickets. A far cry from the 1,400 folks who packed the Castro for Jane, Debbie, Ann-Margret and other Hollywood golden girls.

OK, now that's out of my system I can press play and get back to the event at hand. Tony Curtis arrived three days before the tribute wearing a huge Stetson hat covering his hairless head. At 83, he was paunchy and now largely confined to a wheelchair. His wife Jill provided the horsepower. She was an Amazon, 46 years his junior, tall, buxom, and strong, with stylish, short-cropped blond hair. Think Brigitte Nielsen.

As she wheeled him over to meet me, Tony offered a firm handshake and a winning smile, joyfully announcing, "I'm so excited to be here," in his distinctive New Yawk accent. He then officially introduced me to wife Jilly and her mother, Sally. I had to laugh. Tony's mother-in-law was younger than me!

As I prepped the gig, Tony and company explored San Francisco. They had a ball. The cameras may have stopped rolling in Hollywood, but that didn't stop Tony from making his own home movies on his iPhone and posting them on Facebook. On his personal page was rollicking footage of the roly poly octogenarian star entertaining folks on the ferry to Angel Island. Or tap dancing in his wheelchair for tourists on Powell Street.

I don't think he gave a rat's ass about his current physical condition; he still retained his childlike curiosity and passion for living. Bernie Schwartz, that poor Jewish kid from the mean streets of the Bronx, was now having the time of his life on the streets of San Francisco.

Tony also seemed to desire a second chance. Rumor had it he had burned a lot of bridges in Hollywood, arrogant in his glory years and, later, a monster during his descent into drug abuse. One of his co-stars, and my movie star confidante, disclosed that Tony frequently smoked crack on the set. She watched in horror as the sweet smell of Curtis's success went up in smoke. Literally.

But that was all behind him now. Older and wiser, he had another shot at establishing his legacy. His memoir was a step in that direction, a personal walk of atonement and an attempt to howl out his demons, page by page. The rest he worked out on an easel with his paints and pencils.

Yet for the evening of the tribute, Tony had only one goal. He was determined to ditch the wheelchair and summon the strength to walk the ten feet to the lip of the stage and acknowledge his fans. Backstage, Jill and Allen Sawyer patiently lifted him out of the chair, and gave him the support he needed to stand up. Again, that star thing happened. The spotlight hit, and out came Tony Curtis, the Movie Star, proudly strutting his stuff and grinning from ear to ear in his Stetson.

Tony Curtis taking in the ovation with Jan Wahl.
Photo by Steven Underhill.

In the on-stage interview, Tony was gentlemanly, often with an undertone of a heartfelt mea culpa. Even though he was in a room filled with his admirers, he was intent on turning the event into his own private confessional.

A few highlights:

On making "Some Like It Hot":
Tony Curtis: There was that famous scene on the yacht where I tell Marilyn, "No girl can arouse me." And she says, "Do you mind if an American girl can try?" So she starts, and before I know it, Marilyn's on top of me giving me tongue sandwiches that I never knew existed. And grinding me like I was coffee... My sweet friends, Marilyn was just like marshmallow. There was a vulnerability that we all loved. It was like she had an open wound and we needed to make her feel better.

On his Oscar-nominated role in the classic on race, "The Defiant Ones":
Tony: They gave the script to my dear friend Marlon Brando. He was busy and couldn't do it. Then they gave it to Robert Mitchum. He didn't want to do it unless he could play the black guy. Kirk Douglas wanted to play both parts. Anyway, they got around to me. I read it and I liked it very much. And I asked who the black guy was going to be, and they said they wanted Sidney Poitier. The big dilemma was he would get second billing. They were going to say, "Tony Curtis in *The Defiant Ones,* co-starring Sidney Poitier." That was lousy. Here was a picture where two guys were equal in terms of size and ability. So I went to them, and said, "Please. You cannot do that. I want Sidney to have the same billing above the title." And they finally gave it to him.

On being married to Janet Leigh, his daughter Jamie Lee, and other matters:
Tony: Well, Janet, I fell in love with her. She was a magnificent looking girl. Beautiful bosoms, long legs. She was on the verge of becoming an important player. She was under contract at MGM, they promised her a lot of parts. And they barely delivered. She was very unhappy. And in that environment, we had a married

life. She was very brave and kind and didn't let these things overwhelm us.

Jan Wahl: When you had your second child, Jamie Lee, did you have any idea she'd be a performer?

Tony: When she was a tiny little kid there was a personality that was popping out of her. She was the most amusing little girl! She'd stomp through the house like she was King Kong. Scared the hell out of me! She'd come storming into my bedroom, go right up to my bed, and just stare at me.... But I loved all my children. I lost a son, Nicolas, to an overdose of heroin. I was devastated at his death. Yet it prepared me for the vicissitudes of life.

Jan Wahl: In the book you describe what you went through with cocaine—in a way that will discourage other people because it brought you down. You hit a bottom.

Tony: I'm 83 years old, and if I've got 15 or 18 more years, maybe that's a lot. So I cleansed myself, so to speak, of all the negatives in life. And now my brothers and sisters, I just want to be able to tiptoe through the tulips.

At that moment, as he exited into the wings, high as a kite from the audience's adulation, he probably could have!

At his book signing afterwards, Tony, now back in his wheelchair, motioned me to his side. We locked eyes and he held my hand. Hard. Not letting go. And he had very big, fleshy hands! Then he said, slowly, emphatically, "My dear Marc, I want to thank you so much. You did a wonderful job. Let me kiss you."

So I got a kiss from Tony Curtis. Not a tongue sandwich, but a tender kiss on my hand.

But that was not the end of our story together. About a year and half later, I got an out of the blue phone call.

"Hello, Marc? This is Preston. I'm Tony Curtis' new personal assistant. Listen, Tony and Jill were very impressed with your editing work for the clips at the Castro. Tony's planning a lecture circuit tour, like what Cary Grant did in his later years. We're calling ours 'An Affair With Tony Curtis.' For the opening, we'd like 15 minutes of snippets of the best of Tony's pictures. Like what you did before but even more voluminous and peppier. Is that something you would be interested in?"

Ummm, yeah!

"Good, how much do you charge?"

"Well my going rate is $40 an hour, but for Tony—"

Preston interrupted me before I (once again) sold myself short. "$40 an hour sounds great!"

Tony Curtis and longtime admirer Marc Huestis, together at last. Photo by Steven Underhill.

Deal done. And 40 bucks an hour! For me it was a small fortune. I had gotten used to surviving (decently) on $20,000 a year in very expensive San Francisco. (Thank god for my rent-controlled apartment and a great landlord!)

In consultation with Tony, there were two things he proudly wanted highlighted. Appearing in the iconic photomontage on the Beatles' *Sgt. Pepper's Lonely Hearts Club Band* album and being the cartoon character Stoney Curtis on *The Flintstones*. Otherwise, I was given carte blanche.

It was the most fun job I ever had. Tony and Jill were delighted by my work. Each morning I'd get an e-mail from Curtis's office in Henderson, Nevada. Preston would report on how thrilled his boss was with the project results.

"Tony wakes up each day looking forward to what you have done. It gives him strength."

I never wanted this job to end. I love editing. It was in my DNA. I fantasized about my dad cutting *Hullabaloo* in the NBC tape room back in the '60s. I wondered what he would think of his son now, completely self-taught in Final Cut Pro, working on my personal computer—for Tony Curtis, movie legend.

However, there was one gnawing concern in the back of my mind. I had seen the shape that Tony was in. I had my doubts this tour would ever materialize. But that was not my department. My task was making this compilation reel sparkle. When I submitted it in April 2010, I received this e-mail from Preston:

"This has been a monumental task and you have no idea how much Tony appreciates and enjoys this. It is an incredible retrospective. TC has been talking about doing this since I first met him. And here it is. Thanks again, Marc."

After finishing this job, I kept checking in to Tony's office for a tour schedule. None was forthcoming.

Then in mid-September, I received a large FedEx package from Henderson. It was a framed, signed and numbered lithograph by Tony Curtis. No note. Odd, I thought.

A week later, on September 29, 2010, Tony Curtis died. The mysterious package now made sense; Tony was tying up loose ends.

I was unable to go to the memorial but I read the press reports. They mentioned a 15-minute clip reel that was shown at the beginning of the service. One article singled out the "Stony Curtis" segment from *The Flintstones* and reported how the mourners burst into spontaneous laughter when it played. At that moment, Tony must have been smiling and saying, "I told you so" from above.

And the reel's credit roll ended with: "A special thank you to our friend Marc Huestis for his wonderful editing work."

Tony had insisted on making these the last words on the screen.

Then it hit me. All that time, Tony and I had really been collaborating on his cinematic obituary. In the back of his mind he knew this would be his way of speaking from the grave at his memorial.

According to Tony's last wishes, several prized possessions were placed in his coffin: His iPhone, Stetson hat, paintbrushes, six packets of Splenda—and the DVD of our clip reel.

So part of me will always lie with Tony. Good night, sweet American prince.

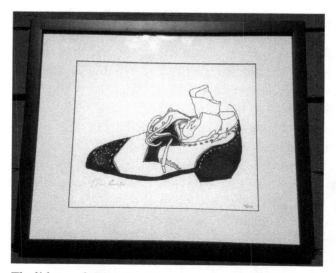

The lithograph Tony Curtis sent one week before his death.

Act 2, Scene 13 – LIVING DOLLS: THE SEQUEL

It's rare that the sequel is better than the original. In the case of snagging Patty Duke, Neely O'Hara from *Valley of the Dolls*, years after celebrating her co-star Barbara Parkins, it was.

My generation grew up in love with Patty. Each week, we'd religiously watch *The Patty Duke Show*, where she played split-screen identical cousins, Patty & Cathy. (Is there really such a thing as identical cousins?)

Whatever. We'd sing along to the classic theme song, some of us with gay abandon: *Our Patty loves to rock and roll. A hot dog makes her lose control. What a wild duet!*

In hindsight, when parsing the lyric, "You can lose your mind, when cousins are two of a kind," could we have been surprised that Patty was bipolar? Perhaps these words were a precursor to Patty's deep dive into mental illness, documented in her best-selling memoir *Call Me Anna*.

I vividly remember the warning signs—Patty Duke's very public meltdown on live national TV in 1970 when she received her first Emmy for *My Sweet Charlie*. After Monty Hall announced the winner, a young woman in a beige maxi climbed onstage. Disheveled, a glazed look in her eyes, she delivered an unforgettable speech. "Thank you *(pause)* and you *(searching the crowd)*. I know you're out there somewhere. *(pointing)*… The best words I've ever learned were hello *(long pause)*, enthusiasm *(long pause)*, and thank you." Then Patty exited quickly.

I told myself, "She must be on drugs!" Little did I know…

I'll also never forget the first time I saw *Valley of the Dolls* (*VD*). I was immediately drawn to Patty's character, Neely O'Hara. The foul-mouthed, booze-dope-dolls-driven Hollywood has-been who comes "crawling back to Broadway." Afterwards, I saw the film a gayzillion times, always reveling in its tacky excesses. And because Neely was such a fabulously vile (and oddly, sympathetic) creature, she had become, along with Joan Crawford in *Mommie Dearest*, one of the most iconic characters in the lexicon of gay camp.

When I did the *Valley of the Dolls* event in 1997, Patty Duke was naturally the first person I wanted to invite. But I learned Patty was allergic to *VD*; if she even heard the words "Valley of the Dolls," she'd break out in hives. What the hell, I thought, it's worth a try. So out went a pitch to Patty. I waited. And waited. Nothing. So Barbara Parkins was booked. I moved on.

But I'm a persistent SOB. The words "giving up" are not in my vocabulary.

Fast-forward to 2009. It began with a small item in the *San Francisco Chronicle*: "Patty Duke is coming to town, replacing Carol Kane as Miss Morrible in the local production of *Wicked*." Why not try again?

Instead of phoning up a manager like in old days, this time I clicked on the Patty Duke website (Pattyduke.com). I refashioned my initial pitch, even addressing her as Anna (her preferred name) and zipped it off to the site's webmaster. To my great surprise, I received an immediate answer from a man named Bill Jankowski.

When Bill called, he sounded young. After Marvin Paige *that* was refreshing. And I quickly realized this friend of Patty was also a friend of Dorothy. I began to sprinkle chats with terms like "girl," and he'd chortle.

Bill was a chit-chatty Cathy, and a wealth of information on all things Patty. He was eager for Anna to get my Castro event proposal. But everything had to go through her husband, Mike Pearce. Bill helped me redo the pitch to hit all of Anna's sweet spots.

I envisioned a grand tribute to a great star, I explained to Mike. An afternoon screening of her Academy Award-winning turn as Helen Keller in *The Miracle Worker* (which Bill and I knew few would attend). Then I began hinting at the main event screening: Maybe, oh, perhaps—*Valley of the Dolls*? I held my breath. Bill had hinted that a *VD* screening was not out of the realm of possibility. Anna had finally made her peace with *Valley* and the self-destructive Neely O'Hara. But make no mistake; she didn't want *that* to be the only thing she'd be remembered for.

I sent the re-tooled pitch. Two weeks later, a response: They'll "consider it." Six weeks later, Mike Pearce had great news: Anna said yes!

Yes! I jumped for joy. It was like the end of *A Star Is Born*: "Ladies and gentlemen, Vicki Lester *will* be appearing tonight!!!"

Everything fell into place quickly. "Sparkle, Patty, Sparkle" was scheduled for Monday, July 20, 2009. (The title was a hat tip to Neely's infamous *VD* line, "I have to get up in the morning and sparkle, Neely, sparkle.") The Monday date meant *Wicked* was not playing and Anna could invite her cast mates. She was especially thrilled to be able to show off some of her earlier work to "the kids." Many of them had no idea who Patty Duke was.

Veteran comic writer Bruce Vilanch, the center square on the revamped *Hollywood Squares*, was booked to conduct the on-stage interview. Matthew Martin and Connie Champagne would reprise their 1997 roles as Neely and Helen. Bill Jankowski agreed to help me compile the Patty Duke clip reel. The event would benefit the National Alliance for Mental Illness and a local sister LBGT organization, A New Leaf, an acknowledgement of Anna's longstanding support for our community. (Anna was one of the few celebrities to attend an early ACT UP meeting—dressed in a pink Chanel suit!)

Several weeks before the event, Bill was flying into San Francisco to see *Wicked*. He invited me along and promised to facilitate an in-person introduction with Anna after the performance. As we settled into our theater seats, I noticed an older couple nearby. Opening the program, the wife let out a shriek. "Oh my gawd," she yelled, "Patty Duke is in this show.

Herb, honey, did you hear me?" I'm sure Herb heard her, as did everyone else in the theater. For whatever reason, Patty's name was not included in the publicity, and few knew she was in this production. Odd, I thought, given she was an Oscar-winning icon.

Except for Patty Duke, I hated *Wicked*. But I was so excited to meet Anna! As Bill led me into her dressing room, I saw a handsome, burly gray haired man on a stool calmly doing needlepoint. It was Anna's husband Mike, a former Army drill sergeant. "That," I thought, "is a real man! She's trained him well."

Anna and Mike both warmly greeted me. Anna was the type of woman who gives you one intense stare and gets you in a second flat. And after she lets you in, her patter is punctuated by the loudest, most life-affirming cackle you've ever heard. And she was so tiny! Four-foot-eleven, to be exact.

The meeting was short, but I felt like I was reconnecting with a long-lost friend. Or a kooky aunt from *Arsenic and Old Lace*. Outside the theater as we said our goodbyes, Anna gave me the tightest hug, shaking my body from side to side. "Christ, I needed that," she yelped. "It's goddamn June and so fucking cold in San Francisco!"

Before the night of "Sparkle, Patty, Sparkle," Anna and I had one last meeting at her temporary digs above Lombard Street. As I rang the buzzer, I could hear all sorts of yapping. Wouldn't you know it, Duke was a dog woman. Three small furry friends greeted me, including a dachshund named Bogie—a hot-dog dog losing control.

I sat down to a doggie lickfest, trying to focus on business. "This is going to be so much fun!" Anna exclaimed, jumping up and down like she had bees in her bonnet and ants in her pants. "Wait, wait. I have to show you something!" Out came a Neiman Marcus shoebox. Anna unwrapped the tissue like a kid on Christmas. She shouted "tah-dah!" and proudly revealed the tiniest pair of black and white patent leather spats. "Aren't they perfect for the Castro? I want you to know, Mike and I shopped long and hard to find these."

The day of the tribute, the matinee of *The Miracle Worker*, as predicted, barely drew an audience. As I arrived outside the theater, an attractive man was sitting on the sidewalk, staring at the event poster. He was sobbing uncontrollably.

I asked if he was okay. He lunged up and hugged me so tightly it was suffocating. "Thank you so much for doing this," he gasped and gulped. "This lady," he said, emphatically pointing to the poster, "This lady has done so much for the world. If you only knew." His hug lasted a good minute. When the weeping man finally let go, a woman next to him whispered in my ear, "That's Anna's son, Mackenzie."

Anna had two sons, Sean Astin, "Sam" in *The Lord of the Rings*—whom she called "the Hobbit"—and Mackenzie, "Mac," best known for the '80s sitcom *The Facts of Life*. Having read Anna's book, I knew their childhood was less than idyllic. And because of my childhood with Marija, the Continental Gypsy, I knew fully well what it was like to have a mother in show business who also suffered from mental illness. It takes its toll. Mackenzie was certainly unhinged that afternoon, and I could only imagine the baggage that had to be unpacked. Still, it was obvious that he worshiped his mom. And hard hugs sure ran in that family!

The evening event was a dream come true. All those years I had been fantasizing about Neely O'Hara—and here she was, live and in person, standing in front of the Castro, greeting fans who had lined up hours before! Anna looked terrific in an elegant gray and white pinstriped blazer, white pants, white stockings— and the adorable black and white shoes. At 62, she courageously looked her age. Her gray-blond hair was subtly coiffed and her face was natural with just a smidge of tasteful make-up.

Anna was so damned playful. At the preshow reception, she greeted the guests like long lost friends. She also spent time listening to a plethora of stories from folks struggling with their own demons. One woman took me aside afterwards, her voice trembling. "I have bipolar disorder. You can't imagine how special it was to me to meet Patty Duke. She held my hand as I told her about my battle with mental illness. Then she turned to my wife and thanked her for staying with me. No one has ever said that before."

From left, Mackenzie Astin, Patty Duke, me, and Mike Pearce.
Photo by Steven Underhill.

At the main event, and after the clip compilation, Anna entered triumphantly. Proudly escorted by Mackenzie, she tearfully mounted the stage like a prodigal daughter.

As the theme music from *The Patty Duke Show* faded, Bruce Vilanch piped in with a quick-witted quip.

Bruce: This is such a thrill for me because we have so much in common. A hot dog makes *me* lose control.

Patty Duke: *(lets out a howl)* For years I wanted to find the writer of that song and ask him how a hot dog can make him lose control.

Patty and Bruce then got down to business.

Connie Champagne, in Neely O'Hara drag,
comes face to face with Patty Duke.
Photo by Steven Underhill.

Some highlights:

On "Valley of the Dolls":
Patty Duke: I don't mean to pander, but this is the truth: I
hated *Valley of the Dolls*! I hated everything about it except Sharon
Tate. I was mortified when someone would say they had seen it.
I would say, "I'm sorry." But the gay community has brought me
to not only liking the movie, but also love that it is not serious.

Valley of the Dolls brought you here tonight, and for that I can only be grateful.

On working with Judy Garland on "Valley of the Dolls":

Patty: We were already in the process of filming for a month or so, when the decision was made to hire Judy to play Helen Lawson, next to me, who was playing Judy. But nobody was allowed to say that. Oh, there were similarities—

Bruce: Judy, Neely. They didn't name her Florence.

Patty: *(cackles)* At any rate, the very first day with Judy, it was going to Mecca. She was charming and *funny*. Oh so funny! But she was having a problem with alcohol, and I don't know about other things. And the director, Mark Robson, who was the meanest son of a bitch I ever met in my lifetime, he kept this icon, this little sparrow, waiting. She had to come in at 6:30 in the morning; he wouldn't even plan to get to her till 4 in the afternoon. She didn't mind waiting. What I minded was that there were gentlemen around her that supplied her with wine and other things. So that when she was finally called to the set, she couldn't function very well. She crumbled. She was fired, and that was devastating. She should never have been hired in the first place, but she needed the money. Anyway I worshiped her. She made me laugh every time she looked at me!

Patty ended the interview with these heartfelt words: "I just want to leave here tonight letting you know how very important it is for us who perform and go out in the community and try to be of some service *(holding back tears)*, how very important it is that you continue to call upon us, and send us your love. God bless you and thank you!"

It was a note of grace by an ultimate survivor. Anna had had a rough life. But like Helen Lawson, she was a barracuda. She had taken the punches; coming left, right and below the belt. Anna/Patty had survived *Valley of the Dolls*. And so much more. She had made peace with her past, finally embracing it with love and a sense of humor.

That resilience was equally apparent as Anna accepted a proclamation from Mayor Gavin Newsom, who declared July 20, 2009, Anna Pearce/Patty Duke Day in San Francisco.

Patty Duke showing off her proclamation
with Bruce Vilanch.
Photo by Steven Underhill.

As the audience stood to give Patty a prolonged and heartfelt standing ovation, I wondered why Neely O'Hara was so important to many of us? Particularly gay men? Because in our own ways we have all been through hell. Some victims of homophobia, some victims of our own struggles with booze and dope. Like Neely in her famous breakdown, we have raged against the world, screaming alone in our own dark alleys.

Anna's ownership and celebration of this character she once loathed made us all feel better about ourselves. And it made Anna quite happy too. It was liberating. (Faye Dunaway, take a note from your fellow Oscar winner and learn to embrace *Mommie Dearest!*)

After the event, I stayed in touch with Anna and Mike. On my 55th birthday, I brought another of my Castro honorees, Ann Blyth, to see *Wicked.* I introduced the two diminutive stars afterwards. Veda Pierce and Neely O'Hara, famous bad girls of the silver screen, together at last! They got on famously, acting like long lost two of a kind cousins who had just been reunited. Watching them together was the best birthday gift ever.

Mike and Anna, aka Patty Duke, meet Ann Blyth.

For years afterwards, Anna never blinked an eye when I asked for favors. When I broke my heel, she sent autographed photos to my "miracle worker" doctors. When I did an event with Patty McCormack, whom Patty Duke was named after, she recorded a special greeting.

Privately, and at the time not for public consumption, I had also known that Anna was suffering serious health problems, and that the prognosis was not good. Yet when death came on March 29, 2016, it hit hard. She died of sepsis, just like my mom.

I loved Anna, and felt drawn to attend her public memorial. I finally had a driver's license, so I took a long road trip from San

Francisco to Coeur d'Alene, Idaho, where she and Mike had lived for many years.

The ride was slow, circuitous, filled with a myriad of landscapes: The snow-capped Sierras, the forlorn desert towns of Nevada. In Idaho, there were ever-changing vistas: moonlike craters, emerald green valleys, rich black soil, furrowed fields of potato farms, huge weeping trees. Over several thousand miles, I had plenty of quiet time to reflect on Anna's spirit and legacy.

As I filed into the memorial service among hundreds of others, there was a montage of Anna's life in pictures on the church's large screen. And then suddenly a photo from our Castro show. I started to sob.

Folks had come from across the country to pay their respects, each with their own personal stories—testaments to Anna's generous heart. Behind me, a deaf man spoke in a loud voice, his belabored words punctuated by convulsive crying. He was an actor in Coeur d'Alene community theater, he said, and Anna had attended several of his performances. I imagined the powerful impact *The Miracle Worker* might have had on him. Near me was a troubled fan who had attempted suicide and was subsequently treated for depression. Anna had been one of the few who listened to her.

Son Mackenzie slowly ascended to the podium to give a moving eulogy: "She took her own story and gave it to the world, telling each and every other person so afflicted that they were not alone in their suffering. There are people alive today who would not be, had my mom not had the audacity to put into print what had been too taboo before."

Mac was a different man from the broken one at the Castro years earlier. He seemed renewed, redeemed, recovered. His final words: "I ask that you take Anna with you today, and to go forth and to speak freely to others about your experiences as she did about hers. Anna be with you." Like a liturgy in a Catholic mass, the crowd repeated "Anna be with you."

But it was Melissa Gilbert, who had played Helen Keller to Anna's Annie Sullivan in a TV version of *The Miracle Worker*, and followed Patty Duke as the president of the Screen Actors Guild, whose words touched me most deeply. "Anna had guts and moxie. She was small but mighty. And those tiny shoes are going to be hard to fill."

Suddenly, I thought back to those little black and white shoes in the Neiman Marcus shoebox. I recalled the look of triumphant joy Anna had on her face as she presented them to me with a riotous "tah-dah" and then ecstatically slipped them on.

Yes, indeed—those tiny shoes would be hard to fill.

Act 2, Scene 14 – THAT FINAL BOW

In my 20 years and over 50 shows at the Castro, I've been fortunate enough to work with many of Hollywood's brightest lights. Yet I'm equally thankful for the many offbeat stars I've hosted: *Hedwig* genius John Cameron Mitchell, impish Alan Cumming, idiosyncratic Candy Clark, kooky Edie Adams, irreverent Rutanya Alda, singular Joey Arias. And the one and only Justin Vivian Bond, whose early work originated in San Francisco.

Traditionally, legions of gifted performers have started in the Bay Area. But most eventually move away *from* here to New York and L.A., where the action is. Still, some *have* chosen to stay behind. Those talented creatures, many drag artistes, have made my nights at the Castro "only in San Francisco" events. They are my family, and I carry them close to my heart.

One such person deserves a full-on tribute: Arturo Galster.

What to say about Arturo? To paraphrase Helen Lawson in *Valley of the Dolls*, "That kid's really got it." In spades.

Arturo was the Agnes Moorehead of my mercurial stock company, going back to the days of the 181 Club in the mid-80s. He hosted my premiere Castro event, *The Stepford Wives*, and was the local star attraction at eleven of my subsequent extravaganzas, sharing a bill with John Waters, John Cameron Mitchell, Karen Black, Patty McCormack, Carol Lynley, and Ann-Margret—the last one playing a man!

He could do anything. Arturo's Castro performances channeled Marlene Dietrich, Conrad Birdie, Endora from *Bewitched*, Tim Gunn from *Project Runway*, and most famously, Patsy Cline. He was the reigning queen of the understatement, saying more with a sly arch of an eyebrow than others could muster in a lavish production number.

Arturo Galster, a reigning queen with many looks.

Arturo was more than a showbiz colleague; he was a dear friend and fellow long-term HIV survivor. That's a bond only those in that exclusive club can truly understand. When we were together there was little discussion of our status. We simply exchanged knowing looks that silently said, with equal parts sarcasm and gratitude, "Damn, girl. You're still here?!"

Smarturo (his nickname) was brilliant. He spoke fluent German and Japanese. He was also an astute therapist, able to diagnose a person's whole psychology in one or two droll words. Once, when I was my usual morose and depressed self, he asked me how I was. I responded, "I've been better." Without missing a beat, he shot back, "When?" That one word said more than a full $200 session with a shrink.

All that said, Artie was, first and foremost, a party gal. For years it was adorable. Then it wasn't. We lived in the same neighborhood and I'd often spy him exiting our corner store clutching a brown paper bag with a big ol' bottle. Or two or three. Sometimes he appeared agitated, fidgety—possible signs of other insidious chemical hellions. I've seen that look before: In the mirror, during my Tina days.

Like many artists, he struggled to make ends meet, getting hired and getting fired from a string of day jobs. Becoming an Airbnb host finally gave Arturo financial stability. But it also enabled his alcoholism. Now he'd get sloshed and show out-of-town guests a wild time in the "real" San Francisco, away from the yuppies and the techies. Drinking became part of the job.

Cracks were beginning to show. Soon, Arturo would uncharacteristically miss rehearsals, making up bullshit excuses. We all knew what was going on.

While playing Hedwig in a local production, Artie shaved his head. It was not a pretty look. The once ever-young Arturo now looked quite old and tired, a shell of himself. It seemed a physical manifestation of deeper problems, and when I spotted him on the street, I thought to myself "This is not going to end well."

During this period, Arturo was involved in a string of liquor-fueled verbal spats, prone to physical violence, and out-and-out rage. One drunken Saturday night in August of 2014, Arturo dragged his Airbnb guests off to the playground at Dolores Park for a late-night party. While on the swings, he mouthed off to a stranger. The guy slugged him. Artie's guests interceded and helped him home. Two days later, they found him slouched on a seat in his bedroom. Dead. He was 55.

The first autopsy reports were inconclusive. His head injuries were not the cause of death. The report also revealed that Artie had an enlarged heart. It was a perfect metaphor for the man.

His sudden tragic death rocked our world. It was a curtain closing. We had lost a true genius and a kindred soul. Many of us had been hardened by death during the AIDS crisis, but this one felt like the beginning of a second wave of passings. Not from a virus, but due to demons lurking inside us. As Danny Nicoletta succinctly put it: "The brighter the star, the darker the shadow."

I quickly stepped up to help facilitate a memorial. After all, during the AIDS crisis I had become Memorials 'R' Us, quite good at producing them. Artie had even performed at a number of them. And since Artie had headlined at the Castro so many times, his would be held there.

A group of friends and colleagues emerged to organize the event including Artie's best girlfriends and confidantes, Helen Shumaker and Barbara Liu McDonald. In days, $6,000 was raised through crowdfunding to pay the rent on the Castro Theatre and finance the memorial. Everyone was all in. Even the Palestinian family who ran the corner store where Artie bought his endless supply of booze donated. "That man kept us in business for years," the father said. "It's the least we can do."

On September 22, 2014, a little more than a month after his passing, our tribe gathered, en masse.

His logical family joined hands with his biological family. Friends flew in from as far as Japan to pay tribute. The evening became a religious experience. Two male members of the San Francisco Ballet led a solemn opening processional. One silently walked with a large portrait of Arturo. The other, dressed as Patsy, proudly carried his ashes.

As host D'Arcy Drollinger brought up friends and family to offer testimonials, and act after act performed, it became obvious this was a celebration not only of Arturo, but also of our collective past. There were lots of wrinkles and gray hair in the room, but our spirit was still punk rock.

Arturo represented a golden period of performers who created purely for the love of it. But times had changed. The current RuPaul obsessed generation now saw drag as a career move, complete with branding and merchandising. Well, good for them; a girl's gotta eat. But the spontaneous spark that ignited our scene, where drag performers were cultural outlaws, is now being buried, along with our beloved Arturo.

Poster for Arturo's memorial.
Photo by Daniel Nicoletta.

Once we were youngbloods; now we were old school. Or dead. And the city we had spent much of our lives building was now becoming increasingly difficult to recognize. Our generation was being evicted, literally and symbolically. We had left our heart in San Francisco, but that enlarged heart was now on life support—endangered by greed, gentrification and gigabytes.

This memorial was more than just last rites for Artie. It was a last hurrah for our community.

The iconic Mickey and Judy spirit, which inspired so many of us to put on our raucous, exuberant, defiantly iconoclastic, gender-fuck, counter-culture, no-budget shows, was fading away. Our time was passing. Sure, that passage had been going on for quite some time. But Arturo's sudden demise put an exclamation mark on the closing sentence. Now, what?

Act 2, Scene 15 – DEUS EX MACHINA
OUT OF THE STREETS AND INTO THE WOODS

I keep having this dream. It takes place at my childhood home in Bethpage, New York. But it's not the ramshackle mess after my father left, when my mother gave up all pretense of keeping up with the Joneses. In this dream, we have a happy home. The house is newly renovated, beautifully painted. The lawn is emerald green and perfectly manicured. My parents love each other. My mother smiles, laughs, even breaks into spontaneous song. My sister, still in pigtails and crinolines, plays with imaginary horses. My brother and I carry on quite a lively and loving conversation. The invisible curtain that separated us is now gone.

But there's one catch in the dream. The house has been sold. The new owners have yet to move in. Our happy family is in the basement, resigned to leave. But not me. I am determined to hold on, to hide—to stay, even though I am no longer welcome. My brother begs me to vacate. But I am intransigent, immovable, and adamant.

At that point I usually wake up.

I realize now that this dream was prescient. Deep down I knew my days as the Castro impresario were numbered. I had muddled through a string of failures. I had booked almost every star I could. I had sunk the shit out of the SS Poseidon and milked *Mommie Dearest* to death. My audiences were now dwindling—and many actually dying. But I was still holding on, unable to break away.

Barbara Parkins once gave me a piece of shockingly simple but sage advice. "If it doesn't taste good, spit it out!" Don't get me wrong. For almost two decades, I loved what I did. It tasted good. But the delight I felt in dancing with the stars was now becoming past tense. I wasn't enjoying this line of work anymore. Yes, what I once savored now was sour.

I just couldn't go on anymore. And sooner or later, life teaches you that you are not as talented or gifted as you once thought. Or to misquote Rick Blaine in *Casablanca*, you realize that your accomplishments don't amount to a hill of beans in this crazy world. You accept that life goes on without you.

But before the without you part kicked in, it was time to explore the life within. I decided it was finally the moment to come face to face with who I am—to reconcile all the bad things in the past, let go of them, and move on.

And there was another thing (literally) within me, lurking deep inside, that I had not properly processed: My life-threatening virus, now in check. I had lived over half of my adult life with the specter of AIDS shadowing me.

In the early years of the epidemic, HIV was a death sentence. Through the advocacy of groups like ACT UP and multiple drug regimens, some with horrific side effects (Crixivan + Norvir begone!), this death sentence had been commuted. Through the luck of the draw, I had survived. But the psychological scars linger. My fears and inner screams were simply suppressed by one blue Truvada pill a day.

So many friends had died. We fetishize them; memorialize them in flowery Facebook posts. We talk incessantly about the good old bad days of AIDS, we who are left with survivor guilt, personal stigmas withheld and unspoken memories. We fear being chastised if we dare verbalize the feelings that lie within. "Girl, life goes on, get over it." Or "Christ, are you playing the AIDS card again?"

I was a survivor, but a wounded warrior, with post-traumatic stress disorder that had not been properly treated.

At this point, I started to think deeply about the phrase "Get a life." Although I had endless adventures and countless encounters with celebrity, I felt empty. I realized that I was a workaholic, my sole concern being my next gig and whether I would make enough money to keep going.

I was so consumed by being a professional that I shut out the normal intimacies of the soul. And the heart. All those years of substituting love with sex. Those thousands of orgasms without one memorable one. Well, maybe one: with Phillip in 1983.

And I found myself doing my own walk of atonement. Over the years, I had made scores of enemies. I often joked that someone would get rich setting up tollbooths at all the bridges I had burnt. Sure, some of the combative rage was fed by crystal meth. But even after I quit, even after I had made good progress in controlling my anger, it still sometimes erupted.

Long story short, I didn't like the person I had become. And there were more yesterdays than tomorrows. I was getting old. Yet I was stagnant, not knowing how to change.

Then fate intervened. My brother Henry died.

Henry and I were never close. Though we shared a room through my teenage years, we barely spoke. He was a shy and troubled child, beaten down by my mom, who blamed his unplanned birth for her miserable life. I realized belatedly that he took on the role of our protector, watching out for my sister Michele and me. But he barely had any friends, and was lost.

Henry was of age to be drafted during the Vietnam War. But he enlisted in the Air Force, thinking that would be the safer option, rather than being sent to the front lines. Regardless, he served much of his tour of duty in Vietnam, but luckily away from battle.

While Henry was on duty overseas, I was marching against the war. After he returned, we never had conversations about his experiences in 'Nam. In fact we never had conversations about anything. But I could tell that his wartime traumas weighed heavily on him. He was even more unsociable, withdrawn. The term wasn't in common usage back then, but Henry also suffered from post-traumatic stress disorder.

He had a brilliant mind. After earning his bachelor's and master's degrees in electrical engineering at Washington University, he spent most of his adult years working in Saudi Arabia. I think it was his way of escaping; he was as far away from home as possible. He did finally return stateside—after my mother's death in 2000.

In those later years, he was a loner, becoming slovenly and obese. He developed diabetes. He was increasingly unconcerned about his physical appearance. He stopped showering. Once he came to visit me in San Francisco. We went out to the Chinese restaurant near my office. I was a regular and had a chummy relationship with the waitresses. When I introduced them to my brother, they looked me in the eye, and in broken English commented, "Oh, you two. Very different skin, yes, very different skin."

Upon his return to the U.S., Henry moved to Washington state and tried for years to find employment. He had no luck. His connection with the world around him diminished.

As gay men, we sometimes proselytize that we are misfits, outsiders in a heterogeneous world. But at least we have our community. My brother had no community, few friends. He was a real outsider, an orphan of society, wandering the planet, unable to fit in.

After almost a decade of rejection and unemployment in the U.S., Henry made one last attempt to re-enter the real world. He accepted a one-year gig back in Saudi, the one place that appreciated his gifts as an engineer and was willing to overlook all the rest. There he died suddenly, at the age of 60, on Nov. 1, 2011. Ironically—or maybe not—the same day as my parents' wedding anniversary.

I heard the news from my dad over the phone. I had just flown to New York and was heading out to Stony Brook to see him. My visits with dad were infrequent, so it was surreal that Henry would die the day of a rare family get-together.

It was determined that the cause of death was sepsis due to complications of his diabetes, obesity, and a bad heart.

A bad heart? My brother had a heart of gold. He was a better man than I will ever be.

My sister Michele was charged with his estate; a job she did meticulously. First order was getting Henry's body back. A word to the wise: Don't die in Saudi during Ramadan. Virtually everything closes up for a month. Despite the best efforts from the State Department, and the pleas from my sister, his body was frozen and stored for weeks.

Finally, his remains were shipped back. On a crisp December day, Henry was given a beautiful burial at Calverton National Cemetery in Long Island, with full military honors. I was surprised how moving it was. I sobbed when they played a recording of "Taps" while two soldiers locked eyes in an intense gaze and folded the flag atop his coffin. There was closure. His pained, lonely life had come to an end. At last he was resting in peace. At my sister's suggestion, on his gravesite was inscribed, "Henry Huestis. Sgt. USAF, Vietnam, Beloved Son and Brother. He Was a Good Soul."

Henry lived his life as a pauper. He stayed in the cheapest hotels. While in Washington state, he inhabited a small, run-down apartment. He would look out for others—he paid for my mother's funeral—but he barely spent money on himself. Because of his spartan life, Henry had amassed a small fortune. I was shocked.

Yet looking back, it made perfect sense. Henry was so fearful that he would be penniless and alone in his retirement; he never allowed himself to enjoy any of his savings.

I have a joke: "Had I known my brother had so much money, I would have been nicer to him." That's black humor with a grain of truth, mixed with a helluva lot of guilt and regret.

Out of the blue, I had been bequeathed a life-changing sum. I was left with an existential question. Should I just sock it away for an emergency, like my brother did? Or should I really change my life?

At first I viewed this inheritance as some form of art grant. It was always a dream of mine to mount the Peter Weiss play *Marat/Sade*. So I joined forces with Russell Blackwood and Thrillpeddlers, an avant-garde theater troupe I was quite fond of, and our co-production opened in July 2012. The show was a critical success, but came in at a loss. And I still felt unsatisfied.

Truth be told, I had become discontented with life in San Francisco. It was now a tale of two cities, that of the newly rich and everyone else. Our favorite places were closing. The art scene was no longer vibrant; it's hard for artists to create when you work two jobs just to pay your rent. Tent cities were popping up with the newly homeless.

And though at one time I took great strength and solace in the LGBT community, the issues within its ranks that captured the headlines left me cold. I didn't want to get married, have children, or enlist in the military. Call me old-fashioned, but that's how I felt.

Okay, they say that money can't buy you happiness, but it sure can help. With this new financial infusion, I had the once in a lifetime opportunity to do what he was unable to do: To *really* change my life. Since my HIV diagnosis, I had assumed I was living on borrowed time. So the option of saving my inheritance and waiting until I was, say, 80, to make good use of it seemed silly. There was a lesson to be learned from Henry's death: Be here, now! And move forward, dammit.

The first change was simple. I learned how to drive a car. I won't bore you with the details, other than to say I was a terrible driving student. It took the patience of Job, but my good friend Greg Cruikshank put up with me on road trips when I got behind the wheel. After months of lessons, several thousand dollars, hired and fired teachers, and a failed road test, I finally got my license on July 26, 2013. At the tender age of 58, I was now a bitch on wheels—and the proud owner of a grey 2008 Hyundai Elantra I named Carlotta.

For years, I was yearning to get out of Dodge. Now I could drive myself out. I was determined to find grace in the healing arms of Mother Nature. My inheritance was not large enough to buy a house in much of California. But in my fantasies, there lingered a desire for a place, however tiny, to call my own. Even if it was a shack, it would be *my* shack.

I found a website called Tinyhouses.com and began my quest in earnest. That led me to the 50cabins.com, which specialized in properties in the Lake Tahoe area. I loved the alpine, pristine beauty of the outdoors. And I always had a thing for knotty pine. When I had pointed my mom in that direction many years ago, I had a secret desire to live there myself.

The site offered cabins for inordinately cheap prices. And they were cuter than shit. These Forest Service cabins had been built in the early and mid-20th century, specifically for working folks to get out of the city and have a summer place to enjoy the beauty of nature. You couldn't own the land, which was part of the National Forest. But you could own the cabin, or, as it was called, "the improvement" (a perfect name for my desire for change).

There was one in particular that I fell in love with immediately. It was located in Kyburz, California, whose claim to fame was a roadside sign saying, "Welcome to Kyburz, Now Leaving Kyburz." It was a three-hour drive from San Francisco, 30 minutes from Lake Tahoe, elevation 5,000 ft., right off the American River.

This rustic cabin had checkerboard asbestos floors, a wood burning stove, a stone barbeque pit, knotty pine, and furnishings straight out of *Better Home & Gardens*, circa 1960.

It looked like a vacation set for *Mad Men*. The price (after inspection deductions) was $67,000. You couldn't get a closet in San Francisco for that amount. I could afford that, and have enough left over to taper off from event producing.

There were downsides: The cabin only had running water from mid-May to mid-October. And since no agent could mortgage the "improvements," you had to pay the full amount upfront.

Could I take this leap? Live part-time in the mountains? I went back and forth in my mind, weighing the pros and cons. Many laughed at the prospect of Grizzly Huestis, predicting that I would last two months tops. Then, they'd sing that line from the theme song from *Green Acres*: "Dahlink, I love you, but give me Park Avenue."

*Check out those floors! Who could resist
this 50Cabins.com listing photo?*

But some were supportive. Greg came up several times to help scout the place. We even broke in the first time when my agent couldn't find the key. That ordeal made the little Kyburz cabin all the more exciting. A secret and forbidden hideaway. My dad thought it a good idea. He was especially happy I wasn't just going to blow my brother's money in Vegas. He also saw it as a solid investment in my future—and a step toward maturity. It's never too late to become an adult at the age of 58.

So I did it. I bought my little cabin in the mountains. I named it "My Brother's Keeper" and dedicated it to Henry. I even set up a small altar to him. His spirit lives with me; I am forever indebted to his generosity.

So here I sit, almost three years after moving into the cabin, typing this memoir.

I'll be forever grateful to my brother Henry, who provided me with an opening for a new life.

I now live half my life in the quietude of the Sierra Nevada. I closed my San Francisco office and packed away the decades of memorabilia and hundreds of photos of me with every legend that I lured to the Castro. The only reminder of my past life as an impresario on display is the lithograph Tony Curtis sent me a week before he died. I'm alone, mostly, just me and the trees and the birds and the bees. And my precious pussies—now my little Edie, and before her, Katrina, who gave me 19 years of unconditional love and now is buried behind the cabin.

Life comes full circle. When I do have company, my most frequent cabin guests are Gregory and Beaver Bauer from the old Angels of Light days. These folks who over 40 years ago showed me an alternative way of life and art, and are now sharing and enjoying another evolution of mind and spirit.

I pinch myself each day. I can't believe I actually *own* a small piece of happiness. I never owned anything before. Some people crave villas in Tuscany, or mansions in Beverly Hills. I feel blessed to have a small cabin in the Sierras.

I've learned new skills: warding off bears, foraging for morel mushrooms, fishing for rainbow trout, and fixing my stream-fed water system. And I look so butch casting a rod or turning a big pipe wrench.

It's a respite from the problems of society and the modern world. Light years away from President It. And close to my mom's gravesite.

Today, I'm playing a version of Granny Clampett, doing my laundry by hand and then hanging it out to dry in the crisp mountain breeze while saying "hey" to the critters. I don't miss having my name in the papers or my picture taken with Debbie, or John, or Jane. If starfucking is what defines identity, we're all in trouble. I'm also trying to be a better brother to my sister, and a good uncle to Sean and Ryan.

My mom would often scoff when I spoke of movie stars, claiming "the only stars that exist are in heaven." So now I delight in the illumination, not of the spotlight, but of the shining stars above. I marvel at the constellation of Perseus, and wish upon the sporatic shooting star that flashes in the northern sky. Corny, huh?

I'm still speed free, and now occasionally have a glass of wine at dinner. It's relaxing, and there's no Craigslist to tempt me into debauchery.

And I love, love, *love* driving. It's a newfound freedom. Nothing pleases me more than going all Joan Didion and hitting the road. Play it as it lays, minus the gun. I love speeding down long, dusty, deserted roads, breathing in the smell of desert sage, and marveling at the magnificent vistas of the wild, Wild West.

As I go full speed ahead at 80 mph in Carlotta, I try not to look into the rearview mirror. If I get stuck reminiscing, I'll miss the real point: The good old days are yesterday, today and tomorrow.

Don't get me wrong; I still have dark days, still prone to depressions. And honestly if I were to die now, I'm ready. I'm not afraid. I have seen enough death to last a lifetime. Just one thing, if I kick the bucket (an apt country metaphor), don't write on Facebook, or declare at my memorial "Rest In Power." Just say "Rest In Peace." Peace is what I want, and I think I've earned it.

In the meanwhile, who knows what the future holds? If ever another legendary star crossed my path, I might just get out my bag of tricks, put on my impresario hat, and once again sparkle. Never say never.

But for now, a whole new world has opened up before me, full of curiosity, surprise, and uncertainty. I think back to that high school yearbook inscription penned by my mentor, Mr. Yesselman: "I wish you much happiness, but little contentment." Well, I now have a little bit of contentment and it makes me happy!

So, after years of excitement, sadness, tragedy, uncertainty, triumph, fulfillment, confusion and blessings, the curtain is finally closing on Act Two.

But don't go too far; Act Three is about to begin!

#

MARC HUESTIS CASTRO THEATRE EVENTS 1995-2018

- *The Stepford Wives* with Sick & Twisted Players (July, 1995)
- *Poseidon Event-Ure* with Carol Lynley (Nov., 1995, July, 2012)
- *Heat* with Sylvia Miles (May, 1996)
- *The Nutty Professor* with Stella Stevens (July, 1996)
- *A John Waters X-Mas* with John Waters (Dec., 1996, Dec., 2003)
- *Valley of the Dolls* with star Barbara Parkins (July, 1997)
- *Gypsy Rose Lee's Home Movies* presented by Erik Lee Preminger (Nov., 1998)
- *A Carrie White Christmas* with Piper Laurie (Dec., 1998)
- *Christmas with Christina Crawford* with Christina Crawford (Dec., 1997)
- *Summer Beach Party* with Troy Donahue & Sandra Dee (July, 1998)
- *The Bad Seed* with Patty McCormack (July, 1999, Oct., 2011)
- *A Judy Garland Christmas* with Lorna Luft (Dec., 1999)
- *New Year's Blow-Out on the SS Poseidon* with Carol Lynley and Stella Stevens (Dec., 2000)
- *A Tribute to Billy Wilder* with Edie Adams (April, 2000)
- *Ho Down with Karen Black* (July, 2000)
- *Can't Stop the Music* with Thelma Houston (July, 2001)
- *The Exorcist* with Linda Blair (Oct., 2001)
- *Viva Ann-Margret* with Ann-Margret (Feb., 2002)
- *Too Darn Hot* with Ann Miller (July, 2002)
- *Joan Baez & Reno Together at Last!* With Performances by Baez & Reno (March, 2003)
- *Create Peace* An All-Star Benefit (July, 2003)
- *A Hedwigged Out X-Mas* with John Cameron Mitchell (Dec., 2003)
- *Sing Along Wizard Of Oz* with Munchkin Margaret Pellegrini (March, 2004)
- *Ladies & Gentlemen Prefer Jane Russell* (July, 2004)
- *A Judy Garland Christmas* with Margaret O'Brien (Dec., 2004)
- *The Unsinkable Debbie Reynolds* with Debbie Reynolds (July, 2005)
- *Mildred Pierce with Ann Blyth Live!* (July, 2006)
- *To Kill a Mockingbird* with "Scout" Mary Badham Live interviewed by Armistead Maupin (Nov., 2006)
- *Bad Boys of Project Runway* with Santino Rice (July, 2007)
- *A Disco X-Mas* with Randy Jones (Dec., 2007)

- *Romeo & Juliet* with Olivia Hussey Live! (Feb., 2008)
- *A Salute to Miss Mitzi Gaynor* (July, 2008)
- *A Tribute to Tony Curtis* (Nov., 2008)
- *Sparkle, Patty, Sparkle* with Patty Duke Live (July, 2009)
- *Justin Vivian Bond* in Concert (Feb., 2010, April 2011)
- *Poltergeist* with JoBeth Williams Live (Oct., 2010)
- *I Bought a Blue Car Today* with Alan Cumming (July, 2010)
- *A Victor/Victoria Valentine* with Lesley Ann Warren (Feb., 2011)
- *I Dream of Barbara Eden* with Barbara Eden (July, 2011)
- *Love Story Valentine* with Ali MacGraw (Feb., 2012)
- *She's Got Balls* with Miss Coco Peru (April, 2012)
- *Mother's Day with Mommie Dearest* with Rutanya Alda (May, 2012)
- *A Tribute to Natalie Wood* with Lana Wood (Nov., 2012)
- *Joey Arias: Love Swings* (Feb., 2013)
- *The Color Purple* with Margaret (Shug) Avery (Feb., 2014)
- *Putting on the Ritz* with Rita Moreno (March, 2014)
- *Romeo & Juliet* with Leonard Whiting (Feb., 2015)
- *A Tribute to David Bowie* with Candy Clark (March, 2016)
- *Vertigo* with Kim Novak (May, 2018)

These events have not only received local publicity, but attention in such national venues as *The New York Times*, *L.A. Times*, *Variety*, Liz Smith, *The London Times*, *Out Magazine*, E!'s *Gossip Show*, *The Village Voice*.

Celebrities who have participated in Huestis' galas (both here and out-of-town) in the past include Alan Cumming, Ali MacGraw, Ann-Margret, Ann Blyth, Ann Miller, Armistead Maupin, Barbara Eden, Barbara Parkins, Bruce Vilanch, Candy Clark, Carol Doda, Carol Lynley, Christina Crawford, Debbie Reynolds, Edie Adams, Eddie Muller, Erik Lee Preminger, Harry Belafonte, Hector Elizondo, Jack Lemmon, Jane Russell, Janeane Garofalo, Jeffrey Sebelia, Jerry Lewis, Joan Baez, JoBeth Williams, Joey Arias, John Cameron Mitchell, John Schlesinger, John Waters, Justin Vivian Bond, Karen Black, Kim Novak, Lana Wood,

Lady Bunny, Lesley Ann Warren, Leonard Whiting, Linda Blair, Lypsinka, Margaret O'Brien, Margaret Avery, Mary Badham, Michael Musto, Mike Farrell, Mitzi Gaynor, Munchkin Margaret Pellegrini, Olivia Hussey, Miss Coco Peru, Patty Duke, Patty McCormack, Patricia Clarkson, Piper Laurie, Randy Jones, Reno, Rex Reed, Rita Moreno, Rutanya Alda, Sandra Dee, Santino Rice, Sissy Spacek, Stella Stevens, Sylvia Miles, Thelma Houston, Tony Curtis, Tony Kushner, Ted Casablanca, Troy Donahue, and Varla Jean Merman. Local luminaries include Arturo Galster, Connie Champagne, D'Arcy Drollinger, Heklina, Juanita More, Joan Jett Black, Marga Gomez, Matthew Martin, and Paula West.

Photo by Steven Underhill

CPSIA information can be obtained
at www.ICGtesting.com
Printed in the USA
FSHW010526180619
59169FS